Emily Dickinson

When a Writer Is a Daughter

Emily Dickinson

When a Writer Is a Daughter

Barbara Antonina Clarke Mossberg

INDIANA UNIVERSITY PRESS

Bloomington

Manufactured in the United States of America

Library of Congress Cataloging in Publication Data

Mossberg, Barbara Antonina Clarke, 1948-
    Emily Dickinson: when a writer is a daughter

    Includes index.
    1. Dickinson, Emily, 1830-1886—Criticism and inter-
    pretation.   I. Title.
PS1541.Z5M67   811$'$.4   80-8633
ISBN 0-253-31948-X   AACR2

1   2   3   4   5   86   85   84   83   82

No one can decline enough
                    —Gertrude Stein

Our best poets write poetry full of holes
                    —Alice Walker

I want this poem to be a weapon
I give it authority
To kill
                    —Olga Broumas

. . . dont you know that "No" is the wildest word we consign to Language?
                    —Emily Dickinson

To
My mother and father
My beloved portable audience
Who read this poem and said, "How did you *know*?"

The Audience

My daughter wrote me a poem.
I thought: my daughter wrote this
Writing poetry when she could be making money
Working in advertising
I tell her if you're too good for advertising there's always TV
You can't think that is below you.

I tell her maybe if it were stories I could help
Poetry I don't know about.

But I can't say anything.
She's very sensitive.

So what is she doing with her life, this daughter?
All this college, and no job,
I don't think she wants one, believe me she could have one.

My brother was a dancer
Went on the stage
And see where he ended up
What you need is a job.

My daughter likes nice things
She'll never be happy without money.

Still, it's very nice,
My daughter wrote me a poem,
Calls me a skinny giraffe,
Says she is my daughter.
Why is she always telling me she is my daughter,
What is she trying to convince me of?

Well, I don't think it will sell.
But it is nice to get a letter.
My son doesn't write me.
Of course
He has a job.

Bloomington, Indiana
13 June 1975

Acknowledgments

I am grateful to many people for their contributions to this book in its various stages of development from 1973–1980. A few: Owen Thomas turned me to Emily Dickinson; David Bleich, Willis Barnstone, Don L. Cook, Lewis Miller, and J. Albert Robbins were formative influences; Martha O'Nan's invitation to address her class on what I had learned about gender and creativity in my work on Dickinson as a woman writer led to the formation of "the daughter construct." Directly and indirectly I have profited from the support of the burgeoning feminist studies of woman writers which accompanied me as I wrote; they soothed my initial feelings of heresy (when I began, the "daughter" and mother-daughter relationship were not on the literary or critical map) and their work illuminates a tradition and context for such a study. E. M. Broner, Cathy M. Davidson, Elaine Hedges, Deborah Holdstein, and Suzanne Juhasz gave signal advice and encouragement.

I am especially indebted to Susan Gubar, first, and Sandra Gilbert—muses who fronted the Anti-Muse with courage and faith—for their inspired, inspiring scholarly generosity which has made such a difference to this work. Other contributions I felt as deeply: the legacy from scholars whose ideas about Emily Dickinson were constant presences as I conceived and wrote the book. To them and the community of Dickinson's readers I felt accountable. Our spirited dialogues about her work shaped and stimulated my own reading and appreciation of the poems, and are reflected in the book. We all are indebted to Thomas H. Johnson for his editing, to Jay Leyda and Richard B. Sewall for the biography, and I in particular to S. P. Rosenbaum for his *Concordance* (now we need one for the letters).

I wish to thank George Wickes and the University of Oregon Graduate School and English Department for financial and editorial support (especially heroic typing); Susan Metzger at Harvard University Press for permissions help and textual advice; Mrs. Helen Thurber for her kind permission to use the Thurber cartoon; Lena Cronqvist, for generously allowing me to dress this "daughter" in her painting "Modern" for the cover and Lars Grimgarn for the cover photograph; my son Nicolino, for forgiving me, and for my understanding of the "cocoon" poems; my family, who know more about Emily Dickinson than they ever wanted to know—and whose doubt, anguish, and good sense were at least as crucial as their abiding faith, commitment, and *help*. Above all, I was blessed to have Christer, who collaborated at every stage, suffering and rejoicing, and without whose love and support the book could not have been written, nor with as much joy. To him, my family and friends, I cannot adequately express my gratitude: but they know.

Finally, it is a special joy to work with the writings of Emily Dickinson, which only become more meaningful and enjoyable with each new reading. I have limited myself to a fraction of the poems, to serve primarily as examples, a kind of guide to the way the poems as a whole can be understood and appreciated. It is my hope and intent that readers accompany me with Dickinson's complete poems, that we return to them, again and again, with fresh surprise, delight, awe, and humility: for of *them* it can never be said "we are finished." My gratitude for that.

Poems and letters reprinted by permission of the publishers and the Trustees of Amherst College from *The Poems of Emily Dickinson*, edited by Thomas H. Johnson, Cambridge, Mass.: The Belknap Press of Harvard University Press, Copyright 1951, © 1955, 1979, 1980 by the President and Fellows of Harvard College. From *The Complete Poems of Emily Dickinson*, edited by Thomas H. Johnson. Copyright 1914, 1929, 1935 by Martha Dickinson; Copyright renewed 1942 by Martha Dickinson Bianchi. Copyright © renewed 1957, 1963 by Mary L. Hampson. Reprinted by permission of Little, Brown, and Company. Thurber cartoon, © 1933, 1961 James Thurber. From *My Life and Hard Times*, published by Harper & Row; also in the *Vintage Thurber*, Hamish Hamilton Limited, The Collection Copyright © 1963.

Contents

"She Has the True Emily Dickinson Spirit Except That She Gets Fed Up Occasionally"

Introduction

The image of Emily Dickinson as remorselessly pure and eccentrically ascetic is so entrenched in the American imagination that James Thurber could draw a cartoon for *The New Yorker* of a Dickinson *manqué*—a woman who comes close to embodying the "true Emily Dickinson spirit" but who has human frailties. The "true" Dickinson spirit never gets "fed up" nor, we imagine, would she stoop to any such colloquial mood. A contemporary version of this image of Dickinson is William Luce's compelling box-office hit, *The Belle of Amherst,* where her chastity, duty, and self-sacrifice are canny, even naughty: Dickinson is Puck, a sassy saint whose spice spills over from her cakes into her retorts.

Indeed, the popular image of Emily Dickinson appears to bear more likeness to figures out of folklore or popular culture than to any actual person: Eve, Rapunzel, Cinderella, Snow White, Gretel, Dido, Alice, the Peter Pan of a Puritan Sleepy Hollow, the Little Match Girl starving outside a prosperous Yankee culture . . . not a woman so much as an archetypal hodgepodge of our culture's attic trunk of feminine roles. In large part, this is Dickinson's doing. She wrote of anguished virginity, crazed or passive confinement, unconsciousness and awakening, persecution, abandonment, dissolution and transformation, fearful and futile flights. She dressed only in white and lived in legendary, conspicuous seclusion in her "father's house." She renounced "All," which included the orthodox joys and frustrations of motherhood and the shopping trip, but not poetry—everything, it seems, *but* poetry. Her actual fifty-five years of life are reduced to the image of an existence untainted by mature female sexuality or common human qualities and yes, frailties. If she lived, it is in our imaginations as a kind of neuter saint.

Even scholarship, until very recently, has tended to preserve and protect the image of Dickinson as an "innocent, confiding child" or a "girl" her readers are supposedly "in love with"[1] or at least treat chivalrously. In 1964 Clark Griffith explored Emily Dickinson's tragic vision and her traumatic relationship with her father—thereby taking her seriously as a woman—but his argument was taken as an insult to Dickinson's honor that scholars felt obliged to avenge. It was asked, "ought one to think of fair play when a critic . . . characterizes Emily Dickinson as neurotic, erotic, laconic, and scared?",[2] yet these are terms that apply to most modern artists, not to mention most people at given moments. But the protective response has persisted. In 1968 a critic set forth "to defend Emily Dickinson's integrity—and hence her sanity."[3] John Cody and others have argued persuasively that such defensive attitudes are products of misplaced gallantry based on prejudices about mental illness,[4] but such attitudes may also reflect a gallantry based on a prejudice about "girls," which holds that girls are not neurotic, nor do they get "fed up," nor are they conscious of and angry about their culture's restraints upon them.[5] Emily Dickinson does seem to arouse paternalistic feelings in those who like their daughters spicy but pure, by virtue of her apparent need of her father's protection and by her literature of inquisitive innocence. But many of her poems are undeniably laconic and express neurotic, erotic, and scared—that is to say, *human*—sentiments. A real woman wrote the poems—a woman with long, kinky, graying hair, bad eyes, a thick waist, freckles on her bosom, and a skin rash—and they reveal a uniquely accessible, immediate, and intimate portrait of this woman.

The irony of the Dickinson myth is that like her less steadfast counterpart in Thurber's cartoon, she did get "fed up," in the most traditional of ways for women, and more than occasionally—fed up with "women's work":

> . . . *my time* [*is considered*] *of so little account—and my writing so very needless—and really I came to the conclusion that I should be a villain unparalleled if I took but an inch of time for so unholy a purpose as writing a friendly letter—for what need had I of affection—or less than they all—of friends—mind the house—and the food—sweep if the spirits are low—nothing like exercise to invigorate—and help away such foolishness—work makes one strong, and cheerful—and for society what neighborhood so full as my own? The halt—the lame—and the blind—the old—the infirm—the bed-ridden—and superannuated—the ugly, and disagreeable—the perfectly hateful to me—and these to see, and be seen by—an opportunity for cultivating meekness—and patience—and submission—and for turning my back on this very sinful, and wicked world. Somehow or other I incline to other things. . . . The path of duty looks very ugly indeed—*[6]

This is not the whole picture, of course, nor is it my purpose only to reveal a new, neglected side of Emily Dickinson. Jay Leyda once said, "There is little need to expand on the harm done Emily Dickinson by the sentimental picture of 'our Emily'. . . In a word, the sentimental picture *isolates* her—and thus much of her poetry—from the real world."[7] Any harm, it seems to me, from imposing a romanticized notion of nineteenth-century femininity onto Emily Dickinson, is done to us, for perpetuating a dehumanized picture of her deprives us of appreciating her ability to express the life we live, the world we still inhabit. Her complaints and moods are not very feminine in the conventional nineteenth-century sense, nor do they conform to the image of Dickinson as a girl about whom we may not use the words laconic, neurotic, erotic, or scared, a girl with whom we are in love. But they place Dickinson on the human map. And Dickinson's greatness lies, I think, in how she charts this landscape.

She makes an art of the complaint: it is one of her literary specialties. Rather than gloss over a bad mood, she maps it out. In other letters housework is "pestilence," cooking is a "prickly art," and when she finds herself forced to engage in these activities, she looks about the kitchen, crying, "My kitchen, I think I called it. God forbid it was or ever shall be my own–God save me from what they call households" (*Letters* II, p. 453; III, p. 827; I, pp. 97–100). In fact, Dickinson often deliberately presents herself as a chronic complainer, whether about her invalid mother ("the infirm" mentioned above), the Puritan work ethic, Christian values, God's choice of a "Son" to represent him, her parents' preferential treatment of her brother, her alienation in her household, or her chores—to name a few of her peeves. Appearing to cherish and indulge her own irritability, Dickinson cultivates a rebellious pose, professing to be wicked and unrepentant, as if to *dissociate* herself from the qualities characterizing the feminine ideal. Indeed, Dickinson exploits her "fed up" moods for the opportunity to show off her linguistic virtuosity. But if she takes liberties with syntax and vocabulary to distinguish herself as a writer, these cases of rhetorical "flash" still express anger, frustration, indignation, scorn, arrogance, and resentment. Dickinson is witty and dramatic in her writing, but she reveals an ego with hypochondria, obsessed with being considered insignificant, powerless, dependent, deprived, and oppressed. Just as often, Dickinson's literary persona is confident, arrogant, stubborn, proud, boisterous, ironic, sarcastic. She enjoys flexing the poetic bicep, snarling to reveal a witch-like venom. She is a combination of "poor little me" and "heh-heh-heh."

It is important to remember that however she may represent her plight as a woman, Dickinson was never a drudge, never contended with society's sneers as a barkeeper's daughter, never felt shame because of illegitimacy, never endured the thousand hardships experienced by many women. As a "Yankee princess," a self-styled invalid, she was indulged and catered to by family and staff, including her sister Lavinia. She enjoyed the privileges of upper-class life, and unlike her father and brother she did not even have to work. She could pursue her intellectual and creative life more easily than most. Thus it is all the more significant that when she does pursue her intellectual life in poetry, she should identify herself as a tragic heroine or beleaguered child out of some fairy tale. Dickinson's "fed up" letters and poems not only provide evidence of her humanness but of her particular problems as a mature woman poet, struggling for a voice in a society that tries to "shut her up" in the "Prose" of conventional female behavior:

> *They shut me up in Prose–*
> *As when a little Girl*

> *They put me in the Closet–*
> *Because they liked me "still"–*
>
> [from 613][8]

It is as a *poet,* then, that she is society's little girl whose literary behavior is a childish rebellion from proper womanly behavior and as such must be quelled by the authorities. She is "shut up" by not being published or taken seriously as a poet, by being criticized for her poetic irregularities, and by the guilt she assumes for undertaking a literary career. Emily Dickinson experienced the effects of feeling torn between two mutually exclusive identities—being, in John Stuart Mill's words, a "contradiction and a disturbing element."[9] She was coping with a formidable intellect, ambition, and creative urge that only alienated her from her family, particularly her mother and sister. She was intensely conscious of her predicament as a woman who wanted a voice, who craved power and immortality, who longed to be "great, Someday" and make her family proud, aware that these were aspirations that could win little sympathy or support in her family or culture, despite her family's prominence and her own access to the leading literary figures of the day.[10]

Recent studies of women have sensitized the reading public to the notion that a writer's gender is significant in direct proportion to the culture's assignation of sex roles. To show a woman's sense of conflict about a literary career, as Sandra Gilbert and Susan Gubar do, for example, in *The Madwoman in the Attic,* is not to impose an enlightened twentieth-century indignation upon nineteenth-century complacency.[11] Rather, our increasing awareness of these issues allows us to hear these early voices more clearly, perhaps more clearly than they could have been heard in their own time. This is certainly true for Dickinson. She never tried to cover up her problems, but brought her case before her reader, calling attention to the circumstances in which she wrote; if readers *today* are reluctant to acknowledge her conflicts or to take seriously the effects upon her of lacking a supportive tradition or environment, we can imagine what it felt like for Dickinson to experience and express such conflicts then.

But we do not have to *imagine,* for Dickinson tells us. In sensational poems we never read in high school or in anthologies, she chronicles the effects such subversive, assertive behavior as writing poetry has upon her sense of her identity. She is "ashamed to own a body," laments her inability to banish "Me from Myself" except by killing herself or going mad, conceives her breast and belly as a "soft prison"—bars and chains she would cut off—and cries, "Amputate my freckled Bosom!/Make me bearded like a man!"

For us to then idealize her renunciation in a way desexes her because it ignores not only the psychic cost but the role such sexual conflict and identification have in Dickinson's poetry. If Dickinson conceived obstacles against her as a woman poet, she also construed these as the very means by which she would cleverly transcend a common female destiny—by stealth, "difference," "small size," and "witchcraft." Thus she never abandoned her female identification in her writing. In this sense her writings are profoundly *sexual.*

What I find remarkable is that in spite of how explicit she is about the trauma she experiences as an unrecognized, resentful, and guilty artist, this is not the voice we have been trained to expect, to look for, or even to value when we read Emily Dickinson.

METHODOLOGY: DE-NEUTERING

Genevieve Taggard, one of Dickinson's first biographers, wrote in 1938: "When Emily Dickinson's letters are carefully assembled and studied, and three or four downright and candid sentences of her own about herself taken seriously, we have a story which tells itself, and a life the poems verify."[12] Although Emily Dickinson specifically makes an issue of the consequences of her female identity, and this was perceived forty years ago, crucial poems and letters on this topic have been ignored or dismissed as trivial, irrelevant, obscure, or inferior; thus we lose an essential component of Dickinson. Adrienne Rich mentions her sense of bewildered betrayal in going back to Emily Dickinson and finding out how much was there that had never been introduced to her.[13] It was not until 1955 that the complete poems were made available by Thomas H. Johnson; yet a quarter of a century has gone by and the critical portrayal of Emily Dickinson still does not reflect the altered image of Dickinson mandated by the complete poems. Jay Leyda has asked, "Is it really possible that we can be shut away from the full work or real personality of so vital a poet? Can *any* false structure . . . forever obscure the real person who wrote those poems?"[14] Simply, yes, if the poems are not read.

I think that key poems, in particular, have been bypassed, not because they are inferior in quality or inconsequential, but because they contradict our notion of an Emily Dickinson poem. In spite of Dickinson's revelations about her dilemma as a woman poet, she is still "shut up," as imprisoned now as she was during her lifetime by our expectations of what she is supposed to be, and not supposed to be, as a woman and as a poet.

In this study, therefore, I depart from Charles Anderson's influential strategy in *Stairway of Surprise* (1960) which is based on a sense that of the 1776 poems, twenty-five are "great," one hundred are "really fine," and the rest are mediocre or "not sufficiently distinguished to linger over."[15] Professor Anderson (and he is not alone) regrets that Dickinson did not do her "writer's duty to her public" by destroying the "miscellaneous sweepings of the poet's workshop," including what he refers to as her "absent-minded scribblings." Therefore he winnows out those poems that are "not excellent": "To cherish all these indiscriminately is the surest way to render her poetic reputation a disservice." What I think we must question is whether Dickinson ever wrote *anything* "absent-mindedly"; whether she never threw out or should have thrown out her own "failures" (assuming we could know a Dickinson "failure"); whether the critic's task is to determine poetic excellence at the expense of poetic meaning; whether her complete poems would in fact injure her poetic reputation; and whether our job is to protect reputations, in this case, by tampering with the evidence. In any case, Emily Dickinson does not need our protection: she needs to be read, and scholarship should facilitate this. The methodology that concentrates exclusively on the "great" poems effectively censors the scores of amazing poems about Dickinson's identity conflict as a woman artist—such as "Rearrange a 'Wife's' affection" or "They shut me up in Prose," quoted earlier—that do not fit what are necessarily subjective criteria for "great" poetry. Such selection could explain why Dickinson is still "shut up" today. We do not have a whole picture of the poet or her work. We have only a neutered version of her achievement, based on less than ten percent of what she wrote!

We have not seen the *woman,* or the woman at odds with herself and her culture, in the poems and letters of Emily Dickinson because we have not been looking for her, nor have we been trained to look for her, as we have been trained, for example, to separate poet from poem in New Criticism. After all, it has only been in recent years that sociological, historical, and psychological feminist studies have been applied to literary studies to impart the significance of gender in the act of creation. It has been a logical step from the pioneering studies by Simone de Beauvoir, Helene Deutsch, and Karen Horney to the sociohistorical work by Martha Vicinus, Gerda Lerner, Ann Douglas, Carroll Smith-Rosenberg, and Nancy Cott, among others, to studies challenging traditional perspectives of women such as Phyllis Chesler's *Women and Madness,* to the literary criticism that establishes the impact of the female mind upon creation and begins to draw a tradition where before there had only been conceived pockets of female literary isolation: Ellen Moers, Elaine Showalter, Patricia Meyer Spacks, Adrienne Rich, Carolyn Heilbrun, Kate Millett, Sandra Gilbert and Susan Gubar, and many others. As works by Suzanne Juhasz, Josephine Donovan, Tillie Olsen, and others make abundantly clear, we can no longer ignore the effects of a woman writer's sense of her own sexuality, or regard her, as we have often done Emily Dickinson, as a poet whose sex is irrelevant to her achievements. When David Higgins analyzes Dickinson's prose, for example, he finds her letters full of "domestic detail" obscuring Dickinson's development as a poet.[16] But letters describing her mornings watching her mother and sister clean house, or her own efforts in the kitchen when her mother is sick, are integrally related to her themes and self-image as a poet. And, if we eliminate these "domestic" letters, we eliminate all there is to provide a sense of her literary development. And while it is true that there were no other "great" women poets in nineteenth-century America when Dickinson was writing, so that her achievement could be viewed as an aberration, it is also true that no one was more aware of her uniqueness than Dickinson herself. We must understand Emily Dickinson's female sensibility not only because she is a woman artist and it only makes sense to do so, but because in her letters, poetry, and life, Dickinson manifests a consciousness of being at odds with her culture and herself *because she is a woman artist.*

I think we do "rearrange" her, amputate her bosom, tear her "Me" from

"Myself," and free her from her "soft" prison of flesh when we read her poetry as if her sex were irrelevant to what or how or why she wrote. To read her as reticent or unconscious about these matters is to read her as neuter, to silence her—in effect, to lose her. Before Richard B. Sewall's 1974 biography, for example, which culminates a century's worth of Dickinson scholarship, we had dozens of major biographies and full-length critical studies, thousands of articles, many volumes of research material, each of which attempted to recreate an aspect of Dickinson's social and intellectual environment that would explain the nature of her life and artistic achievement: her gene pool, her family ambience, the people she knew, the books she read, the sermons she heard, the attitudes she inherited and assimilated, her medical history, and the religious and philosophical atmosphere she breathed. Yet Professor Sewall finds that Emily Dickinson is "not yet ours," nor can she be, "until her hopes and fears and mysteries become as plain to us as Antigone's or Hamlet's."[17] Or as plain as *Sophocles'* or *Shakespeare's*: the point is that unlike these authors, Dickinson has essentially one protagonist, herself; one "plot," her hopes, fears, and problems as a woman artist. What strikes me, in reading through Dickinson's poems as one long "interconnected" piece, as Inder Nath Kher suggests,[18] is how often her poetry refers to her own effort to escape, transcend, or establish her female identity through the writing of poetry. We see her "confident despair" in her decision to renounce a traditional woman's life to write poetry, how ill-at-ease she is in her identity as a poet; characterizing herself to an *Atlantic Monthly* editor as a "Kangaroo among the Beauty" (*L*. II, p. 412), an oddball intruder into the domain of male authors. Every time she takes up her pen she herself is, in effect, amputating her own bosom, tearing her "me" from "myself": in helpless unity, woman and poet each try to struggle out of the other's skin. On the battlefield of her poetry, we see evidence of the struggle in the deleted verbs, camouflaged subjects, stricken syntax, and melodramatic histrionics.

APPROACH

Emily Dickinson's self-consciousness, feelings of subversiveness, identity conflict, and secrecy belong to a "new" tradition, as Suzanne Juhasz puts it, of other women writers, and studies in the context of her female identity are only logical.[19] But her case is unique and demands a new approach. We have not been able to construe—certainly, we have not been able to agree upon—the relationship between Dickinson and her poetry. The life her biographers have set forth does not seem to illuminate or inform the *poetry* very clearly, and both the life and the poetry are open to various interpretations. This in itself would not present such a problem if the poems were not so often hard to decipher, ambiguous, allusive, symbolic, and structurally designed to tease or mislead. The fact that they are frequently fashioned as riddles or puzzles makes us suspect that the technical difficulty the poems pose may be calculated to intrigue. Our sense that the poems contain and are hiding some key revelatory information is strengthened by Dickinson's references to her "Secret" and by the facts that she adopts a persona in the first person and that her lyrics seem autobiographical.

The poems might well be a private version of Dickinson's life, then, but the self-portrait is of a childhood and adulthood often tormented with parental and social abuse, neglect, and deprivation, as well as grief, madness, loss, and doubt. This self-portrait contrasts dramatically with the majority of her biographers' interpretations of her life. Richard Sewall, for example, adopting a middle ground, finds it necessary to discount the impression that Dickinson's parents were villains or that Dickinson was tortured or mad; but because the poetry sometimes suggests the contrary, several studies are premised on a psychotic Emily Dickinson and a tyrant father. And in spite of the difficulty of the poetry, the feelings in the poems are so vividly recreated that readers have not been able to refrain from inferring that the poems derive from felt experience. We are put into the position of wondering whom to believe, the persona or the biographers; and if we believe the persona, we still do not know *what* experience informs those poems. We also do not know why Dickinson would want to put a distance between the poetry and the experience from which it derives. Finally, our puzzlement over the source of the poetry is compounded by the fact that in form and content the poems are unique. Nothing like them had appeared before in our literature. In fact, the poetry departed so much from the conventional ways in which poetry was known, generically and stylistically, that early readers denied it was "poetry," and the first editors thought it prudent to doctor the poetry to make it conform more to readers' expectations.

Thus, the poetry's very uniqueness prompts people to turn to the life of its author. But when we turn to Dickinson's life to verify the suffering and help explain the meanings behind the bold departures in form and attitude from traditional poetry, we see only the grin of a Cheshire cat: a sharply witty, extremely shy New England woman, immersed in the orthodoxies of living at home, baking her father's daily bread, and caring for her invalid mother. Hard as we have looked, we find no evidence of deprivation or enforced incarceration. What we do see, however, arouses our suspicions that there is a mystery to be solved. At some point in an apparently happy childhood, something happened so that the droll, cheeky, precocious child became withdrawn and could not even stay in school because of homesickness, depression, and mysterious ailments. As she matured, she maintained the outward manifestations of a child in dress, deportment, and lifestyle, and gradually withdrew from a normal social life, shunning friends and strangers alike, and confining her interactions with the world to notes and letters. She wore white, kept to her room or the upper floors of the house unless no one was about, and wrote poetry at night. The stream of voluminous, gushy letters of her early years dwindled to a trickle of aphoristic telegrams as the years progressed. She gardened, sewed, read, and played the piano. In later years, as a recluse, she would not let old friends see her "face to face," but permitted her voice to be heard through a door that was left ajar.

Dickinson's seclusion, her habit of dressing in white, her scurrying from the faces of friends and strangers, and her reported eccentricities have inevitably drawn psychologists to her case, while most of Dickinson's critics appear uncomfortable with the aesthetic implications of a neurotic poet. Thus while case studies have been made, the most notable being those by John Cody and Clark Griffith, other scholars have assumed that the experience the poems veil is a traumatic love affair—or two—that motivated the poetry and Dickinson's curious lifestyle. If the identity of the lover(s) were discovered, the reasoning seems to go, the meaning of Dickinson's life and poetry would be clarified, her sudden poetic flowering would be explained, and individual poems could be explicated.

The problem with this approach is that a different lover is advocated in each study, and with convincing documentation; even when agreement is reached on one lover, there are conflicting interpretations about that lover's role. As early as 1938, George Whicher protested that not all the theories could be true; since then, even more theories have been advanced.[20] We cannot agree on one; and if we agree that none are true, we are left without an explanation for the "love" poetry and the emotional anguish the poems depict. Responding to this stalemate, David Porter suggests that we "not be troubled by the refusal of the *life* to explain the *poetry*," and Inder Nath Kher urges us to simply focus our attention on the poems.[21] In one way, I agree: it is clear that we have not adopted a successful strategy to clarify the relation between the biography and the poetry. I, for one, am ready to accept that *all* the "lover" theories are true to some degree. But what I would like to suggest is that whom Dickinson loved is ultimately beside the point.

Knowing that Dickinson had relationships with various people does not tell us which particular experience generated the poetic output or informs the poetry. Dickinson first began saving her poetry in 1858. In the poetry written between then and her death in 1886, I, like Albert Gelpi, find no substantive development in the poetry in style, outlook, imagery, or theme.[22] Dickinson was ambivalent throughout her career and vacillated between moods of doubt and certainty over her prospects for eventual greatness, but there is no progressive development in her attitudes toward or depiction of love, death, immortality, or herself. She expressed herself at the end in essentially the same idiom she began with; after her Valentine Sermon, her format, imagery, even line and poem-length, remain virtually unchanged. Events are abstracted to be given universal import and to confirm her world vision. Identifying a lover will not help us interpret the poetry *because the themes and attitudes expressed in Emily Dickinson's poems are not informed by her adult experience*. They were already formulated by the time she began writing, when she was fifteen or younger.

THEORY: THE DAUGHTER

I am not suggesting that there is no relation between Dickinson's experience and the poetry she wrote. On the contrary, I think it is both possible and necessary to establish the relation between the biography and the poetry, but in order to do so, we must look at the years in Dickinson's development during which her aesthetics and her attitudes toward experience were formed. That is, we must turn to her childhood.

Focusing on these years illuminates an aspect of Dickinson that has been overlooked—her identity as a daughter. This identity is significant not only because it shapes her poetic stance, but because Emily Dickinson's primary relationship with her parents was never transcended in her life, her letters, or her poetry. Economically and socially dependent upon men, nineteenth-century American women, in this sense, were "girls" all their lives. But the "daughter" is the "girl" who relates to others and conceives of herself only in terms of her relationship to her parents. Typically, this identity is temporary, only the first in a series of identities that the woman will adopt, adapt to, or incorporate into her self-image as she matures. Subsequent identities are a function of the breaking away from the parents to acknowledge the primacy of friends, relatives, lovers, spouses, children, work, or religion, when the dominant self-image as daughter becomes submerged or eclipsed. But Emily Dickinson never progressed beyond her primary identity as a daughter functioning in reference to her parents: she never left home ("my Father's Ground"); she retained her adolescent dress, hairstyle, behavior, mannerisms, and attitudes; she never developed a significant relationship that would take her away from the child-parent matrix, but projected onto all relationships the parent-child construct she had established with her parents, perpetuating her identity as a little girl.

The question, of course, is why. Inability or lack of desire to transcend the daughter role can suggest several different circumstances: her experience as a daughter was so secure and idyllic that she could not bear to leave home; she harbored an antipathy for other culturally acceptable identities for women such as wife, mother, or Sister of Charity, and was therefore trapped in her original identity as Daughter by default; the original relationship between the daughter and the parents was not satisfactory in some elemental way, and the unfulfilled daughter tried to recreate or project this primary relationship onto other people in the hope of their giving her the parental nurture she craved. In this last case, because her parents were the source of her permanent regression, she expressed her ambivalence towards them by remaining a Daughter but refusing to be dutiful. In her letters and poems Dickinson proffers all three explanations to account for her life. Practically speaking, remaining a daughter may have been the only way to keep herself free from responsibilities so that she could write poetry. Her seclusion may have been her only means of being her true self.

Thus, while the poet complains of her "small size" and says she yearns to "grow," only lacking the knowledge of how to go about it, the woman did not permit herself to grow up and out of her daughter role in life or art. In her poetry, Dickinson perpetuates her identity as a little girl to her absent mother and tyrant father, extending her childhood even through her afterlife, to a schoolyard heaven where God never naps and recess never comes. In fact, in her poetry she appears to nurture and even extol the repression, dependence, frustration, and deprivation of childhood. Whether Dickinson exhibits a dutiful sensibility—timid, self-sacrificing, anxious, eager to please, seeking parental approval, dependent, and vulnerable—or a rebellious sensibility—jaunty, angry, scornful, ironic, convinced of her own uniqueness, power, autonomy, and superiority—she is a daughter trying to commune with and break away from a patriarchy that eclipses women.

But while Dickinson's poetry is informed by a daughter's consciousness, we do not have to imagine that Dickinson's childhood actually took the form the poetry describes. The daughter identity became a metaphor for her feelings and experience as an adult woman poet struggling to develop a voice in her patriarchal culture. In fact, Emily Dickinson's poems about her art and life give evidence that she was convinced the childhood she depicts is the breeding ground of poetry. As long as she retains this daughter's sensibility, she will be motivated to use language to give herself the power, independence, glory, and autonomy that she lacks in her father's house.

We will probably never know whether Emily Dickinson's mother ever entertained a desire to become a writer, but if she had shown even the slightest propensity to be intellectual or literary, it would have changed Dickinson's life. Influencing Dickinson more than her dominating father's suspicious attitude toward "modern Literati" was a mother Dickinson defined as not "caring for thought," having "low" and "narrow" intellectual faculties, and being too busy for letters (*L*. II, pp. 475; 517–18; I, p. 241). Not that any of this was Mrs. Dickinson's fault, but it condemned her in her daughter's eyes. This was the mother to whom a husband-to-be wrote the following courtship letter, only one of many in which he enumerated his specifications for what a wife should be:

> *I passed Tuesday evening of this week, in company with Miss Sedgwick, the Authoress of "Redwood" & "New England Tale," at a party. . . . She had an interesting countenance—an appearance of much thought, & rather masculine features. And I feel happy at having an opportunity of seeing a female who had done so much to give our works of taste so pure and delicate a character—and a conscious pride that women of our own country & our own state, too, are emulating not only the females but the men of England & France & Germany & Italy in works of literature— we are warranted in presuming that, if they had opportunities equal to their talents, they would not be inferior to our own sex in improving the sciences. Tho' I should be sorry to see another Mmd. de Stael—especially*

*if one wished to make a partner of her for life. Different qualities are
more desirable in a female who enters into domestic relations—and you
have already had my opinions on that subject—*[23]

The irony is that Mrs. Dickinson's dutiful adherence to the spirit of her husband's domestic requirements deprived her children—in the eyes of her daughter—of a mother who could teach them "to grow." An adult Emily Dickinson
claims, "I never had a mother;" she runs home to Awe, when a child in trouble
("He was an awful mother, but better than none"); "How to grow up I don't
know." That her father, as the above letter shows, felt that women ought to be
given the same opportunities as men to develop their potential—for the glory of
the country, no less—and yet failed to recognize his own daughter's literary
talent, or to encourage her in a literary career, is only a further irony.

Dickinson proved her father wrong, of course: a "female" could juggle a
domestic and literary life. She stayed home and played the role of the dutiful
daughter, a "reticent volcano," a "calm bomb." In secrecy and defiance she
forged the poetry that would make her great. But the idea that a woman faced
an either/or decision—write or marry—and the notion that marrying and writing
required different attributes, haunted Dickinson, and the effects on her identity
of growing up as a daughter in this household with this set of parents were
profound. Refusing to conform to the nineteenth-century feminine ideal her
mother represented led to identity conflict that was further intensified by the
lack of a role model upon whom Dickinson could pattern herself to become a
poet.

I believe even Dickinson's aesthetics, her unique uses of language, spelling, grammar, and rhyme, and her unconventional and irreverent themes, reflect her need to establish an independent identity from her mother; they defy a
tradition and past that make duty "ugly" for daughters, and conformity fatal.
Thus in one way, the fusion of Dickinson's poetry and daughter role constitutes
a strategy to outwit her female destiny. Yet what particularly interests me is that
the ideal feminine characteristics she rejects in her mother and feels to be so
antithetical to poetry—chastity, humility, service, devotion, "wifehood," martyrdom—are the terms in which Dickinson depicts her role as a poet. In fact
the dutiful persona of the poems bears an uncanny resemblance to the portrait
of Mrs. Dickinson that can be gleaned from the family letters and biographical
accounts. While the daughter dissociates herself from her mother to the point
of preferring to be regarded as motherless, as a poet she conducts herself as her
mother's daughter, after all. And while she opposes and even confronts the
logic of her father's authority, scorning his worldly importance as a lawyer and
legislator, she reveals herself as "Cato's daughter" as well. In her poetry she is
disputatious, litigatious; she brings suits, posits loopholes, presents legal ar-
guments, appeals judge's decisions, sports with logic, and uses business and
legal terminology. Thus while Dickinson often declares herself as a rebel or an
orphan in control of her own life, powerfully parentless or at odds with parents,

her experience as a daughter directly informs the way her poetry is written and the kinds of poems she writes.

To analyze Emily Dickinson's poetic rendering of her experience as a daughter, it is necessary to reconstruct her actual relationship to her parents to determine their role in her development. Critics have thus far given attention to Emily Dickinson's father, appropriately enough, since he appears as a prominent force in the poems and letters. But Emily Dickinson's mother has been ignored, perhaps for the same reasons we only now look at Dickinson's response to her female experience. Since Mrs. Dickinson was not important to society, we assume she was not important to Dickinson. Dickinson herself is largely responsible for this conclusion, denying as she does that she ever had a mother and leaving her out of her poetry altogether. But psychologists have shown the significance of the mother in any person's development, especially a woman's; and the daughter who tries to erase her mother's existence reveals that there is indeed a significant mother-daughter relationship to be examined. I am more interested in probing the significance of the way Dickinson presents her parents than arriving at an "objective" portrait of the two elder Dickinsons. Her erasures of her mother, and her making her father into a comitragic tyrant buffoon at cross-purposes with himself, do not necessarily reflect a particular Dickinson parental pathology, but rather, are the result of what I call a "daughter construct," which Dickinson exploits in order to create.

PART ONE

The Case: The Identity Poems

"I seek, and am, Emily"

The Self-seeking Persona

Emily Dickinson arrives as an intellectual and sexual refugee from an age in which she felt she could not speak, could not be heard—an age which tried to "shut me up in Prose," she says, "As when a little Girl/They put me in the Closet–/Because they liked me 'still'–" (613). Identifying with the bird which society ludicrously forces into the pound (for the "treason" presumably, of "singing" instead of being "still"), Dickinson says that through the voice of her *poetry* she can escape "at will" that strange captivity in the nineteenth-century patriarchal closet she called simply "Prose," or "my Father's house." While her poems speak of her experience in this Closet, they are uncannily "modern," as if they were written out of the context of her age and its events, attitudes and perspectives. During Dickinson's most creative, poetically productive years, 1860–1865, America was engaged in a civil war and saw its head of state assassinated; but Dickinson's seclusion during this violent era is legendary. She clung to the apolitical, aworldly interiors of her "father's house" and garden in Amherst, Massachusetts, and would not be budged. She held fast to a microscopic, idiosyncratic, alienated vision in her poetry.

And yet the nineteenth-century experienced by her contemporaries is present in large degree in Dickinson's poetry, particularly the civil war and the events of those years: the battles, victories, defeats, even the plight of a body that must continue to function despite the loss of its head. Saboteurs lurk; there are constant funerals. But the strife that Dickinson describes is inner. What Dickinson has done is to take the civil war and the politics of secession, division, and conflict *inside* her father's house—and inside the mind of an individual in captivity there. In these poems we see an almost incapacitating self-consciousness and yet a compulsive exhibitionism, a brain debilitated, a sensibility ruptured, a soul "bandaged," a self bickering with an alien, antagonistic other self or selves; frequently this self is fragmented into halves or thirds of various states of animation, consciousness, and gender.

Taking her metaphors from the century at hand, she borrows from the theatrical as well as the martial: her conflict is vaudeville. Her poems about identity are set in the creative mind's eerie and cobwebbed backstage, a psychic circus where the poet is owned by a ringmaster and comprises the entire troupe: bearded lady, sideshow freak, disembodied voice, lady sawed-in-two, trained animal, and helpless performer who "speaks" at her master's command.

Even more arresting than Dickinson's sensational depictions of self-image and creative psyche are the attitudes she expresses toward identity and the voice. Identity is an uninhabitable region of chasms, fissures, and gaping holes; it is a pursuing hound, intolerable and inescapable. It is withheld from the persona during her lifetime. It is a function of a fatal relationship with a male owner or master. The self in these "identity poems," as I call them, is dispossessed and a possession, dependent, bidden, and obedient, whereas the selves within are autonomous and rebellious. Finally, we encounter the notion that such psychic trauma is necessary to the poetic voice.

A developmental psychologist such as Erik Erikson might argue that the ability to dramatize this kind of identity chaos is indicative of an exceptionally strong ego;[1] and indeed, in spite of a "cleaved" brain (and even because of it) the poet shows herself able to create. But the *content* of these poems is about an ego in crisis, and the style and structure of the poems reflect a trauma of articulation. This is all the more significant when we realize that Emily Dickinson is talking about herself. She is the divided country whose president has been assassinated; she is the heroine of the gothic terror story; she is the bearded lady. Her poems about civil war and identity conflict are metaphors for her own struggles with her identity as a woman artist.

It is true that Emily Dickinson herself denied that her lyric "I" had anything to do with her. "When I state myself, as the Representative of the Verse—" she told Thomas Wentworth Higginson, "it does not mean—me—but a supposed person" (*L*. II, pp. 411–12). But her disclaimer can be seen as a function of her ambivalence toward her own identity. In the mental landscape in Emily Dickinson's poetry, the persona is seen dodging yawning chasms and fissures as she flees the hound Identity, running from the self down the mind's "corridors" whose terrors surpass "Material Place" (670); identity is the Spider to the persona's Little Miss Muffet. Or else the persona wistfully lives without identity, as in "At last, to be identified!" (174). This poem presents the predicament wherein she is helpless to identify herself; its emphasis on "at last," suggests the intensity with which the speaker has yearned for recognition during her life. Only when she dies (and goes "Past Midnight! Past the Morning Star!/ Past Sunrise!") is she "identified." And though, significantly, she does not say as what, I strongly suspect that she means as a poet, since it is most probable that she will be identified as a writer only after her death, at which point her poems will be discovered. Dickinson essentially lived as an unknown, as regards her "true" identity as a poet, and in this poem, she presents a consciousness that has waited a lifetime for such identification.

These poems, which thematically vacillate between the persona's dread of self-revelation and her chafing to have her identity revealed, betray a particular ambivalence with regard to her self-image as a poet. Indeed, Dickinson seems to define poetic identity in terms of a woman's dependent role in her culture, a function of a man's notice and initiative. It makes sense that poetic identity would have to be conferred, and by men: the publishers, editors, and mentors responsible for delivering Emily Dickinson to a public. Dickinson uses the same terminology for poetic and sexual identification, showing that from her perspective, her career as a poet takes the same social configuration as a traditional woman's life. Her dominant image as poet is one of passive, patient protest against her helplessness, as a woman, to identify herself, or be identified when and on what terms she chooses.

Her feeling of dependence is addressed in many poems. For example,

> *He found my Being—set it up—*
> *Adjusted it to place—*
> *Then carved his name—upon it—*
> *And bade it to the East*
>
> *Be faithful—in his absence—*
> *And he would come again—*

[from 603]

But further evidence of this conceptualization of the poet self at the mercy of an omnipotent father/husband figure or "owner," and only a *receptacle* of identity, is "My Life had stood—a Loaded Gun—" (754). Like "At last, to be identified!" and "He found my Being," the metaphysical ballad narrates the occasion on which she gets identity:

> *My Life had stood—a Loaded Gun—*
> *In Corners—till a Day*
> *The Owner passed—identified—*
> *And carried Me away—*
>
> *And now We roam in Sovereign Woods—*
> *And now We hunt the Doe—*
> *And every time I speak for Him—*
> *The Mountains straight reply—*
>
> *And do I smile, such cordial light*
> *Upon the Valley glow—*
> *It is as a Vesuvian face*
> *Had let its pleasure through—*
>
> *And when at Night—Our good Day done—*
> *I guard My Master's Head—*

'Tis better than the Eider-Duck's
Deep Pillow—to have shared—

To foe of His—I'm deadly foe—
None stir the second time—
On whom I lay a Yellow Eye—
Or an emphatic Thumb—

Though I than He—may longer live
He longer must—than I—
For I have but the power to kill,
Without—the power to die—

I consider this allegory of identity to be one of Dickinson's most significant
poems, particularly because it illuminates Dickinson's attitudes toward herself
as an artist and the nature of the identity crisis described in so many of her
poems.[2] In her most brilliant metaphor for her poetic power as a woman, she is
a gun; potentially explosive, but again dependent, manipulated, passive, inanimate, and owned, an object whose "life," now past, has been as a tool, and
whose identity and value are a function of her serviceability as a weapon—and
her master's desire to use her. But although she is essentially passive, controlled, and activated at her owner's whim, she can be fatal if discharged. Her
power is latent and implied, however: without a master, she is impotent.

Structurally, the poem builds on the concept of power. Power is initially
defined as the ability to confer identity. Traditionally this power is dramatized
by the male figure who awakens female sexuality, as in Sleeping Beauty and
Prince Charming; but Dickinson gives the tale type a twist by having a "gun"
awakened to kill. As the persona becomes increasingly autonomous and animate, power is redefined: it becomes a function of an obedience that transcends
the master's ability to give orders.

As the poem begins, the persona is unrealized and useless until she is
"carried away"—out of control, possessed—and thus acquires "life" doing "The
Owner's" bidding. This definition of "life" is all the more telling when we
consider the use to which she is put and thus "lives": she can "speak." A gun
"reports" or speaks when it fires; of course, "speaks" also suggests the poet's
voice. The ability to "speak" in both senses depends upon the owner's need to
discharge his will. Because she can speak, the persona is able to establish a
more integrated relationship with her owner: the gun and the owner act in
harmony. This sense of a team spirit is reflected in the persona's identification
with her master to the point where she adopts a plural identity ("We hunt the
Doe—"). Although the persona feels no sense of division between herself and
her master, she reveals an essential ambivalence toward the poet self. Her
identity depends upon her ability to speak, but she is helpless to speak without
her owner, a fact that diminishes the poet's sense of autonomy when she creates.

Several interpretations are possible of this relationship between unrealized potential (for destructive power) and the activator of this potential. On the most basic level, the gun could represent a life that is unfulfilled without a relationship with a more powerful, masculine "master" figure. Then from the poet's perspective artistic potential requires the muse or inspiration to "carry one away." In this sense the Owner could represent those external events or forces that stimulate poetry, such as death or love. The notion of the Owner's power has sexual implications in that the masculine lover is traditionally seen as the bringer of fulfillment and identity to the as yet sexually unfulfilled woman. In each of these cases, the life as a loaded gun indicates a feminine persona. But the identity of this feminine persona is ambiguous because of the gun analogy. At the least, it would suggest that the feminine identity, like a loaded gun, has potential for power and destruction. A challenge to society's ideal woman is offered: the traditional woman lives a life standing in the "corner," but once identified, she is a dangerous tool of aggression and hostility. This image would not make sense unless we remember that as an artist Dickinson could see herself as a tool for expressing the anger of an omnipotent being such as God who would work *through* her. She is the medium of His wrath and His word, a kind of "hit man" as His spokesperson, shooting by speaking. But what makes this poem so interesting is that Dickinson will argue that the owner is ultimately not as powerful as the supposedly dependent artist. The owner is as helpless without the gun as the gun is without the owner. The gun becomes increasingly animate in stanzas three and four as a function of the owner's dependence as a hunter on the gun; his identity depends upon being able to use and possess it. Although the gun is only a tool, the phrase "My Master" implies a willing submission, a sensibility of will, on the gun's part. This supportive posture denoting the will of the gun is reinforced by the sinister image of the persona, whose "smile" is as destructive as an erupting volcano. The persona is ebullient with pleasure at the honor of guarding her master's head. She has all the loyalty and devotion of a dog or true soldier: duty is more desirable than personal comfort. The persona is increasingly prouder of the closeness she shares with her master. Her boasts about her eagerness to enforce wrath suggest a naive as well as hostile sensibility.

The necessity of protecting the Owner's head is a crucial concept in the poem. If the Owner cannot "speak" without the gun, and speaking is a function of the brain and motor system, perhaps the Owner and gun are integral parts of *one* sensibility. The Owner is the brain and the gun the complying body mechanism. Such division does characterize many poems. We see the persona's consciousness operating on intellectual, emotional, and physical levels, each controlled by an autonomous pesonality with its own specific gender. For example, there are a male Brain, neuter Mind, and female Heart, and a female Soul (which is ordered about by the brain and told to speak—see poem 410.) This colony of consciousness naturally wreaks havoc on the persona's sense of identity. Such dichotomy seems to be operating in this poem; only here there is the effort to reintegrate the varying aspects of consciousness. That the head must be guarded by the gun persona would indicate that the ability to speak (whether by writing poetry or shooting) functions as a means of mental defense. For some reason, the mind feels both angry and vulnerable: it attacks to protect itself. The Master/Owner figure is the persona's informing consciousness. The Owner has control over emotions, which suggests that the Owner is an artist objectifying and giving voice to anger and power. Speaking then is a defense in the most literal terms.

One implication of the notion that Dickinson's ability to speak protects her mind (or, in the image of the poem, that the gun's ability to kill protects her master) is that poetry is an important factor in the realization of identity. The ability to speak and have identity are shown to be synonymous functions, in that the gun and the Owner have equal power. If identity, or self-realization, depends upon speaking/shooting—that is, writing poetry—the *poet* is both gun and Owner. A gun does not work if the trigger is not pulled: the mind works upon the voice as a kind of finger.

Stanza five hints at the nature of the identity the persona wants to establish: an aggressive, destructive capability designed to strike out at foes, especially foes that threaten the mind of the informing consciousness ("To foe of His—I'm deadly foe"). The persona assumes, by way of her ability to speak, the identity of a judge or final arbiter. This status gives her legal authority and sanction to act out the destructive impulses of her mind-owner. She is both judge and executioner: punishment is meted out by speaking. It is as a poet, then, that she is able to strike out with impunity.

But in a larger sense, the power to create the word (to speak) is fatal. The persona achieves immortality, by virtue of the fact that she does have the "power to die." As a tool, of course, she does not have the power to live or die. But the relationship between "I" and "He" pivots on reversals of power:

> Though I than He—may longer live
> He longer must—than I—
> For I have but the power to kill,
> Without—the power to die—

He must live longer because He has the "power to die" as well as the power to confer life and identity. Dickinson was apparently fascinated with this paradox of artistic power. In an earlier poem she concluded: "Dying—annuls the power to kill" (358). Her persona has been rendered inanimate and lifeless by crisis, but has the consolation that one can undercut the power to kill by dying, in other words, by stripping the power of the killer and making him consequently impotent. Yet the power to kill is an attribute of the poet; Dickinson's persona in "My Life had stood—" conceives this power as a sign of *lack* of power. In both poems, the power to kill or create is undercut because this power depends upon being identified and brought to life. Thus, to be alive is to have power: and the corresponding power to die is a greater power than the power to kill and the ability *not* to die (that is, the power to create and the ability to become immortal). If, as I have asserted, the "I" in the poem refers to the artist's creative powers and "He" to her controlling mind, it would make sense that though the creative abilities endure once they are set into motion, they require the mind to set them in motion, or pull the trigger. The inference is that identification activates creative power; but this power to create (or, conversely, kill) cannot die of itself because (1) the product of creation, the word, is immortal, and (2) it possesses no power of its own to activate itself or deactivate itself. Only the mind can die, but the poetry it produces, while having the power to kill, lives on.

Finally, this poem sheds light on the nature of Dickinson's preoccupation with identity as it relates to her art. The persona's mind is male and "owns" her; the persona's relation to it is strictly passive and in this sense, traditionally "feminine," even as a gun. Identification as poet or even woman is shown to be out of her control. She can only project something outside of her (word, bullet) when she is recognized for this purpose. She has no inherent sense of identity or purpose herself, and even if she does, she cannot act on it. The conceptualization of the self as split into parts underscores the identity problems caused when one regards the brain as an autonomous bully one is at the mercy of, especially when one is so obviously vulnerable and hostile. Furthermore, if poetry is a masculine tool which the woman artist must use to express and realize herself, then having a gun speak for her only reinforces and perpetuates her ambivalent feelings as a supposedly passive woman. She gains power by writing poetry (shooting for her master), but her identity as a woman runs in direct conflict with her creation of poetry. Therefore, "speaking" for Dickinson creates psychic chaos.

What this poem most significantly represents, then, is an array of conflicting attitudes toward art and the self, which result in severe identity conflict. According to this poem, speaking is a powerful and destructive activity for women. Poetry is not creation so much as it is annihilation, and the poet is consequently portrayed by Dickinson in ambivalent terms. The poet is conceptualized as an enthusiastic, grateful killer, perhaps because Dickinson has projected onto her persona venomous impulses of revenge that can only be safely discharged through the word. One can speculate about what this means: as a woman, Dickinson is not supposed to be "fed up" or even potentially dangerous. She must not be a real woman after all, if she writes poetry and thereby expresses power and anger. Thus, in her poem, a persona is created who speaks, but who speaks helplessly, and "for him." She expresses *his* will, not her own, although she is in full accord with "his" wishes. Such maneuvering is a kind of legal defense for the "gun" aspect of her poetic career, but it also indicates that she feels she has no identity or voice apart from an Owner/Master. She cannot be autonomous as a poet.

DISPOSSESSED: WHEN IDENTITY IS ALIEN

The kind of psychological damage a woman incurs who insists on being a poet is seen in the first stanza of poem 1737:

> *Rearrange a "Wife's" affection!*
> *When they dislocate my Brain!*
> *Amputate my freckled Bosom!*
> *Make me bearded like a man!*

Dickinson fantasizes that her own autopsy will reveal her true nature as masculine, presumably because she has been writing poetry, which until her death will have been a "Big . . . Secret." The anguish and hysteria the persona feels can be seen as reflective of Dickinson's conflict as an unrecognized and guilty woman poet.

While "Rearrange a 'Wife's' affection!" dramatizes the ambivalence the persona feels about her sexuality as a poet, "I felt my life . . ." describes her alienation from her very being:

> *I felt my life with both my hands*
> *To see if it was there—*
> *I held my spirit to the Glass,*
> *To prove it possibler—*
>
> *I turned my Being round and round*
> *And paused at every pound*
> *To ask the Owner's name—*
> *For doubt, that I should know the Sound—*

[from 351]

Thus she describes herself pathetically, or comically, trying to feel for herself with her hands, looking into a mirror to apply the traditional test for breath by holding a glass over her mouth to see if vapor, evidence of expiration, appears. Each of these tests relies on externally derived evidence. Having to resort to these tactics reveals not a physical but a psychological numbness. As in "My Life had stood," she is possessed by an unknown Owner, dispossessed of herself: the result is her sensation of being dead, in "Heaven."

Dickinson describes this existential dilemma in other poems. She hazards a hesitant "I am alive—I guess—" (470), but as she suspects, when she regards herself in the mirror, her eyes confront only "wastes" (458) and "Blank . . . steady Wilderness—." Regarding herself in the mirror, the persona comes to the awareness that the perceived and perceiving selves are as interdependent as the owner/subject relationship in "My Life had stood" or in "Drama's Vitallest

Expression" (741). In these poems, identity is fate—in fact, a "hound" one cannot escape:

> *This Consciousness that is aware*
> *Of Neighbors and the Sun*
> *Will be the one aware of Death*
> *And that itself alone*
>
> *Is traversing the interval*
> *Experience between*
> *And most profound experiment*
> *Appointed unto Men—*
>
> *How adequate unto itself*
> *Its properties shall be*
> *Itself unto itself and none*
> *Shall make discovery.*
>
> *Adventure most unto itself*
> *The Soul condemned to be—*
> *Attended by a single Hound*
> *Its own identity.*
>
> [822]

The extent to which consciousness is traumatized is stressed by the depersonalized references to the self. Consciousness is presented here in emphatically neuter terms: "It" or "itself" dominate the poem not only by repetition but by the syntax.

"COULD IT BE MADNESS–THIS?"—DAILY ANARCHY

Dickinson's topical treatment of identity casts light on her split, fragmented, or plural sense of self; sexual inconsistency and division; the self as alien to "itself"; and the distance from the self expressed in terms of pronoun substitutions (he, that, one, some, this, we, it, her). What is especially significant is that these pronouns refer to the inanimate as well as the animate. Such reference to a vegetable self implies that consciousness and mental and emotional faculties are inoperative. Furthermore, many of the poems are characterized by a dead persona, and often there is no persona at all, suggesting a kind of mental absence or madness. These symptomatic aspects of Dickinson's persona often appear in poems that deal either explicitly or implicitly with madness, which seems to be the result, or extreme degree of, identity crisis.

For example, in "I never hear that one is dead" (1323), Dickinson describes the "Daily mind" tilling its abyss—her term for the artist who utilizes her consciousness of pain. This mind "Had Madness . . . once or twice": and consciousness *causes* the madness. A similar configuration is seen in 410, where consciousness plays a role which renders the mind and voice inoperative:

> *The first Day's Night had come–*
> *And grateful that a thing*
> *So terrible–had been endured–*
> *I told my Soul to sing–*
>
> *She said her Strings were snapt–*
> *Her Bow–to Atoms blown–*
> *And so to mend her–gave me work*
> *Until another Morn–*
>
> *And then–a Day as huge*
> *As Yesterdays in pairs,*
> *Unrolled its horror in my face–*
> *Until it blocked my eyes–*
>
> *My Brain–begun to laugh–*
> *I mumbled–like a fool–*
> *And tho' 'tis Years ago–that Day–*
> *My Brain keeps giggling–still.*
>
> *And Something's odd–within–*
> *That person that I was–*
> *And this One–do not feel the same–*
> *Could it be Madness–this?*

Again, we see a drama of identity conflict, narrated by the artist persona. There is a division in the self's consciousness between "I" (master), "my Soul" (female), and "my Brain." Not only is the operating self split into three parts, but there is civil war: the parts are not cooperating, and the master persona is not in control. As before, the artist is revealed as dependent on a speaking mechanism. When she orders her soul to sing, much as the Master/Owner compels the gun to speak in poem 754, presumably to preserve her mental faculties, the soul cannot comply ("She said her Strings were snapt–"). The role of the soul is analogous to the poet's gun "speaking" which can discharge bullets or lullaby. But because the soul has been ravaged, she cannot help the informing consciousness celebrate surviving a "Day." Her helpfulness sapped by the very forces the persona has defeated, the soul can no longer guard the Master's head. Needing to defend the vulnerable mind, the self sets out to repair the soul. But she too is overcome by "horror" and is blinded ("blocked my eyes"). Meanwhile the brain is a passive onlooker who only laughs. Indeed, the brain appears to be the ultimate victim, because the soul's inability to sing causes the brain to succumb to hysteria. A chain reaction ensues so that the self—the narrator of the poem—records itself mumbling "like a fool." It is indeed able to narrate what has transpired, but we see the cost. The self is detached from the Brain, which has been rendered permanently useless. Even with this sense of detachment, the giggling Brain gives the persona the sense that "within," things are still "odd." "That person that I was–and This one–do not feel the same–". She wonders if this sense of dissociation from her former self is "Madness." When pain or suffering are too intense, the ability to "sing" is lost, and one's psychological condition becomes aggravated. Peace is a product of singing, speaking, and shooting: it is a function of art.

In this light, it is interesting to note that the persona's ability to speak or sing has not been affected by the brain's debility. For Dickinson, poetic ability is not a function of consciousness or intellect; the brain is necessary neither for speaking nor seeing. In both this poem and "My Life had stood– . . ." the owner of the self is shown to be dependent on a speaking or singing mechanism for a "voice" that expresses and identifies the self. Singing in turn depends upon being identified (in "My Life had stood–") and being healthy (in "The first Day's Night"). The schism in consciousness is between the parts of the self we ordinarily associate as integral aspects of the creative process: brain, eyes, voice, mind. Although Dickinson has elsewhere argued for madness as "wholesome" (1333) and "divinest sense" (435), her use of madness in the majority of poems shows it disorienting the senses and leaving the self so stricken that self-expression is impossible.

"To try to speak, and miss the way" (1617) is one of Dickinson's last poems. At fifty-four years old, Dickinson is still describing the problem of trying to express herself (as a man); she feels unable to because her soul is a "Mutineer" who refuses to be subjugated. The compromise that the self makes is that it then tries, instead of "speaking," to conceal its problems:

> *To try to speak, and miss the way*
> *And ask it of the Tears,*
> *Is Gratitude's sweet poverty,*
> *The Tatters that he wears–*
>
> *A better Coat if he possessed*
> *Would help him to conceal,*
> *Not subjugate, the Mutineer*
> *Whose title is "the Soul."*

In spite of its "bandaged moments," Emily Dickinson's soul has autonomy: it speaks, hears, stands, entertains visitors, and shuts the door. It is her persona's antagonist ("My Soul–accused me–And I quailed–", 753), perhaps because she wants to "own the art within the soul" (855).

This division of sensible organs includes the heart. Numerous poems describe her rather comic predicament at the mercy of an autonomous heart: "Heart!" she implores, "We will forget him!/You and I–tonight!" (47). Her heart has its own consciousness (78, 1290, 1413), doubts in "sweet skepticism" (5, 1413), speaks after "great pain" (341), is attended by a whimpering hound (186), and is itself "subdivided" (655). Not only is the heart a willful personality whose support she must enlist in order to function, but it can be an alien presence that dispossesses her. In "Father–I bring thee–not Myself–"(one version of 217), for example, she describes herself jilted first by being invaded, and then ruptured by an alien heart. We see her approach God, not on her own behalf, but for her heart. Her heart is a tyrannical being whose supremacy she accepts. In poem 1354 the physical and psychological anatomy is shuffled so that the heart is the "Capital of the Mind," which by itself is a "single State," but which the heart expands into a "Continent." The Mind's diminished role in the functioning of the persona is shown in "The Mind lives on the Heart/Like any Parasite" (1355).

Presenting the soul, heart, and mind as distinct entities is a convention, and the dialogue between flesh and spirit, for example, is a traditional literary form. But Dickinson conceives heart, mind, and soul as vying factions of a paralyzing civil war within the poet. The chronicles of the war within herself rage through the poetry. No side wins, no issue is resolved. The strain results in what she describes as the death of identity; little remains except a disembodied voice, the voice of impasse and defeat, as in poem 1576:

> *The Spirit lasts–but in what mode–*
> *Below, the Body speaks,*
> *But as the Spirit furnishes–*
> *Apart, it never talks–*

Again, we see the dependence of the voice upon an outer force, the spirit and flesh essentially detached, a trauma of identity and alienation that the pronominal disorder and syntactic structure reflect:

> *What would the Either be?*
> *Does that know–now–or does it cease–*
> *That which to this is done,*
> *Resuming at a mutual date*
> *With every future one?*

In fact the pronouns are so depersonalized (the Either, that, it, which, this, one) that the poem hardly makes sense. Such writing illustrates the kind of obscurity that has both frustrated and challenged Dickinson's readers. But this is not to say that each pronoun, beginning with the awkward "the Either," does not have a specific reference. The poem is a metaphysical discussion of the relationship between the body's speaking apparatus and informing consciousness.

As even this poem makes clear, the artist is able to record, often with diarylike precision, the various stages of madness, crisis, disorientation of senses, and ruptures within her mind. She can "sing" even while her mind or brain is supposedly inoperative. Thus we have poems such as "I felt a Cleaving in my Mind" (937), "I felt a Funeral, in my Brain" (280), "I stepped from Plank to Plank" (875), "If ever the lid gets off my head" (1727), and "I've dropped my Brain–My Soul is numb–" (1046).[3] For example:

> *I felt a Cleaving in my Mind–*
> *As if my Brain had split–*
> *I tried to match it–Seam by Seam–*
> *But could not make them fit.*
>
> *The thought behind, I strove to join*
> *Unto the thought before–*
> *But Sequence ravelled out of Sound*
> *Like Balls–upon a Floor.*
>
> [937]

We must remember that the persona is narrating her defeat in putting her mind back together, using the domestic imagery of sewing up her torn thoughts. She is disoriented, unable to integrate what she has been ("thought before") and was ("thought behind"). In "The first Day's Night" (410) she had described the dilemma in similar terms: "That person that I was–/And This One–do not feel the same–" and she concluded that this was "Madness." "I felt a Cleaving," like "The first Day's Night," shows that she is able to function as an artist despite, or perhaps because of, the dysfunction of her brain, her mind, and even her soul.

Dickinson often uses domestic imagery to describe her interior landscape, juxtaposing environmental catastrophe and feminine solutions. Just as she tries to sew up the rent fabric of her mind, in poem 858 she is tempted "to stitch it up"—a comic idea given the enormity of the ruptures and her suicidal state of mind. Within are chasms, fissures, gaping sides of tombs, and growing turbulence. To repair herself, however, would mean "Death" to "Him," a masculine component within her that needs psychic wounds. Because of "him" she must endure a life of mental pain and divided consciousness.

Therefore while the voice of the poet is anguished, it is operative, and even seems to be fueled by the distress caused by its own fragmentation and ruptures in sensibility. We see this in "A doubt if it be Us/Assists the staggering Mind" (859); and in "Had we our senses/But perhaps 'tis well they're not at Home" (1284). In "If ever the lid gets off my head" (1727), a poem about madness and mental debility, the persona is shown to be unable to control her brain, a "fellow" who will go "where he belonged!" and the world will then see "how far from home/It is possible for sense to live/The soul there–all the time."

In "I felt a Funeral, in my Brain" (280), she hears "Mourners" treading "till it seemed/That Sense was breaking through–" and "I thought/My Mind was going numb." The persona is so detached that she is able to describe the burial of her consciousness and senses. It is important to note that the deceased is plural, "some strange Race" which is "wrecked, solitary, here." In other words, the persona describes the death of a multiple self. She continues:

> And then a Plank in Reason, broke,
> And I dropped down, and down–
> And hit a World, at every plunge,
> And Finished knowing–then–

The persona is able to chronicle her own demise, to record her experience after death and madness, when her reason and sensory faculties have "Finished knowing." No longer able to think or to remember, she is yet the survivor as the artist. Poems proceed in aftermath when the mind is debilitated: the artist is totally detached from her informing consciousness. It is a humiliating, if comic, situation Dickinson describes. In fact, even "Myself" is a sneering antagonist she appeals to in vain (904). Consisting of bullying "Me's" who taunt her with her lack of control over them by saying "Thou hast not Me, nor Me," "Myself" is an "it." In the face of the self's jeers, the narrator is humbled into obsequious acknowledgment of vulnerability: "My need–was all I had–I said."

Dickinson describes the objectification of the self through art as a function, then, of a divided sensibility where the persona actively seems to rid herself of her alien antagonistic self. In "Me from Myself–to banish–/Had I Art–" (642), she puns with the word "art" to equate therapeutic skill with a poet's abilities. It is through her poetry that she can flee the intolerable division within. However, to destroy this enemy called "Myself" is futile:

> But since Myself–assault Me–
> How have I peace
> Except by subjugating
> Consciousness?

Much as she has a sensibility of schism, she never harbors the illusion that she can be separated from all her alien selves. Thus there can be no solution to her dilemma as she defines it. She is stuck with her sense of herself as a despised alien being, for without this consciousness, the self loses meaning and disintegrates: "And since We're mutual Monarch," there can be no resolution unless one of the selves abdicates: "Abdication–/Me–of Me?" She is trapped in a plural identity by her need of her alien self: her psychological conflict is perpetuated.

Although the persona interprets her heart's, soul's, and brain's anarchies as a defeat for her senses, and although she may reject herself in substantive ways (268, "Me, change! Me, alter!"), she also acknowledges her "need" of a consciousness tormented by antagonism directed against itself. In this way, her identity conflict is revealed as necessary to her art. This is why "Myself" cannot be destroyed, miserable as "he," "it," or "they" make her. Describing the persona's mind as engaged in civil war may be a metaphor for the creation process that depends upon identity conflict. As long as the war manifests itself in madness and dissociation of sensibility, the general-poet exists. Therefore peace can never be declared, or the "self" banished, because the conflict fuels the poems.

The incongruity of a speaker who relates disaster stories about herself could reduce the dramatic power of the poems unless the persona is seen as the prevailing poet. The poems have argued that the ability to speak is a function of the voice's estrangement from the brain. The rejection of the self that induces identity conflict also creates the distance necessary for art which objectifies—or banishes—the self.

I have felt it important to establish the terms in which we may consider Dickinson's supposed person as representative of herself, because examining her poetry as the voice of one persona introduces compelling evidence of Dickinson's identity conflict. But once we identify Dickinson with these peculiar and even pathological poems, we are faced with trying to understand why she conceptualized her plight in these terms. We need to know why she portrays identity as a function of a relationship with a master who owns (if not tortures) her, why identity is synonymous with madness and death, why consciousness is fragmented, disjointed, inanimate, masculine, and so divided into autonomous organic senses that it becomes dysfunctional, why the interior landscape is a surrealistic badlands of ruptures and chasms where brains giggle and funeral parties shuffle over a grave in which the poet lies, clinically taking notes of the proceedings.

What experience are these poems metaphors for? We turn to Dickinson's life to see; and if the identity crisis so forcefully portrayed in the poems is merely an artistic ploy, we must explore the implications of an aesthetic theory that insists on a self in crisis. Dickinson continued the civil war in her poetry, making the most, from a poet's point of view, of every interior skirmish, every humiliation, every wound, every death. She once said that her poems were "full of Opera," and as in operas, again and again the poet heroine gets up after being mortally wounded to sing arias about her plight. Why in these terms, and why at all?

PART TWO

The Daughter Construct

"And I wonder who I am,
And what has made me so"

A Portrait of the Poet-to-Be

Emily Dickinson's letters provide invaluable insight into the imagery and ideology of the identity poems. Although scholars such as David Higgins are frustrated with the content of the letters ("The trouble with Emily's letters is that they are so long, so full of domestic detail. Only at rare moments are there glimpses of the poet-to-be"),[1] we cannot dissociate her formative poetic development from her descriptions of her feelings when she is washing dishes or playing hooky from the Sewing Society or watching her sister dust the stairs. Her "domestic detail" is not incidental or even antithetical to her poetic achievement. Perhaps for other writers it could be argued that the world of the house is but a transient stage in their literary development, having superfically little to do with the formation of their artistic sensibility and evolving career. But Emily Dickinson had no years other than her domestic ones.

It may seem incongruous that Dickinson could transcend a conventional destiny as a woman to write a new kind of largely unsentimental, unconventional poetry when she was so immersed in the orthodoxies of living at home, caring for her invalid mother, and baking her father's daily bread. But the letters in which Dickinson reveals her feelings as a daughter provide a clue to her self-image as a poet, and we can only feel fortunate that they are "so long." However, Emily Dickinson did share David Higgins's notions about the incongruity of the poetic being juxtasposed with the domestic: no one was more worried than she that "domestic detail" might obscure the mind of the poet. Although her household routine did not prevent her poetry, her letters show how her position as daughter threatened her poetic identity. A major theme of her early letters is how inappropriate it is for a person of her capabilities and poetic sensibility to be confined to the feminine-domestic realm of experience. Yet her poetic aspirations made havoc of her self-image as a woman. The identity poems showing Dickinson's sense of herself as a neuter freak differ only in degree from letters in which she describes her mind and spirits at war over her refusal to accept the role of a traditional woman, in her house or out of it.

Therefore, the "domestic"—we may even say feminist—letters she wrote during her formative years, which do not seem either relevant or important to her critics, express Emily Dickinson's sense of the fundamental dilemma of the woman who sacrifices a feminine life in order to be "great." These letters depicting her rebellious sensibility as a daughter not only give us a portrait of the "poet-to-be," then, but provide a portrait of the mature poet as well, whose problems are so vividly represented in the identity poems.

Emily Dickinson's identity as a daughter is defined by her relationships with her parents; by tracing first her relationship with her mother, then that with her father, the pattern of the daughter construct will emerge, a construct that encompasses not only the significance and genesis of the identity poems, but the configuration of Dickinson's life and poetry as a whole.

The Mother Matrix

I Never Had a Mother[2]

Emily Dickinson's mother, the first "Emily Dickinson," lived until her daughter Emily was fifty-one years old, and was the person with whom the younger Emily shared the most intimate—perhaps even the *only* intimate—contact of her adult daily life. The last ten years of her life, Mrs. Dickinson was an invalid tended exclusively by her daughter Emily: mother and daughter literally constituted the other's community. The two occupied the upstairs day and night.

Yet we tend to overlook the reality of their relationship, because Dickinson obscures its nature and even its existence. In the poetry, Mrs. Dickinson seems to be absent in name, concept, theme, image, metaphor, and biographical fact. And in the letters, she fares no better. We glimpse her only occasionally, and then as the butt of jokes or the target of overt and covert complaints. She is patronized by her daughter as a mouther of clichés, one who does not "care for thought" (*L*. II, p. 404). But, most interesting of all, even though we see Emily Dickinson complaining about her mother, she also describes her, paradoxically, as absent. There are explicit denials of her very existence: "I never had a mother"; "I always ran Home to Awe when a child, if anything befell me. He was an awful Mother, but I liked him better than none". Dickinson has no one but her sister to dress her, to tell her right from wrong; she even asks an editor she has never met to advise her "how to grow" since she has "none to ask"; and she complains to her brother, "how to grow up I don't know" (*L*. II, p. 475, 517–18, 508, 403–4; I, p. 241).

It is not surprising, then, that most studies have dismissed Mrs. Dickinson as irrelevant to her daughter's development as a poet. So cleverly has Dickinson covered up her mother's import that scholars poring over her work for clues to the mystery of how she ever became a poet have come up with every influence but her mother. Only John Cody, who as a psychiatrist knows better, has dealt with Mrs. Dickinson as a significant figure, and his approach is hypothetical—from the viewpoint of the analyst to whom Emily Dickinson has presumably come for help with her psychosexual psychoses. More recently, Jean Mudge and Richard B. Sewall (1974) have paid attention to the mother—and her ostensible relative insignificance. Jean Mudge establishes a link between mother and daughter on the basis that each liked to stay at home, was inclined to be homesick, and had a green thumb.[3] But there was more to this maternal legacy than these shared traits, and the mother's role in Dickinson's poetic development remains obscure. In the light of what we know about the significance of a mother in any person's development, especially a woman's, we should not take a daughter at her word when she says she never had a mother. Understanding the mother-daughter relationship is crucial if we are to determine how the seeds of Dickinson's childhood experience flowered later in her letters and art, for the mother has great impact on the development of a child's social and sexual identity. Therefore the fact that we are told there *is* no mother, particularly in light of the identity poems, becomes doubly significant.

There are several circumstances which mandate a re-examination of the role her mother played in Dickinson's development. Emily Dickinson's first recorded words were spoken during her first trip away from home, when she was two. Enroute to her aunt's, in the midst of a lightning storm, her request was polite but to the point: "Do take me to my mother."[4] But Emily was being sent to visit her aunt because Mrs. Dickinson was recuperating from the birth of Lavinia—a trauma for Emily in itself. When her mother died, Dickinson spoke of her own "sorrowing gluttony"; and her last recorded words about her mother, written soon after her mother's death, were, "To have *had* a Mother—how mighty!" (*L*. III, p. 892). Dickinson's emotional attachment to her mother is indicated by the value she places on the word "mother": " 'Mother'! what a name!"; and " 'Mother,' to me, is so sacred a Name, I take even that of the 'Seraphim' with less hallowed significance—"; and "Oh, Vision of Language!" (*L*. III, pp. 747, 752, 748).

Coming at the beginning and ending of her life as they do, these statements frame an otherwise blank or vandalized mother-daughter portrait. While I am examining Dickinson's attitudes toward her mother and the attempts she makes to deny her, we should keep these latter statements in mind, for they are variants, not contradictions, of "I never had a mother" and "Awe" was "an awful Mother, but . . . better than none" (*L*. II, p. 518).[5] Together, the statements reveal that it is a *longing* for a mother that Dickinson expresses; Dickinson's ambivalent attitude may be a function of her yearning either for her primal relationship with her mother,[6] or else for a mother she has never had.[7]

As John Cody has pointed out, such a viewpoint may be supported by the scores of poems in which Dickinson speaks of being deprived of food: "I had been hungry, all the Years" (579); "Deprived of other Banquet/I entertained Myself—" (773);

> *It would have starved a Gnat—*
> *To live so small as I—*
> *And yet I was a living Child—*
> *With Food's necessity*
>
> [from 612][8]

In these deprivation poems, the idea of starving is linked with the childhood experience, and statements in her letters corroborate this association: "The ravenousness of fondness is best disclosed by children. . . . Is there not a sweet wolf within us that demands its food?" (*L*. III, p. 777). Dickinson's association of food, love, and childhood is significant in what it reveals about her attitudes toward—and her experience with—her mother. The references to a hungry childhood give weight to Dickinson's portrayal of herself as a motherless child, especially when she alludes to childhood maternal loss, as she does in a late letter: "No Verse in the Bible has frightened me so much from a Child as 'from him that hath not, shall be taken even that he hath.' Was it because it's dark menace deepened our own Door? You speak as if you still missed your Mother" (*L*. III, pp. 751–52). Why would Dickinson imply that she felt she suffered from feeling she "hath not" as a child? Did she feel her own "Door" was darkened by maternal absence? Her confession is in response to her correspondent's talking about her mother in a nostalgic way ("You speak as if you still missed your Mother"). Dickinson follows with a confession about her feelings concerning her own mother's death—she cannot "conjecture a form of space without her timid face" (*L*. II, p. 508).

Mother, love, and food are more or less inseparable concepts in the infant's mind. Developmental psychologists stress the importance of the mother-child interaction during breastfeeding and weaning: food becomes a mode of mediating the relationship. Dickinson explicitly will equate food and love: "Tenderness . . . is the only food that the Will takes" (*L*. II, p. 445); "God keeps His Oath to Sparrows–/Who of little Love–know how to starve–" (690); "Affection is like bread, unnoticed till we starve, and then we dream of it, and sing of it, and paint it. . . ." (*L*. II, p. 445; II, p. 499). Perhaps Dickinson's response to lack of nurturing love is to "dream . . . sing . . . paint it": to use her conscious imagination to ease her hunger. Her letters and poems can be her "dream-song portraits" of hunger and maternal loss. Such an interpretation has a basis in some psycholinguistic theory. The child's gradual acquisition and use of language reflects the dynamics of the early mother-child relationship which revolves, logically, around food and nurture. Language, we think, is first used as a response to the child's sense of separation from, or hunger for, the mother: the word is both an acknowledgment of loss and an instrument of power.[9] Certainly, in her poems and letters Dickinson uses language in both these ways. Out of the "earliest catastrophe" we know—being weaned, according to Erikson—comes our motivation to use words and our permanent sense of mourning and nostalgia.

Dickinson may be inventing the childhood depicted in the poems and letters, but it is significant that in her imagination, deprivation (especially oral) and childhood are associated. Even if Dickinson's description of her deprivation is metaphoric, so that the food she lacks can be God's spiritual grace, for example, or society's esteem and encouragement, her persona is the unsatisfied hungry child—her pain is drawn in terms of a malfunction in the mother-child relationship.

Since there is no empirical evidence that Dickinson ever was physically starved, we are faced with surmising that Dickinson lacked primary forms of nourishment, which reflects on her relationship with her mother. And in fact, psychologists have concluded that Emily Dickinson did experience maternal rejection. John Cody argues that Dickinson expresses a yearning for a mother because her mother "cruelly" rejected her at some crucial stage in her development.[10] However, as Erik Erikson admits, the psychologists' "occupational prejudice is the rejecting mother . . . ; 'Mom' is blamed for everything."[11] The problem with psycholinguistic theory is that since so much stress is placed upon the mother's role, the mother is inevitably the villain, just as the butler is always the culprit in a murder mystery.

I am not saying that her mother was not a crucial factor in Emily Dickinson's literary development, but I think that it was what Mrs. Dickinson *represented* as much as her actual behavior that made Dickinson into a self-declared orphan claiming to reject or not to have experienced maternal nurture. As Dickinson's letters show, she was only too aware of her mother's significance. Not only was she dependent upon her mother for nurture and guidance, but as daughter she was expected to identify with her mother in physical, social, and sexual ways. While her older brother Austin could anticipate emulating a man who was important in the eyes of the world, a local and national public figure (Edward Dickinson was a U.S. Congressman, prominent in the affairs of Amherst College and in town and state politics), Dickinson's same-sex role model was perceived by Dickinson as an "anxious-dependent" servant of her family who was dominated, disregarded, weak, passive, dull, occupied with petty charity and housework, and conventionally pious. Friends describe Mrs. Dickinson as too busy for letters, fluttering, timid, meek, and plaintive. Apparently she did at least once display "decision of character" and an "air of authority and *independence*"—in her husband's words—and Edward Dickinson thought that unusual enough to report it to the world, "with amusement."[12] Knowing that the growing daughter cannot help but identify with her mother at least physically and emotionally, we must try to imagine the pain it caused the daughter to see her mother belittled and patronized, dismissed as a physical and emotional invalid whose attempts at mothering "failed sadly" and whose life was so insignificant that her son is reported to have said that her death barely "caused a ripple."[13]

Mrs. Dickinson was the prototype of the "ideal woman," as Dickinson's father once remarked, "modest and unassuming."[14] Describing the traits a woman should have, Edward Dickinson included amiability, virtue, prudence, and benevolence—not power, authority, independence, initiative, or a willingness to risk—and not moods of anger, selfishness, or stubbornness; not those qualities that Dickinson cultivated for her self-image in her letters and poetry. Edward Dickinson's opinions of what a wife should be—and he was explicit in these opinions from his courtship on—were acted upon dutifully by his wife. Mrs. Dickinson, Sewall writes, "apparently fitted without friction into the traditional pattern of dominant husband and sweet submissive wife, with both [spouses] recognizing a still higher authority, duty—to each other, children, community, and God."[15] It is this masculine ideal of femininity, so successfully assumed by her mother, that Dickinson rejected. Sewall writes, "Just how dominant Edward became and whether his wife's submissiveness became so abject as to degrade her in the eyes of the children . . . are questions that still, I think, remain open."[16] According to conventional nineteenth-century standards, Dickinson's mother was a "perfect" wife; but Emily Dickinson saw the world's contempt for this dutiful woman whose conformity was held against her (so that her husband scoffed when she acted with self-confidence). Dickinson confronted the paradox that although her mother lived up to society's ideal, "it was in the bosom of her family"[17] that she was most unappreciated, neglected by her husband and ridiculed by her children.

The tragic irony is that Mrs. Dickinson's adherence to the spirit of her husband's domestic requirements deprived her children—in the eyes of her daughter Emily—of a mother who could teach them "how to grow." The qualities that made her a perfect wife and mother were the very qualities that made Dickinson believe she was not adequately nurtured and that being a wife was not a suitable occupation. We can see how duty conflicts with mothering when we consider a book that Edward Dickinson gave to his wife when Emily was three years old. Entitled *The Mother at Home: The Principles of Maternal Duty*, the manual promulgates maternal "duty," which entails not encouraging vanity by acting too approving; children must never be allowed to think that they are great. Rather, the mother must be sure that the children obey and that all tendencies toward insubordination are checked. As a dutiful wife, Mrs. Dickinson was bound to have taken its precepts seriously; Jean Mudge tells us that the book's pages are worn and pressed with flowers. John Cody says that "For Abbott," (the author of the book), "the obedience of the child—even if bought at the price of fear, a sense of sin and unworthiness, and the suppression of natural impulses—is the mother's highest achievement."[18]

Thus we will see Dickinson summing up her childhood experience in terms of disobedience and maternal reproof, which she had the insight to see was delivered only perfunctorily; of course, this did not foster Dickinson's respect for her mother's authority. Dickinson wrote, "Two things have I lost with Childhood—the rapture of losing my shoe in the Mud and going Home barefoot . . . and the mothers reproof which was . . . more for my sake than her weary own for she frowned with a smile" (*L.* III, pp. 928–29). Disobedience elicits attention from the mother, which is necessary for the child, even if the attention is manifested in dutiful disapproval. Again, we see Dickinson's insight into the limitations placed upon her mother in her dutiful role when she gives an excuse for her sister's not having written a letter: "Vinnie's middle name restrained her loving pen" (*L*. III, p. 691). Lavinia's middle name was "Norcross," her mother's maiden name. Thus the mother's conception of duty keeps her from writing letters and expressing literary affection.

But what, then, was Emily Dickinson going to be, and with whom was she to identify, if not this self-same wife and mother whom society, church, parents, and school were all training her to become? When Dickinson wrote "how to grow up, I don't know," she was expressing the dilemma resulting from her reluctance to identify with her mother and grow up dutifully as a conventional woman. In her perpetual daughterhood, she rejected her mother's role by not becoming her, and Dickinson's "mourning" a mother should therefore be viewed from the perspective of her literary ambitions.

Emily Dickinson's literary occupation enabled her to escape her mother's fate. Generally speaking, children use language as a proclamation of "separation anxiety"; the child can also use language to express herself in her own right, for better or worse. Psycholinguistic theory stresses that the acquisition of language serves a dual, conflicting function. The word brings the child back into communication with the parents and society, and it also provides the means by which the child can assert her autonomy and independence. She can express herself as an individual, defined by her difference—or separation—from those around her, distinguishing, in Emerson's phrase, the "Me" from the "Not Me."[19] The mother's absence, whether real or contrived, then, enables the child to discover that the mother-nurturing figure is the "Not Me." In Emily Dickinson's case, we see that she used language to separate herself from her mother, while at the same time her informing consciousness as a writer functioned as a mother-hungry daughter.

Throughout her letters, Dickinson engaged in a verbal struggle to dissociate herself from her mother. Emily Dickinson insisted, for example, that her correspondents know that her mother meant little to her. When her father died, home was no longer "home" to her, in spite of her mother's presence. To Higginson, she explained, "When Father lived I remained with him because he would miss me–Now, Mother is helpless–a holier demand–" (*L*. II, pp. 526, 538, 542; III, pp. 716, 675). The impression she gave was that she indulged her father willingly, while she had to take care of her mother whether she wanted to or not. Although she committed herself to her mother's care, she emphasized the emotional distance between them in her letters. While we see that Dickinson had been traumatized by her father's death, she was able to describe her mother's last moments, and was even gently witty, associating her mother's favorite saying ("like a bird") with the death: "It never occurred to us that though she had not Limbs, she had *Wings*" (*L*. III, p. 746). It seems incredible that Dickinson could have been detached enough to be witty about death and about her mother's paralysis. Similarly, when her mother had a dental problem that made her face so swollen she could not see out of one eye, Dickinson describes her face as "a face that would take a premium at any cattle-show in the land . . . Doubtless we are 'fearfully and wonderfully made,' and occasionally grotesquely" (*L*. II, p. 428).

In a further effort to dissociate herself from her mother, Emily Dickinson made her mother largely absent from her chronicles of her intellectual and spiritual life. When Dickinson does mention her, it is with gentle humor as she records and makes fun of her mother's use of clichés: *cold as ice, like a bird, turn over a new leaf* ("I call that the Foliage Admonition") (*L*. I, pp. 111, 137–38; II, p. 622)—asserting her independence and disapproval of her mother's limited mental and moral conventionality, especially regarding expectations for women which the other tries to enforce. For example, when Dickinson transgresses some expectation for feminine obedience or cleanliness—what she will call acting like a "boy"—and is told by her mother to "turn over a new leaf," Dickinson equates the mind using the cliché with the mind urging her to sexual conformity in ladylike behavior. In the process of pointing this out, Dickinson juxtaposes her own poetic sensibility against her mother's common mind, so that the reader can discern the intellectual and artistic difference between the two Emily Dickinsons. Dickinson told Higginson her mother did not "care for thought" and referred to her mother's disappointment in a lecture which was "too high for her unobtrusive faculties" (*L*. II, p. 454; I, pp. 116, 137–38). Mocking her mother's narrow piety and sense of propriety was a way of promoting her own superior mental capabilities. Thus she documents sophisticated and witty conversations of hers that her mother considers "very improper" in order to show how shallow her mother is; she writes to Mrs. Holland that she and her brother were talking about the "Extension of Consciousness, after Death and Mother told Vinnie afterward, she thought it was 'very improper.' She forgets that we are past 'Correction in Righteousness'–I dont know what she would think if she knew that Austin told me confidentially 'there was no such person as Elijah!'" (*L*. III, p. 667). Other letters patronize her mother. Spending her time on "Mother's dear little wants" consumes her whole day. She has to read to her, fan her, comfort her, and explain "*why* 'the Grasshopper is a Burden'–because it is not as new a grasshopper as it was–this is so ensuing, that I hardly have said, 'Good Morning, Mother,' when I hear myself saying, 'Mother,–Good Night–' " (*L*. III, p. 675). Dickinson was fifty when she wrote this complaint, and fifty-one when she complained of her "Gymnastic Destiny" in taking care of her mother (*L*. III, p. 687). When she was forty, she was insisting that she was "so hurried with Parents that I run all Day with my tongue abroad, like a Summer Dog" (*L*. II, p. 333). The fact that Dickinson was still defining herself as a rebellious daughter at an age when her contemporaries were grandmothers indicates the extent to which Dickinson was aware of her mother in her life.

When her mother died, Dickinson tried to come to terms with the meaning of their relationship by comparing her feelings for her mother with those for her father. After making witty remarks about her mother's ascent to heaven, she then groped for a more appropriate way to talk about her. Using her father's legal terminology, she wrote her cousin that her mother "was scarcely the aunt you knew. The great mission of pain had been ratified–cultivated to tenderness by persistent sorrow, so that a larger mother died than had she died before . . . Mother was very beautiful when she had died. Seraphs are solemn artists" (L. III, p. 750). Her mother gained in Emily Dickinson's esteem when she died, not only because she had suffered, but because of Emily's role in taking care of her: "We were never intimate Mother and Children while she was our Mother– but mines in the same Ground meet by tunneling and when she became our Child, the affection came–" (L. III, pp. 754–55). Mother and daughter were unable to love each other *as* mother and daughter: it was only when Mrs. Dickinson was paralyzed out of the role of mother that she "achieved in sweet- ness" and became "larger" with tenderness to her daughter (L. III, p. 771). When the mother became the child, she was no longer threatening. Also, perhaps the role that Mrs. Dickinson had felt duty-bound to play as perfect wife had made her "small" by not allowing her to be sweet or tender. Dickinson makes an implicit criticism of the way mothers are taught to raise their children. Interestingly, Emily Dickinson found love for her mother when the daughter was cast, even against her will, into the mother role, and was allowed to nurture: perhaps this is what she means by "Mines in the same Ground meet by tunnel- ing." The "same ground" Dickinson could refer to is their shared female sex- uality, which if taken to its most elemental figurative significance (mines are explored beneath the surface) embodies the ability to nurture, as well as to be nurtured.

Thus we see that Dickinson's references to her mother before Mrs. Dick- inson's death are offhand tolerant remarks and ironic records of the mother's disapproval, while the references afterwards reflect the effort to come to terms with her mother as a human being. It was apparently safe to be serious about the meaning of the mother-daughter relationship once the mother was dead: it was while Dickinson was intimately involved with her mother's care that she felt acknowledging their closeness threatening to Dickinson's self-image.

Dickinson's mourning her mother—even though she had denied having one and had mocked her—only makes sense if we understand that she felt she had been deprived of a mother who could give her the emotional support and guidance she needed to become "great," not just after her mother died but when she was growing up. Dickinson clearly wanted to become Somebody other than her mother, and writing poetry was her way to do it.\She made her association of poetry and an esteemed identity clear in a letter she wrote to her sister-in- law. She followed a discussion of one of her poems, and its prospects for publication, with these words: "Could I make you and Austin [her brother]– proud–sometime–a great way off–'twould give me taller feet" (L. II, p. 380). Emily Dickinson felt chronically "small" in the eyes of the world in terms of importance, just like her mother. She could not turn to her mother for a role-model or even ask her how to become larger, because her mother was small herself; Mrs. Dickinson did not know how to become somebody "taller," and what is more, did not even share her daughter's aspiration to be something other than a dutiful wife and mother. In this way Dickinson *was* deprived of a mother, and consequently turned to a male editor of an important literary journal to tell him she "never had a mother" and to ask *him* "how to grow" to get those "taller feet" (*L*. II, p. 404). Thomas Wentworth Higginson of *The Atlantic Monthly* functioned, then, as a surrogate literary mother figure: because he had the power to identify her as a poet by publishing her, he could effect her growth and stature. Dickinson did want to grow up. She simply did not regard becoming what her mother was as "growing." Dickinson's unequivocal denial of her mother is her way of assuring Higginson of her need of him. To say she had no real mother provided a rationale for her request for *his* guidance and nurture. When she proclaimed herself an orphan to him ("I never had a mother") she was not being unfair to her mother so much as she was describing her dilemma as an ambitious woman without a role model or a mother adequate to her needs.

As Phyllis Chesler (*Women and Madness*) and others have begun to point out, the tragedy of the mother-daughter relationship is that women (daughters all) have been denied the mothers they need.[20] The daughter's perception of the mother's status as "nobody" is a source of humiliation to her because naturally she identifies with her mother; thus instead of empathizing with their mother's plight, women turn against their mothers in rage and resentment, for it seems to every daughter that her anatomical destiny is her mother's fault. This notion is only substantiated when the daughter perceives her mother trying to enforce her own degradation (compliance to the role of woman) upon her, in effect, betraying her. In this context, we think of Joseph Lyman, a family friend of the Dickinsons, who praised Mrs. Dickinson's effort to teach the "domestic arts" to her daughters; Richard B. Sewall quotes this point as evidence that Mrs. Dickinson was a good and loving mother.[21]

Emily Dickinson's rejection of "maternia" took several forms. We have seen her denial of her mother's existence and her general detachment toward her mother. Just as important is her insistence upon herself as an orphan in her letters and the poetry. She is a defiant orphan, dispossessing herself of parents as often as she is dispossessed. Freud has noted that children may claim they are not their parents' biological children, but actually the children of other parents who are rich and famous. People indulge in such fantasies to give themselves more status, usually in the sense that they assume their "real" parents are royalty or aristocracy. But Dickinson's fantasy was that she had no mother at all (*L*. II, p. 508). Her real parents were distinguished enough (that is, her father was), but it did not matter. Her status as Edward Dickinson's daughter was not enough: she could never be anything *more* than a famous man's wife or daughter (*L*. II, p. 368).

In one poem, Dickinson fantasizes that she *does* adopt her mother's identity after all by entering into a kind of marriage:

> *I'm "wife"—I've finished that—*
> *That other state—*
> *I'm Czar—I'm "Woman" now—*
> *It's safer so—*
>
> *How odd the Girl's life looks*
> *Behind this soft Eclipse—*
> *I think that Earth feels so*
> *To folks in Heaven—now—*
>
> *This being comfort—then*
> *That other kind—was pain—*
> *But why compare?*
> *I'm "Wife!" Stop there!*
>
> [199]

Just as Dickinson let her correspondents know that she was not to be identified with her mother, she lets us know that she is not to be identified with the role of wife or woman, even though she might appear in those roles and even though she is supposed to feel the status they allegedly confer. She sets off the words "Wife" and "Woman" in quotation marks to show that while she is equating herself with those titles as roles or concepts, they are essentially foreign to her—"quotes," as it were, from society's voice, states of being that society prescribes. We see her in a dilemma, then, because she is trapped in an alien identity as a "woman," and having "finished" her girlhood, has burned her bridges behind her. She finds herself "on the other side" (whether it is death or marriage is not specified). The analogy between marriage and heaven in the poem is a particularly ambivalent celebration of the identity of the married woman. The metaphor of death (going to heaven) is superimposed onto marriage so that a woman's supposed "happy ending" in marriage is her literal demise as well.

Whether the persona is dead or merely married is not made clear, but the poem's humorous ambiguity on this point signifies that marriage or maturity is a kind of death for a woman. Ironically, the woman is betrayed by her own body, because she has obviously matured to the point where she specifically resembles a "woman" and has the potential to be a "wife," even if she does not want to be one. Her self feels separate from "this soft Eclipse," which is a barrier between the state of girlhood and womanhood, between life and death: it is either a rounded feminine body (breasts, belly), or a grave. "Soft eclipse" is a remarkable image juxtaposing sexuality and death; her use of "eclipse" suggests that the mature female body is a kind of moon covering up a much larger sun (which Dickinson always portrays in the poetry as masculine and powerful). This could mean that Dickinson feels her life as a *girl* is a powerful Sun her newly "soft" body covers up, traps, or hides. But this is only a function of society's limited perspective. It sees only her "soft Eclipse," her matured femininity, not her "Sun," or her potential to be great.

PUBERTY: THE AWFUL PRECIPICE ("I AM ASHAMED TO OWN A BODY")

Even though the persona claims she has left girlhood behind, all she has really left is an identity with which she can feel at ease. Being a daughter may be a painful state, but Dickinson does not want to be a "woman." If she does not want to be a "woman" or "wife"—or circumstances prevent her—there is no other identity for her to adopt. The above poem shows that she is neither a girl nor a woman, but poised precariously in between, trying desperately to maintain the façade that one identity or the other belongs to her. The result is a lack of identity as well as identity conflict. Dickinson's ambivalence toward both girlhood and wifehood characterizes a primary mode of rejection of her mother. Helene Deutsch's work on "Girlhood" is illuminating in this regard. The period just before a girl enters puberty is the time in her life when she is most free from the identity of girl or woman. There is an absence of pressure to conform to a sexually determined role; girls at this time, unrestrained by social expectations/restrictions for women, are lively, aggressive, and independent. (However, Deutsch attributes the passivity which follows to be an innate trait of the female sex, not a matter of social conditioning.)[22] Significantly, it is this sexual limbo in which we often find Emily Dickinson's "supposed person" in the poems and letters. In these writings, she retains the sensibility of an eleven- or twelve-year-old, on the brink of maturity, precocious, defiant, and rambunctious. But because she does not go beyond this stage to become a "woman" or "wife," she experiences the pain, discomfort, and insecurity we see in "I'm 'wife.'" Perhaps because this refusal to become a woman is a conscious or unconscious rejection of her mother, we see Dickinson presenting herself in this stage in terms of conflict and guilt. In fact, she defines herself in the letters as alienated because she is wicked and wicked because she is alienated. If she does not get the emotional nurture she needs ("You can be president, Emily Dickinson") she interprets it as a sign that she does not deserve it. The only explanation the child can find for this lack of encouragement is that she is a girl. After all, her brother Austin is expected to be "something"; she and her sister and mother are not.

Thus we see that when puberty looms and Dickinson slowly gains her "soft Eclipse," she reports herself on the edge of psychosis; she is alienated from her body which is betraying and dooming her, and she conceives of herself as evil because she will not resign herself to a role as a "woman" in society. Ostensibly, the crises she went through between the ages of eleven and fifteen were a response to her inability to convert to Christianity in spite of the intense social and family pressure to do so:[23] "I feel that I am sailing upon the brink of an awful precipice from which I cannot escape & over which I fear my tiny boat will soon glide if I do not receive help from above" (*L*. I, pp. 30–31). The metaphor more accurately expresses her feelings about her own body rushing headlong into womanhood.

Her battles with Christianity and society, resisting pressures to yield and to conform, constitute a symbolic parallel to her ambivalence toward her own body, as well as toward her mother, who was the deeply religious one in the family. Her poems which say "I am ashamed to own a body," "Me from Myself— to banish–/Had I Art," (642) could be read as an orthodox spiritual preference for the soul: but it is more probable that Dickinson's religious philosophy is a function of her feelings about her own femininity. Dickinson feels that her failure to convert will doom her ("I hope you are a christian for I feel that it is impossible for any one to be happy without a treasure in heaven. I feel that I shall never be happy without I love Christ" [*L*. I, pp. 26–27]), just as she feels that her body is taking her toward a "darkened" destiny as a "woman." This fear of imminent eclipse is manifested in the doomed battles against the self and the resulting identity crises that we see in the "identity poems", even in the poem "I'm 'wife' " (199) discussed above. Therefore Dickinson's deliberate decision not to convert—to damn herself—can be understood in the light of her unwillingness to leave the limbo of preadolescence and her desire to forestall becoming a "woman."

Consequently, the guilt Dickinson expresses about her religious noncon- formity is significantly unconvincing. For example, although she has said that "I feel that I shall never be happy without I love Christ," we also see the following:

> *I was almost persuaded to be a christian. I thought I never again could be thoughtless and worldly–and I can say that I never enjoyed such perfect peace and happiness as the short time in which I felt I had found my savior. But I soon forgot my morning prayer or else it was irksome to me. One by one my old habits returned and I cared less for religion than ever.*

She implies that she has once said "yes" to religion and society, and has known the "perfect peace" of conformity (the safety and comfort we see in "I'm 'wife' "), but she cannot be persuaded to yield. She is stubbornly deliberate in her refusal, even as she is suspiciously casual about the reasons for her abandon- ment of peace (which she cannot really remember), and the reasons she suggests in retrospect are inappropriately trivial for such a far-reaching decision ("or else it was irksome to me"). On the one hand, then, she refuses to acknowledge the possibility that she herself can be religious or happy—that is out of the ques- tion, *for her*—but on the other hand, she believes that what is so impossible, unpleasant, or unimportant for her is crucial for other people. In this way, she alienates herself not only from formal religious structures, but from her social world, even at the price of unhappiness and crisis. The fact that she feels she will not and cannot be happy unless she loves Christ, and yet still refuses to do so, indicates that she is trying to fate herself. It is as if she wants to create the impression that it is too late for her to reform or that she was not meant to be happy. It mitigates the impression that her unhappiness is a deliberate decision at the same time it separates her from those who conform. We see her bidding for love and autonomy at the same time.

Dickinson's appearance of helplessness and uncertainty in her letters signals that while Dickinson needed to rebel—or to be seen rebelling—she did not want to seem to take the initiative in her rebellion. Her resigned fatalistic attitude, which must have frustrated her female correspondents by its lack of logic, continued through the letters of her early teenage years as she dangled the possibility of her conversion before her correspondents, to whom her acceptance of Christ was so important. A pattern surfaces in the way Dickinson describes her dilemma. She complains of an "aching void in my heart which I am convinced the world will never fill"; she acknowledges a remedy for her suffering ("I continually hear Christ saying to me Daughter give me thine Heart"); she rejects the remedy ("I am continually putting off becoming a christian"); and she pronounces herself evil ("I feel that every day I live I sin more and more . . ."). She never explains the crucial stage between perceiving a solution and rejecting it. Her lack of real concern and distress shows her true feelings about being saved. That she is not "hopeful" is clear from her description of a revival meeting:

> *It seemed as if those who sneered loudest at serious things [not unlike herself] were soonest brought to see . . . how near heaven came to sinful mortals. Many who felt there was nothing in religion determined to go once & see if there was anything in it, and they were melted at once.*
>
> *Perhaps you will not beleive [sic] it Dear A. but I attended none of the meetings last winter.*

The irony of her final remark is akin to her statement which follows her fear for her fate if she does not convert: "I am continually putting off becoming a christian." It is not hard to believe that Dickinson attended none of the revival meetings that winter, because, according to her letters, as one of the "loudest sneerers" she might "melt at once," and she is afraid she will be "inclined to yeild [sic] to the claims of He who is greater than I."

In conceptualizing the issue of religious conversion as a "to yield" or "not to yield" construct, Dickinson exposes her sensitivity as a daughter. She responds to social pressure as an authority to rebel against; and given that any figures who urge conformity upon her, whether they be her actual parents, teachers, friends, or Christ himself, will be met with disobedience, she is by her own definition a rebellious, wicked daughter. What stands out most from her letters is that there is never any question of a desire to actually submit herself "willingly" to Christ:

> *It was then my greatest pleasure to commune alone with the great God & to feel that he would listen to my prayers. I determined to devote my whole life to his service. . . . But the world allured me & in an unguarded moment I listened to her syren voice. From that moment I seemed to lose my interest in heavenly things by degrees. Prayer in which I had taken such delight became a task & the small circle who met for prayer missed me from their number.* [L. I, pp. 30–31]

When she is warned by her friends of the consequences of staying away, she is resigned and firm: "I had rambled too far to return & ever since my heart has been growing harder." Even as she admits that she "ought now . . . give myself to God," she serves "Mammon." To do what she "ought" is to give herself up; and by refusing to do so, she automatically judges herself evil. In other words, doing what she ought not is her way of *keeping* herself. If she is dutiful and yields, she will lose herself.

A final example of Dickinson's attitude toward conversion is her response to being taken away from school by her father. If Mary Lyons' goal at Mount Holyoke Academy had been to win conversions, Dickinson's education had been a failure. On leaving, Dickinson thinks that her "fate will be sealed, perhaps. I have neglected the *one thing needful* when all were obtaining it, and I may never, never again pass through such a season as was granted us last winter" (L. I, pp. 67–68). Now that it is too late, of course, she can say that she regrets her decision, and when her friends plead that it is not too late, even now, she is forced to acknowledge that "It is hard for me to give up the world." She does not want to be saved (to enjoy perfect peace and comfort): this established, she now "never can [say] with sincerity" that she only desires "to be good." Thus Dickinson emerged from the crisis of her early adolescence with a hard-won identity as the unredeemed, only half-repentant sinner. She had flaunted her soul's peril in the faces of her worried friends like a child who loves the attention it receives when it rushes near the street. When she says, "I love to buffet the sea—I can count the bitter wrecks here in these pleasant waters, and hear the murmuring winds, but oh, I love the danger!" (L. I, p. 104), she reveals that it is peril she values, as long as the peril is incurred by saying "no" to those who urge conformity—and peace—upon her.

It was a religious crisis which confirmed in Dickinson a sense of her rebellion. But her refusal to conform by yielding to social pressure can be understood to constitute a major mode of rejection of her mother and her mother's destiny. As the elder Dickinsons saw it, it was a woman's duty to be religious, and Emily Norcross Dickinson was extremely dutiful in this regard. John Cody suggests that the fact that Emily Dickinson's religious crisis occurred at the onset of puberty is not a coincidence; it represented her rejection of her physically maturing body.[24] Rejecting her mother's religion was another way of warding off her mother's anatomically defined and confined destiny. Her identity crisis is a function of being afraid of "yielding" to her mother's fate: she is urged to a particularly feminine form of social conformity at the time her body is mandating physical and sexual conformity as a "woman." She cannot say "no" to her body, but she can say "no" to religion for the specific reason that to say "yes" constitutes submission to a Father and Son. Saying "yes" to Christ is to say "yes" to the oppressive maternal matrix—the same kind of submission to a patriarchal order that has effaced her mother in her role as wife and mother. It is submission itself that Dickinson conceives as her destiny as a woman; and it is submission that she rejects. Refusing to yield to family, school, and peer pressure, then, Dickinson is attempting to ward off the inevitability of being a "woman," and in the process, she defines the world—the feminine world—as the "Not Me." Her need to assert her autonomy and independence in a public way is so great that she would rather "doom" and damn herself than be eclipsed as a dutiful "woman." This renunciation effectively "stops" her identity from progressing to woman or wife. To say "yes" to her maternal matrix would relieve the pressure, but it would doom her (*L.* II, pp. 924, 617), and Dickinson's efforts to distinguish herself out of the context of social and sexual expectations constitute in her mind the onus of disobedience.

According to Erikson, the identity which is presumably emerging for a woman at fourteen or fifteen (when Dickinson is writing these letters) bridges the gap between childhood and womanhood, the time when the bodily self and the parental images are given their cultural connotations. The gap cannot be bridged and an identity cannot be achieved if the child does not accept "coercive" social roles—in this case, religious conformity. Erikson stresses that children "need a sense of achievement that has meaning in their culture."[25] Dickinson cannot be "coerced" into becoming a good "woman" (i.e., religious, submissive) because when a destiny is limited, it leads to "severe conflict" and "unexpected naughtiness or delinquency." Erikson continues, "in the social jungle of human existence, there is no feeling of being alive without a sense of ego identity. Deprivation of identity, can lead to murder." In this context, Dickinson's refusal to yield takes on added significance in terms of the daughter construct. For Erikson, the oral stage of infant development in which the child takes in food from the mother is when the human psyche learns to trust an external world, ideas, and values—to have, as he calls it, "faith" that what the mother/world gives it is good. A lasting ego identity that enables the person to integrate with larger social structures (marriage, community) cannot begin to exist without the trust of the first oral stage firmly established, and the ability to have faith or trust is impossible unless the infant receives the food, warmth, love, and security it needs. The person must see that what the world urges is nurturing. In this way, religion is "institutionalized trust." Both identity *and* religion are a function of believing that the values of the world can be swallowed without harm. Emily Dickinson shows an awareness of this relationship between childhood and the ability to "trust" what the world gives when she says that George Eliot was denied "the gift of belief" because of her "greatness." Dickinson now "trusts" that Eliot "receives in the childhood of the Kingdom of heaven [the gift of belief]. As childhood is earth's confiding time, perhaps having no childhood, she lost her way to the early trust, and no later came" (*L*. III, p. 700). Because she cannot abide what the world will give *her* (her mother's limited destiny, a sense of achievement that has little meaning in the culture), it is she who cannot enjoy the comfort or happiness of a "lasting identity" which depends upon the ability to trust. She is caught in the gap between girlhood and womanhood as a Daughter in perpetual identity crisis. Both her suffering and her inability to find comfort in the institutions society has erected to provide comfort are the world/mother's fault, and through her letters and poetry Dickinson never lets the world, as Richard Wilbur says, "forget it."

"GOD SAVE ME FROM WHAT THEY CALL HOUSEHOLDS"

Emily Dickinson's early letters illustrate yet another form of rejection of the feminine tradition her mother embodies. Dickinson dissociates herself not only from her mother and her mother's religion, but from other aspects of her domain as well, including housework, good works, and sewing societies. Even though—and perhaps because—these are prescribed activities promoted by her mother, sister, and girlfriends, Dickinson perceives them as obstacles in the way of her determination to be "great someday"—that is, somebody *else* than society expects. Her letters emphasize how she does not fit into or identify with her mother's world. Housework, the center of the feminine existence, is, according to the rebellious daughter, a "prickly art" (*L*. III, p. 827), another "Awful Yes" (*L*. III, p. 924) she must resist if she is to save herself. Outwardly, she conforms to being a dutiful daughter by staying home to take complete care of her mother and attend to her father. But she can distance herself from her dutiful role and retain the integrity of her poetic mind by complaining about how she is abused and how her true talent goes unrecognized in her performance of traditional roles. Through deed and word she synthesizes duty and rebellion: she acts out the role of duty, and rebels in her writing.

Thus when we hear Dickinson's ironic treatment of herself being a poor imitation of a "woman" or "wife" when her mother is sick, or describing her desultory efforts at housekeeping, we also see her resentment at having no time or sanction to write: as she tells a friend, "If it wasn't for broad day light, and cooking stoves, and roosters, I'm afraid you would have occasion to smile at my letters more often, but so sure as 'this mortal' essay immortality [that is, by writing poetry], a crow from a neighboring farmyard dissipates the illusion, and I am here again" (*L*. I, pp. 97–100, 80–85, 227, 264). Her statement to her niece that it is "unfeminine to publish"[26] may be an ironic comment upon the fact that being feminine or domestic means having no time to write, let alone publish. We remember, in this respect, that Mrs. Dickinson is actually described as "too busy to write," a fact which Dickinson makes much of in her letters. She distinguishes herself because she alone takes the time to write, and she alone *can* take the time (*L*. I, pp. 114, 118, 124). Therefore, the poet-to-be is very much present in these letters about domestic life. The portrait she gives of herself is of an artist at odds with tradition and social and sexual expectations: there is nothing she describes that is not meant to turn the reader's attention to the fact that she is forced to do work for which she is manifestly unsuited—that she is a poet whose identity and talent are being temporarily eclipsed by society's mistaken conviction that she is a "woman" like her mother and therefore will do when the "wife" or real mother is taken out of commission.

When her mother is sick, for example, we see Dickinson write a long letter describing herself confronting the "culinary arts," which she claims to have "always neglected" (*L*. I, pp. 97–100). Assuring her reader that she attends to them now only from "necessity, and from a desire to make everything pleasant for father, and Austin [but not her sister?]," she finds herself torn. On the one hand she is being feminine and dutiful, pleasing the men in her family who "clamor for food" by simulating the women's role—providing food and doing housework—and therefore, says she, goes "cheerfully round my work." But lest the reader assume she is *really* cheerful being eclipsed by this maternal role, she confesses that she is actually miserable, and "cries with all my might," convinced that she is "much abused, that this wicked world was unworth such devoted, and terrible sufferings." Humorous as this statement appears in this context, it reveals the precise terms in which Dickinson rejects the maternal matrix. What the world offers her is not good, but "wicked." It is therefore not worth being obedient (that is, trusting). Being dutiful is "terrible." And why? The familiar refrain: she has not been able to write even one letter for weeks, because she is kept so busy with domestic chores. Religious and familial obedience is antithetical to her self-fulfillment as a poet.

In giving this rendition, Dickinson is careful to express herself poetically so that the reader is convinced by style as well as content that she is not her mother and does not belong in the kitchen. She is witty and metaphoric: "Twin loaves of bread have just been born into the world under my auspices–fine children–the image of their mother . . . ," a feat, she says, which is her "*glory.*" To emphasize that making bread is a specifically maternal activity which has been imposed upon her, she relates the process to giving birth; making bread is not only "creation" but it interferes with her poetry just as having children would. She sees a mother's function, then, in terms of self-sacrifice: "Father and Austin still clamor for food, and I, like a martyr, am feeding them."

Providing the "food that perisheth" as she calls it, has kept her from her "mission," which we are led to assume is her determination to provide the food that does *not* perish: the immortal word. Thus cooking for her father projects

Dickinson into her mother's dreaded role, a situation in which Dickinson feels great conflict as a daughter and would-be poet.

Emily Dickinson dissociates herself from her mother's role as housekeeper not only by complaining indirectly about the self-sacrifice involved, but explicitly: "Wouldn't you love to see me in these bonds of great despair, looking around my kitchen, and praying for kind deliverance . . . *My* kitchen I think I called it, God forbid that it was or shall be my own–God keep me from what they call *households*." Her imprecation to God to deliver her from what she considers evil—being an obedient woman like her mother—as well as her free use of religious terminology to characterize her plight ("praying for kind deliverance," "God forbid," "God keep me," "was or ever shall be") is ironic and intended to show, I think, how far she is from a traditional interpretation of good and evil. At another time she writes, " 'House' is being 'cleaned.' I prefer pestilence. That is more classic and less fell" (*L*. II, p. 453). Emily Dickinson considers herself "bad" because she will not love Christ or housework, which are essentially the same thing to the daughter—an alliance between church and home which insists upon *her* self-sacrifice and keeps her from worldly gain. She therefore willingly accepts her image as a sinner as the price she has to pay. Her refusal to take a woman's role in stride only illustrates what she has been maintaining all along about her inability to accept Jesus. Thus she ends her letter in typical fashion by rehashing for the fiftieth time the reasons for her refusal to submit to Christ. She now uses her refusal to happily conform as evidence of her intrinsically evil nature: "I am one of the lingering *bad* ones." She says she knows that according to society she is "bad," because she refuses to do her female duty by loving Christ or housework, but the reason she hates "scaring the timorous dust, and being obedient, and kind," is that such dutiful behavior confers no *status*. She is only "Queen of the court, if regalia be dust, and dirt." Household chores keep her from writing, and she is convinced that only through writing will she ever hope to attain "glory" and status—only by not becoming her mother can she break away from the limitations imposed on her sex. She prefers being "bad" and great to being good and "nobody," and there is no question as she sees it that this division is what it all comes down to for a woman.

Not that she ever thinks this right, of course. In perhaps the most explicit letter she writes to dissociate herself from the feminine world, she complains. Her family takes it for granted that she fulfills her duties, and her time is considered

> . . . *of so* little *account–and my writing so* very *needless–and really I came to the conclusion that I should be a villain unparralleled* [sic] *if I took but an inch of time for so unholy a purpose as writing a friendly letter–for what need had I of sympathy–or very much less of affection–or less than they all–of friends–mind the house–and the food–sweep if the spirits were low–nothing like exercise to invigorate–and help away such*

foolishness–work makes one strong, and cheerful–and for society what neighborhood so full as my own? The halt–the lame–and the blind–the old–the infirm–the bed-ridden–and superannuated–the ugly, and disagreeable–the perfectly hateful to me–all these to see, and be seen by–an opportunity for cultivating meekness–and patience–and submission–and for turning my back on this very sinful, and wicked world. Somehow or other I incline to other things–and Satan covers them up with flowers, and I reach out to pick them. The path of duty looks very ugly indeed– and the place where I want to go more amiable–a great deal– . . . so much pleasanter to be evil than good, I dont wonder that good angels weep,–and bad ones sing songs. [L. I, pp. 81–85]

In spite of the satiric rhetoric, this letter gives vent to Dickinson's feelings as a daughter in her family and community: her bald contempt for what is held sacred; her hostility and resentment against her family; her scorn for the precepts of church, school, and home; her feelings of being imposed upon and misunderstood; and her rejection of the Christian Puritan work ethic, especially as it applies to women. Religious submission is again directly equated here with housework: in Dickinson's mind, church, family, and society are in league against her to prevent her from becoming "great." The most intense antagonism is leveled against her mother, the invalid for whom Dickinson has been caring: halt, lame, old, infirm, bed-ridden, ugly, disagreeable, and perfectly hateful. The qualities that her mother embodies—meekness, patience, and submission, as well as a commitment to Christ—are attributes Dickinson feels to be deserving of contempt: "somehow or other," she writes, "I incline to other things."

The image which emerges from her teen-age letters is of a daughter torn between duty and rebellion, consciously distancing herself from womanly activities. Most significantly, it is in reference to herself as a writer that she alludes to herself as wicked. She equates religious wickedness and writing, for example, when she confesses to correspondents that she is conscious of sinning if she "breaks the Sabbath" by writing on Sunday: out of a respect for religion she finds herself "quite curtailed" from what she describes as her "natural" inclination to write of "many worldly things which would doubtless grieve and distress you." She flaunts her tendency to rebel, insisting to her correspondents, for example, that when people sing hymns in church, she makes up her own tunes; finally, she stops attending church (and baiting her friends) altogether, and a primary mode of rejection of the maternal matrix is complete.

"You Know How I Hate To Be Common"

Dickinson extends her rejection of the maternal world to any convention which she, as a "woman," is expected to submit to: courtship, marriage, church, housework, and Sewing Society. She makes sure that her correspondents see her contempt for these forms of feminine duty: "The Sewing Society has commenced again . . . —now all the poor will be helped—the cold warmed—the warm cooled—the hungry fed—the thirsty attended to—the ragged clothed—and this suffering tumbled-down world will be helped to its feet again—which will be quite pleasant to all" (L. I, p. 84). She is morally critical of such female groups which, although harmless, manifestly help no one and have no import whatsoever on the fate of the world. These groups are the real wasters of time: "I dont attend—not withstanding my high approbation—which must puzzle the public exceedingly. I am already set down as one of those brands almost consumed— and my hard-heartedness gets me many prayers." She signs her letter, "Your very sincere, and *wicked* friend" (L. I, p. 89). In this culture, truth is wicked. She is detached from the "girls" with whom she associates: "The girls 'Musical' met here on Tuesday evening, and we had as pleasant a time as would have expected, in view of the individuals composing the society" (L. I, p. 238). When she describes herself as so put upon by her family that she goes about her work slamming doors and crying into her apron, it is because she is essentially estranged from women's activities, and wants her reader to know it: "Vinnie sweeps—sweeps—upon the Chamber stairs; and mother is hurrying around with her hair in a silk pocket handkerchief, on account of dust. Oh Susie, it is dismal" (L. I, p. 193). It is not just the housework that depresses her—it is her sister's compliance in doing it which is so provoking. Writing a letter provides an escape valve from the pressures of feminine responsibilities and expectations, for Dickinson is afraid of incurring the charge of "Femina insania!" She takes leave of her housework to write: "They are cleaning house today, Susie, and I've made a flying retreat to my own little chamber . . ." (L. I, pp. 204, 297, 238). She is clearly alienated from what "they" do.

Emily Dickinson laments when she sees her sister Vinnie succumb to the daily expectations of the dutiful daughter. Noting that Vinnie is "driven" with household cares, Dickinson says, "We consider her standard for superhuman effort erroneously applied" (L. II, p. 397). She can joke about her sister's fate as a dutiful daughter, but Dickinson feels increasingly alone. Her letters in her mid-twenties confess to loneliness, but if she is "Alone," as she says, it is only figuratively speaking: in spite of the intimate daily contact with her sister, Dickinson claims that she doesn't see much of her because "she's mostly dusting stairs" (L. I, p. 310). Her loneliness and sense of isolation are not induced by a lack of physical proximity to people, but by a lack of kindred spirits. Just as she can be seen to have been orphaned in the sense that her mother is not a role model for success, she is rendered friendless and betrayed by Vinnie's dusting the stairs—and not minding: "Vinnie is happy with her duties, her pussies, and her posies . . ." (L. III, p. 862).[27] Dusting stairs symbolizes the terms of her alienation from a domestic, feminine lifestyle she cannot transform but which she can shirk. This lifestyle that she rejects takes the form of housework in the letters, probably because this occupation literally absorbed her mother and then her sister's life. As Dickinson asked, what kind of "life" is that?

> *I rise, because the sun shines, and sleep has done with me, and I brush my hair, and dress me, and wonder what I am and who has made me so, and then I wash the dishes, and anon, wash them again, and then tis afternoon, and Ladies call, and evening, and some members of another sex come in to spend the hour, and then that day is done. And prithee, what is Life?"* [*L*. I, p. 304]

Even Emily Dickinson's "real" identity as a poet becomes submerged in this mindless routine of "domestic detail," as much as she actively resists it. Her sense of the tedium of dutiful feminine existence is summed up in her statement, "Are the children women, and the women thinking it will soon be afternoon? We will help each other bear our unique burdens" (*L*. II, p. 354).

It is interesting to note that she follows her lines complaining of loneliness because of Vinnie's capitulation to a dusty duty with the statement, "Sermons on unbelief ever did attract me." She directly associates her rebellion from housework with her rebellious attitude towards God and/or the church. And just as Vinnie will capitulate in social roles, she leaves Dickinson alone in terms of her own commitment to Christ:

> *Christ is calling everyone here, all my companions have answered, even my darling Vinnie believes she loves, and trusts him, and I am standing alone in rebellion, and growing very careless. . . they all believe they have found; I cant tell you what they have found, but they think it is something precious. I wonder if it is?* [*L*. I, p. 94]

Her determination to dissociate herself from the feminine world leaves her feeling increasingly isolated: significantly, the days become "like Sundays, and I wait for the bells to ring. . . ."

It is precisely at the point in her letter when she ironically and bitterly notes her estrangement from the happiness and peace of the "good" people ("the faces of good men shine, and bright halos come around them"), that she alludes to her poetry: she has "dared to do strange—bold things, and [has] asked no advice from any" [we remember that she is an orphan in this regard, and she has "none to ask"] "I have heeded beautiful tempters, yet do not think I am wrong." Again, she should consider herself "a villain unparalleled," but she is unalterably at odds with society's concepts of right and wrong, convinced in the face of all opposition from family and society that her "mission" *is* "holy," and that she is *not* "wrong," either to write poetry or to dare to be great. Her aspirations are not sanctioned and run counter to those of members of the

Sewing Society, because she really wants to "achieve" something that has meaning in her culture.

She has written her friends that she will never be happy unless she submits
to Christ, but this is only what she supposes she ought to feel. Her real feelings
about her supposed wickedness in writing are, "Nobody *thinks* of the joy,
nobody *guesses* it . . ." (*L*. I, p. 95). Her only problem is that she has no one to
"instruct" her; so in the American tradition of self-reliance cherished by her
male contemporaries, she instructs herself. The difference between Dickinson's
kind of self-reliance and that of writers like Hawthorne and Emerson, who were
trying to formulate their own tradition and aesthetic as Americans distinct from
a British cultural identity, is that they did not feel that their efforts to do so
were inherently wicked in the eyes of society. Dickinson was totally committed
to her decision to be a writer, and she gladly risked the psychological dangers:
but she also wrote in her room, in secret, at night. For all her complaints, we
must never forget that her outward actions were dutiful. But it is because she
acted out her role of duty that she incurred the biggest risk—loss of her self-
identity.

Over and over again the letters record Dickinson's consciousness of the
odds against her achieving greatness in her culture, and her awareness, specifically, that her ambitions were departures from feminine conventions. At fifteen,
she was already writing "You know I hate to be common" (*L*. I, p. 10); when she
was forty-six she rebuked a friend who had addressed an envelope to both her
sister and herself: "A mutual plum is not a plum" (*L*. II, p. 455). She did not
want to be identified with anyone, nor did she want a conventional destiny. She
was aware that her education was not taken as seriously as her brother's. She
was being taken out of school because she was missed at home; it was felt that
she needed to be home for her own good. In a letter to her friend Abiah Root,
she pleads, even before she has *begun* her formal schooling, "We'll finish an
education sometime, won't we? You may then be Plato, and I will be Socrates"
(*L*. I, p. 10). It is significant that she assumes she must educate herself if she
is to become great. Dickinson's choice of Socrates for her identity reflects her
own sensibility which questions every precept and value held by her contemporaries, not in order to arrive at an answer for herself, but, like Socrates, to
lead others to her kind of reasoning, her kind of questioning of what they are
being "taught"—or not being taught. In other words, she wants to challenge
fallacies in conventional thinking about women, encouraging others to rebel
against a restricting society. For example, when she learned that her friend
Susan Gilbert had missed connections for a ride home from school, Dickinson
interpreted the incident as a victory against a male world in which expectations
of dutiful women were successfully defied: "She's outwitted them all–ha-ha!
Just imagine me giving three cheers for American Independence!" (*L*. I, p.
233). Dickinson champions the ability to act autonomously–that is, defiantly–
and exhorts her friends to resist any attempt to restrict them; in the same vein
she laments her own compliances and dependence as a dutiful daughter as

defeats ("they triumphed, and led me off in defeat," "But I kept still," "but I dared not ask"). At fifteen, she is conscious of being dominated and intimidated, and pleaded with a friend, "don't let your free spirit be chained" (*L*. I, p. 13).

In another letter in her middle age, she reminds her cousin of a secret conference they had once had in which they had strayed from a family outing and instead "decided to be distinguished–It's a great thing to be 'great,' Loo, and you and I might tug for a life, and never accomplish it, but no one can stop our looking on . . . You know some cannot sing . . . what if we learn, ourselves, someday! Who indeed knows?" (*L*. II, p. 345). Here she alludes to her ambition to be a poet as a specifically feminine heresy. Like a "bad angel," she is going to learn to write poetry "someday." She has not been taught how to be "great," but she will teach herself. She seems to be engaged in the process of urging her correspondents to question their destinies and to aspire to greatness. We see her urging Susan Gilbert to believe that they could write a best-selling book like "Ik Marvel's" *Reveries of a Bachelor*; she insists that they could have their own " 'Reverie! . . . just as charming as that lonely Bachelor . . . and you and I would *try* to make a little destiny to have for our own. . . .'" "We are the only poets," she maintains, in a world where "everyone else is *prose*" (*L*. I, p. 144). Poetry is a way to defy convention: if it constitutes rebellion for a woman, it is also the only way a woman can achieve a destiny "of [her] own."

The "poet-to-be" is explicit in her letters about why she values writing as a means to achieve a destiny for herself different from that of a traditional woman. Insisting to her correspondents that it is possible to have a unique destiny—that they can be anything—she asks why she cannot be Eve, "alias Mrs. Adam. You know there is no account of her death in the Bible, and why am I not Eve?" (*L*. I, p. 24). (Indeed, did not Eve take a bite of forbidden fruit to gain knowledge—urged on by the "Evil Tempter?") And why, she asks, cannot she and her friend be David and Jonathan, Damon and Pythias, the United States of America, Judith (the heroine of the Apocrypha), and the orator of Ephesus? It is possible, she says, for with the use of "metaphor" one can transform oneself into anyone one pleases, if only on paper. She never comes right out and declares that she is a poet, but she implies her own familiarity with a metaphor's miraculous powers, and even flaunts her intimacy with metaphor, defining a metaphor to her cousin as if he has never heard of one before, condescendingly: "Don't be afraid of it, sir, it won't bite" (*L*. I, p. 92). She seems to exult in her ability to tame a metaphor, and in a letter to Austin, she lets herself go in an exuberant abandon, equating herself with a dog, a stick, a mosquito, a fowl. It is significant to note in this context that Dickinson makes an issue of the esteem in which she is held by her elder brother, needling him about his assumed superiority: "Permit me to tie your shoe, to run like a dog behind you. I can bark, see here! Bow wow' . . . Permit me to be a stick to show how I will not beat you, a stone, how I would not fling" (*L*. I, pp. 100–101). She will metaphorically assume an identity that has the potential to do harm in order to make him appreciate that she spares him only by choice. She does not feel that he regards her identity as a sister as something to reckon with: therefore he takes her for granted, and her kindness as a symptom of powerlessness or submissiveness. In these ways, her desire for metaphor betrays her dissatisfaction with a girl's identity. She is saying to Austin, then, please see me in terms of my potential (even to do harm) and appreciate me (my capacity to do good). When her parents are gone (and she does not have to play the role of dutiful daughter), she gets "the old King feeling" (*L.* I, pp. 101, 181), and she acts giddy with her metaphoric omnipotence: the possibility of transforming herself even into the lowliest insect confers power, authority, and importance.

But Austin's response is only an irritable confusion over what she is talking about; he asks for a "simpler style" than her metaphoric fantasies. In a sense, Emily Dickinson has made herself vulnerable to her brother by revealing the nature of her literary ambition. She interprets his request as a rebuff for the liberties she has taken with language—the *way* she uses metaphor to simulate powerful and otherwise unfeminine identities. The bitter edge of her reply is turned against herself: she retorts defiantly by using another metaphoric structure, but this time one that will be more appropriate for her brother's tastes: "I'll be a little ninny—a little pussy catty, a little Red Riding Hood . . ." (*L.* I, p. 117). The allusion to Little Red Riding Hood is ironically fitting. Red Riding Hood is the harmless dutiful daughter, who foolishly trusts what society—her mother—gives her by taking in food (Christian dogma) to aid her invalid grandmother in an act of charitable benevolence. Red Riding Hood is not alert enough to notice immediately that a wolf is lying in her grandmother's bed, and were it not for a convenient male in the vicinity, she would have been eaten. In some versions she *is* eaten.

The sad part of this exchange is that Emily Dickinson really had wanted her brother's esteem. She thought by being "poetic" in her writing efforts, addressing him as an equal and even teasing him with her superior linguistic abilities, that she would gain his esteem. She must have felt put down by his letter rebuking her for her flamboyant "style." Although she acknowledges his dismissal with spirited sarcasm, her exuberance is muted: "I feel quite like retiring in presence of one so grand, and casting my small lot among small birds, and fishes—You say you dont comprehend me, you want a simpler style . . . I strove to be exalted thinking I might reach *you* and while I pant and struggle and climb the nearest cloud, you walk out very leisurely in your slippers . . . and without the *slightest* notice request me to get down! As *simple* as you please, the *simplest* sort of simple—I'll be a little ninny. . . ."

Dickinson often attempted to dissociate herself from the traditional feminine world inhabited by her mother and sister by affecting a rebellious spirit in her letters to Austin. She once teased Austin, for example, by threatening to show a letter he had written her to her stern headmistress. She would decide whether or not she would carry out this threat after examining his letter "with sobriety becoming my station, & if after a close investigation of it's [sic] contents I found nothing which savored of rebellion or an unsubdued will, I would lay it away in my folio & forget I had ever received it." After revealing the unseemly value she places on rebellion, she asks, "Are you not gratified that I am so rapidly gaining correct ideas of female propriety and sedate deportment" (*L*. I, p. 62).

The problem for Dickinson is that when she is dutiful Austin does not take her seriously, yet when she is rebellious she is rejected: "If I hadn't been afraid that you would poke fun at my feelings, I had written a *sincere* letter, but since the 'world is hollow, and Dollie is stuffed with sawdust,' I really do not think we had better expose our feelings" (*L*. I, p. 112). To expose herself in terms of her serious ambitions without humor or metaphor is to incur rejection. But she defeats herself in her "naughty" and clever little girl pose, undercutting herself with ironic remarks as "Am I not a very wise *young lady*?" (*L*. I, p. 57). Dickinson constantly battles Austin's preconception of women, confessing that she is afraid he supposes her a "fool" and defending herself as "sensible" and "really quite intelligent." Emily Dickinson's hope is that she will be "an *accountable* being" to him by presenting herself as estranged from her sex (making fun of housework and sewing societies) (*L*. I. p. 116). Through her writing she tries to express the sensibility of the "poet-to-be," who is capable of intelligence and worthy of his esteem. She tries to distinguish herself through her use of metaphor, style, and theme. But her brother's scornful and patronizing reaction shows that her efforts are in vain. We see that Dickinson will give up trying to convince Austin: "I shall never write any more grand letters to you, but all the *little* things, and the things called *trifles* . . . you will be sure to hear." She will be as "simple" and as "little" as he pleases—nay, *demands* (*L*. I, p. 240).

Nevertheless, Emily Dickinson remains candid about her need to be identified out of the context of her sexual role. In a revealing letter about her self-image as a Daughter who wants to be great, she sets out the conflict she feels. On the one hand, she enjoys cooperating in a conspiracy in which she addresses letters for others to send because she is not "herself" but instead is someone who can "loom up from Hindoostan, or drop from an Appenine, or peer at you suddenly from the hollow of a tree, calling myself King Charles, Sancho Panza, or Herod, King of the Jews–I suppose it is all the same" (*L*. I, pp. 228–29). The identities are all the same in that they are male—and incidentally, famous, powerful, and exotic. But on the other hand, Dickinson confesses that part of her personality is Miss Mills from *David Copperfield*, who is withdrawn and cares only for others: the other side of the metaphor-happy multi-personality. The Miss Mills in her "never dreamed of the depth of *my clandestiny*." She continues, ". . .if *I* stopped to think of the figure I was cutting, it would be the last of me, and you'd never hear again from your poor Jeremy Bentham–. . . ." Part of Dickinson's conscience (her internal parents) holds back from her escape fantasies into other personages and possibilities, but she says, "I say to my mind, 'tut, tut,' 'Rock a bye baby' conscience, and so I keep them still!" We note that her conscience, then, is plural: the daughter's rebellion is against her parents. The reference to "them" as a synonym of her frowning mind is evidence of her consciousness aware of division within itself. Part of Dickinson's conflict is that she is keeping the mode of her rebellion—writing poetry—more or less secret. She refers to the secrecy of her omnipotence and "omnipresence," which "nobody guesses." For her, rebellion from the feminine world through heresy, boldness, and assertion—that is, poetry—is the means to a great destiny. But it must be an "eclipsed" rebellion.

HOMESICK ("HOW TO GROW UP I DON'T KNOW"): CHILDHOOD LOST

Emily Dickinson's rejection of the values and destiny of the "dutiful" woman culminates in what has been termed her "withdrawal" or "regression" into childhood. This withdrawal or regression, which manifested itself in Dickinson's adoption of the child persona, dressing as a child and living like a child, more likely can be seen as a refusal to be a "woman" or "wife" because neither identity allows her the possibility of a great career. The most significant form of Dickinson's alienation from the destiny her mother literally embodies, then, is her identity as a daughter, who, like Peter Pan, refuses to obey her body and society by leaving the world of childhood. Peter Pan's "I'll never grow up" is Dickinson's "I wish we were *always* children, how to grow up I dont know" (*L*. I, p. 241). When she is grown, she has only one prayer: that she be a child (*L*. I, p. 211). Even when she is only fifteen, she evinces a nostalgia for childhood in her letters: "How happy we all were." She tries to re-create her childhood in the letters by recalling anecdotes about school; and she reports herself loving to be a child (*L*. I, pp. 14, 206, 104). In her celebration of, and mourning for, childhood, we see not necessarily a refutation of the idea that girlhood is "pain" to her, but rather, a more complex construct in which the idealization of childhood is a strategy to circumvent becoming what she most hated: someone common. To grow up to be a "woman" is to conform. We see this philosophy embedded in a revealing series of letters to her girlfriends in which Dickinson projects—and rejects—the destiny of marriage, which takes away one's identity. She cannot, in her terms, "lose herself" to a man any more than she can "give herself up" to Christ or acquiesce to housework. "I do think it's wonderful, Susie, that our hearts dont break, *every day*, when I think of all the whiskers, and all the gallant men, but I guess I'm made with nothing but a hard heart of stone, for it don't break any" (*L*. I, pp, 194–95). She reminds Susan Gilbert that they must never "yield." The "big future" Dickinson describes awaiting them pivots on a denial of conventional female fulfillment in marriage. When Dickinson's friends get married, she writes them as if they are bereaved (*L*. I, pp. 276–77). Dickinson adopts a defensive, mocking tone about wedding ceremonies. After sporting with a ceremony in which she describes the minister tying the couple into a bow-knot, she says, "I beg pardon for speaking lightly of so solemn a ceremony" (*L*. I, p. 20). When they are "lovers" sighing and twining oak leaves, she describes herself as the "*anti*-enamored" eating sugar and crackers in the house, making the "best of fate" (*L*. I, p. 202). Marriage is a "strange adoption" that happens when one stops running away and submits: "lie still and be happy." She imagines what happens when one does submit, dwelling on the fate of "the wife *forgotten*" who longs to be a girl again. In marriage, the wife is scorched by the "man of noon, *mightier* than the morn, and their life is henceforth to him."

> *How dull our lives must seem to the bride, and the plighted maiden, whose days are fed with gold, and who gathers petals every evening; but to the* wife, Susie, *sometimes the* wife forgotten, *our lives perhaps seem dearer than all others in the world; you have seen flowers at morning,* satisfied *with the dew, and those same sweet flowers at noon with their heads bowed in anguish before the mighty sun; think you these thirsty blossoms will* now *need nought but–*dew*? No, They will cry for sunlight, and pine for the burning noon, tho' it scorches them, scathes them; they have got through with peace–they know that the man of noon, is* mightier *than the morning and their life is henceforth to him. Oh Susie, it is dangerous, and it is all too dear, these simply trusting spirits, and the spirits mightier, which we cannot resist! It does rend me, Susie, the thought of it when it comes, that I tremble lest at sometime I, too, am yielded up.* [*L*. I, pp. 209–10]

This passage delineates why Dickinson thinks that the "Yes" which lurks menacingly within each of us is "Awful," and dangerous. This fear of being eclipsed, or scorched, in marriage is like her fear of submitting to one who is "more powerful" than herself, Christ. In both cases, submitting entails adopting the role of the "woman" or "wife." Childhood is thus a place of retreat from the threat of the world's expectations for women. If her friends insist on capitulating to marriage, she will urge herself, at least, to remember that renunciation leads to a superior destiny. The child persona is in large measure a reflection of Emily Dickinson's systematic refusals to become a conventional woman.

Insisting on being a child in her correspondents' eyes enables her to set herself up as at odds with the world. At the same time, she is released from the pressure of being a "woman." Being a child is a way to disown her body and enjoy that magical neuter state in which sex roles are not yet limiting. When Dickinson did venture into these stereotyped roles, she found herself mysteriously inadequate. Her self-image as a teenager is low; she says of herself disparagingly that she will always "remain the same old sixpence" (*L*. I, p. 21). When it is Valentine's Day, she writes her brother complaining that "your *highly accomplished & gifted elder sister* is entirely overlooked" (*L*. I, p. 63). She stresses the qualities she most values in herself; but these are not necessarily the traits that would win her beaus and male admiration. In this early letter

(1848) she also complains of being homesick. We see a collage of symptoms of the "daughter construct": she is ambivalent about the social roles of women; she wants to rebel; she wants to be home; and she tries to esteem herself in terms other than the ones that are externally imposed by society. As time goes on, she cultivates an anti-social attitude as the naughty child; finding herself obliged to be sociable to visitors, she admits hoping that "all our grand-fathers and all their country cousins will pass away, as insects on vegetation" (*L*. I, p. 257).

Thus we can understand what poses as a paradox in Emily Dickinson's letters. She presents herself as a happily wicked child who is beaten for not working, and who loves to "run fast—and hide away from them all—" (*L*. I, p. 193), and at the same time as a child who insists that she cannot leave her house because she "loves it so." When she is invited elsewhere, she looks at "father and mother and Vinnie, and all my friends, and I say no—no, cant leave them, what if they die when I'm gone . . ." (*L*. I, p. 197). That she mourns for her childhood and refuses to leave home, whether to visit or marry, suggests that in spite of her wicked independence, she is in need of a mother to tell her how to grow.

ANGER IN THE ATTIC

Emily Dickinson's "naughty" persona constitutes another form of her re-jection of the feminine ideal which her mother represents. She presents herself as not pious or kind, but as hostile, vengeful, and angry. In fact she admits that part of her reluctance to deal with the world is her fear that she will do it harm. In some states of mind she cannot stay home, but when she goes out she experiences "suspense," although she is "held in check by some invisible agent" for she returns to the house "without having done any harm!" (*L*. I, pp. 111–12). The feeling that has driven her out of the house is a conscious desire to hurt someone. Dickinson cultivates an image of propensity for inflicting harm. She writes to Austin about his students, "So far as *I* am concerned I should like to have you kill some—there are so many now, there is no room for the Americans, and I cant think of a death that would be more after my mind than *scientific destruction* . . ." (*L*.I, p. 113). She seems to be teasing him by violating his ideas of female propriety, asking for "startling news": "I dont think deaths or murders can ever come amiss in a young woman's journal." She urges Susan Gilbert to "whip" her students as well: ". . . for *my* sake, whip them *hard* . . ." She tells another friend: "I have half a mind to *throw a stone* as it is, and kill barn door fowls, but I wont, I'll be considerate." She fantasizes being a witch: it would be "comfort to have a piping voice, and broken back, and scare little children." Even though she does feel "frightful," she assures Susan, she won't do her any harm; but when she thinks of "those I love," she fears that she will go "hopelessly insane" and will have to be "chained up" (*L.* I, pp. 144–45, 235; I, pp. 175, 182).

In a revealing letter to her uncle, Dickinson again gives expression to her anger. She denounces him as a "sinner" and purports to be planning to kill him. But she ends the fantasy with a disclaimer:

> . . . *no harm done I hope. Harm is one of those things that I always mean to keep clear of–but somehow my intentions and me dont chime as they ought–and people will get hit with stones I throw at my neighbor's dogs–not only hit–that is the least of the whole–but they insist on blaming* me *instead of the* stones–*and tell me their heads ache.* . . . . [*L.* I, pp. 79–80]

Again, we see Dickinson describing the conflict she feels in her role as the ideal harmless woman, which we must remember is her identity in society's eyes. Her ambivalence about this role takes the form of a war in her consciousness between "my intentions and me." The result is an identity in which she is not responsible for herself; there is a division within her between dutiful and rebellious daughter, and if this makes her do harm, it is the fault of whatever causes her conflict. In this sense she is "only a victim of society." She explains her reasoning further.

> *One man pointed a loaded gun at a man–and it shot him so that he died–and the people threw the owner of the gun into prison–and afterwards hung him for* murder. *Only another victim to the misunderstanding of society–such things should not be permitted–it certainly is as much as one's neck is worth to live in so stupid a world–and it makes one grow weary.* . . . *Now when I walk into your room and pluck your heart out that you die–I kill you–hang me if you like–but if I stab you while sleeping the dagger's to blame–it's no business of mine–you have no more right to accuse me of injuring you than anything else I can think of. That we understand capital punishment, and one another too I verily believe– and sincerely hope–for it's so trying to be read out of the wrong book when the right one is out of sight.*

We can read the letter in two ways. Dickinson can be seen as sarcastic when she talks about the owner of the gun as guiltless or the sleep-walker as innocent: it could be a satire on law—fathers and lawyers—and legal logic. But as I have been arguing, it also represents an ultimately logical defense for Dickinson who does feel herself to be a criminal in society's eyes: the crime of murder is only a degree past the crime of hating housework or not going to church. If one sees oneself as victim of forces greater than oneself, as Dickinson does, one is not to blame for the consequences. (We remember that Erikson insists that the deprivation of identity "can lead to murder.") In "My Life had stood–a Loaded Gun" (754), Dickinson specifically describes her persona as a gun held by the "Owner" mind in which the persona serves as a kind of mindless "hit man" for him. As such, being the gun but not the director who activates the gun, she cannot be blamed for what she does to his "foes." The poem, which expresses Dickinson's identity conflict as a guilty woman poet, relates to Dickinson's notion in the letter to her uncle thirteen years earlier that she is not to blame for where her words (or weapons) fall. The implication is that she is only doing her "duty"—serving her master by being a dutiful daughter.

That Emily Dickinson is perversely twisting logic to show the angry effects of "serving," and an identity conflict that has been imposed on her, shows us Dickinson's attitudes toward her own guilt as a rebellious daughter. In her writing, she is the owner of the gun. But she is not to blame for inflicting harm with the word. Her fantasy sketches reveal that the desire to harm (therefore the fear of harming) is quite conscious. Her frustrated aggression is aimed not so much at specific persons as at a nameless enemy which misinterprets her by "misreading" her potential. Doing harm is only a perversion of power—she would much rather do something great. But if society insists that as a woman she is powerless and harmless, she will take her revenge by insisting that she has the potential at least to do some harm—to make society suffer for underestimating her capabilities because she is a woman. Ironically, Emily Dickinson does no harm, but assumes the guilt for her angry feelings anyway. As psychologists have pointed out, feelings and deeds are the same to the superego (the punishing parents). This letter is written by a daughter trying to revenge those parents within her. They are as much to blame for her hostility as she is; but even for the muted rebellion of writing, she punishes herself and puts herself at war because of her "wicked" thoughts. She tells a girlfriend she *is* wicked: "Out of a wicked heart cometh wicked words." This is after her confession that she "hates" time and space because they limit and restrict her: "How I *hate* them–and would love to do them harm!" (*L*. I, p. 83). The context in which this attack on time and space takes place is a series of complaints about housework, family, God (who does not answer prayers), church (it is only necessary because God does not answer prayers), and the Sewing Society (which she refuses to attend). The odds at which Dickinson finds herself in regard to her family, society, and herself result from a series of restraints Dickinson assumes come with her given identity as "daughter." Her letters about her desire to harm and her insistence that she is "not guilty" are justifications for the kind of injustice she feels done to a daughter like herself. The biggest injustice in her mind is her guilt which manifests itself in the division within her consciousness so that she is always at war and never "at home."

Emily Dickinson's letters show her professing a criminal identity which disdains what other people value: she "loves" to be "surly–and muggy–and cross." The "Me" and the "Not Me" are violently unyoked: Dickinson has had to resort to metaphysical reversals in order to separate herself from concepts, attitudes, and activities relating to women that stand in the way of a "great" destiny. In order to make her own "declaration of independence" from her female destiny, she rejects the feminine ideal and stereotype. She could be very sexist in her letters, then: "Women talk: men are silent: that is why I dread women" (*L*. II, p. 473); another time she referred to the "sincere spite of a *Woman*" (*L*. III, p. 929). When Samuel Bowles once rebuked her for her chauvinism toward women, she replied, "I am sorry I smiled at women. Indeed, I revere holy ones, like Mrs Fry and Miss Nightingale. I will never be giddy again" (*L*. II, p. 366).

But if the letters show Dickinson in rebellion from the mother matrix, they do not really deal with the mother at all. In Dickinson's landscape as a poet-to-be, her mother is conspicuous by her absence. Even though Dickinson is physically engaged with her mother on a daily basis, her mother is consciously divorced from the "poetic" emotional sensibility she exposes to others. The absence of the mother in the letters is a direct response to a powerful mother matrix. She has both too much and too little mother: the right *kind* of mother is simply not available. She thus is motherless and resentful of her mother at the same time. In fact her lifestyle fuses such contradiction. She tends to her invalid mother in a dutiful way, and hides her rebellion safely away in letters and a cherry dresser full of poems neatly stitched together. After years of daily contact, it is odd that Mrs. Dickinson never knew who Dickinson really was. Dickinson felt forced to deprive herself of maternal recognition; this is the source, I think, of the poems in which she laments her lack of identity. Even "At last, to be identified!" (174) expresses relief. When she dies people will know who the dutiful nobody really was. Considering Emily Dickinson's sense of need to dissociate herself from her mother's matrix, her ambivalence toward her feminine identity, poetry, patriarchal society, God, church, politics—which have heretofore so puzzled her critics—make significant and coherent sense. For Dickinson, the House of Art is not a "household" and cannot be established by a woman unless she is one of those who "never had a mother" to teach her a woman's proper place.

3

The Father Eclipse

THE CASE OF THE NOTORIOUS FATHER

Emily Norcross Dickinson was not the only one to deny the Daughter recognition as "poet-to-be": Dickinson felt her father to be equally culpable, and if she stresses the absence of her mother in her life as a supportive figure, she gives equal weight to her father as a villainous presence. It is as if the child "touches up" the stern visage of her father by penciling in fangs and poking horns through his top hat. Dickinson's letters make erosions upon her father's public dignified image; they show a Halloween villain whose threat is not to be taken seriously. Granted, Emily Dickinson's account of her father in her correspondence is biased. But it is this bias which informs the poetry. It is readily apparent to the reader of both the poetry and the letters that the father is the central—if not the only—figure in Dickinson's thought. Consequently, Edward Dickinson is one of the most notorious fathers in literary history, his importance an issue which every biographer has had to resolve: how ironic that the man who was "too busy" to "notice" what his daughter did should be a figure of study today solely because his daughter wrote poetry, which he would have scorned on principle, and wrote about him. While there is no question that Edward had a role in his daughter's development, there is also no agreement about what this role was. It probably reflects Dickinson's own ambivalence in her record of their relationship that biographers have been drawn in to take sides. First there is her side, the inevitable "villain tyrant" school. In a pioneering work published in 1964, Clark Griffith advanced the theory of Edward's destructive effect upon his daughter, bringing to the legends and speculation of Genevieve Taggard (1930) a psychological methodology which concluded that Dickinson's "tragic poetry" is the result of her negative experience with her father. This relationship made her apprehensive about entering into a masculine world. Griffith's interpretation is supported by John Cody, a psychiatrist who views Edward Dickinson as clinically neurotic, destructively hostile and resentful toward his family because they kept him from entering the world with an easy conscience.[28] Cody argues persuasively that Edward's ambivalence toward his family produced three emotionally crippled children. Earlier, Taggard had suggested that Edward was responsible for Dickinson's withdrawal from society ("the tyrant formed the child") by forbidding her to accept the courtship of George Gould. For whatever reason, it is believed that Dickinson's psychologically damaged life as a recluse is a direct function of her relationship with her father.

On the other side is the backlash "oh come now" group who conceive it their duty to right Edward Dickinson's reputation and repair it from its malignment by his daughter. This defensive or corrective approach resists the negative image of Edward put forth in the poetry and letters in the light of his prominent and esteemed role in the community. They argue against taking Dickinson's foolery regarding her father too seriously. Richard B. Sewall, the major biographer and proponent of this approach, is committed to dispel the legends, myths, and clichés that have grown up about the father-daughter relationship.[29] He concedes that Edward was a powerful figure, but argues that he was not powerful to Dickinson, who did not take her father's "mild authoritarianism" seriously. But by saying this, Sewall acknowledges the potentially harmful effect the father could have had on Dickinson especially when he adds that given Edward's character, it is "just as well" that he neglected and misread his daughter: "had Edward Dickinson noticed what his daughter was up to, had he nurtured her as his darling genius and tried to impose his will on her creativity, he might have spoiled her or destroyed her. As it was, she survived and wrote. Perhaps it is just as well that he was too busy."[30]

Sewall's thesis is a slight variation of the argument begun by George Whicher in his widely influential 1938 biography when the father's reputation was already in dispute.[31] Whicher sought to give Edward Dickinson an important but neutral interpretation as far as Dickinson's development as a poet is concerned, in order to provide an "accurate" interpretation of Dickinson's personality; but in the process of being "objective" he was forced to dismiss much of Dickinson's testimony as inadmissible evidence. The determination of Edward Dickinson's "true" nature is not important, however—supposing we could ever determine such a thing for anyone—and therefore, defending or blaming him is irrelevant to our purpose. Rather, we need to determine his importance to the poet-to-be; and looking at how and why Dickinson portrayed him as she did, the retaliatory injustice she does to him in her "portraits," gives us a good indication of her feelings as a daughter and of the role he plays—the role she *makes* him play—in her poetic development. We want to know from her point of view how she came to be the poet and live the life she did. If she gives her father a starring role as villain, we must make a serious critical analysis of their relationship from this perspective. This means taking seriously Dickinson's bias, for what is literature, after all, but one biased perspective? The trouble

with a "neutral" approach is that it imposes a neutrality upon figures who were
not themselves neutral. Dickinson may have been self-centered and unfair, but
her biases are the heart of her poetry. The "neutral" approach necessarily
obscures her reality.[32] For example, Whicher agrees that Edward Dickinson
was the "cardinal fact" in Dickinson's life, yes, not as a villain but as a cultured
man of reason, an heroic idealist, a humanitarian sacrificing himself for the
world, an arbiter of "humane living." Insisting that Dickinson's personality can
"only be correctly interpreted" when this father "is taken for granted, beside
her and in her," Whicher reconstructs a symbiotic father-daughter relationship:

> *His gods were her gods: his granite integrity was hers also. . . . Her*
> *defiance of her father was a defiance of what was deepest in herself. . . .*
> *It was in high fun that she delighted to picture herself as a rebel incar-*
> *nate. Precisely because her character was as firmly rooted as his, she*
> *could permit her fancy to frisk. . . . She came to understand him as her*
> *own soul. . . . [While Edward Dickinson made a] sacrificial effort to*
> *sustain for a little time the precarious order of humane living, it was her*
> *part to contribute grace and wit. . . . There were desserts to make and*
> *the piano to be played after dinner.*[33]

The picture that emerges from the above passage is of a delightful ambience,
from rebellion to dessert. We see a stylized relationship, a meeting of enlightened, compatible minds across a drawing room, of hearts in tune, of spirits at
play. Even if this portrait is accurate from the world's point of view, this is not
the picture we get of Edward or their situation from his daughter. Emily Dickinson's letters, especially her early ones, argue vigorously against her father's
noble image: she is persecuted and oppressed by a tragic clown, a tryant buffoon
whom the world erroneously takes seriously and to whom it grants the power to
control her life.

That Emily Dickinson had to make desserts and play the piano—that this
was her worth to her father—that he never knew who his daughter was or could
be—was to her way of thinking a tragic, ironic predicament. To make light of
Dickinson's obligatory and demeaning role in her household as Whicher does,
for example, might make for fine irony on the part of critics who think a great
poet's temporal unimportance or persecution is humorous in hindsight, but it
does injustice to the extreme seriousness with which Dickinson took her dilemma. Whicher's sense of the daughter who delights in the fun of posing
herself as a rebel incarnate seems to be a symptom of paternal wishful thinking;
no nice girl like Emily Dickinson would ever be really hostile toward her father.
She was not *really* unhappy; it was all a joke.

Emily Dickinson cannot be said to be her father's daughter ("his gods
were her gods"), any more than she can be said to be her mother's; but she
could have been, and she gladly would have been, if the daughter had the same

opportunity in her family as the son. This was the rub—the denial of opportunity to realize herself. If Dickinson is defiant, as Whicher states, it is not "in high fun." Her anger is directed toward a father—the masculine world—who does not notice, and will not notice, in what ways she is powerful, just like him: that is, her potential to be his "son." His conviction of the limitations of her sex blinded him to the realization that his daughter had the ambition as well as the intellectual capability to take after him. Her role, to *his* way of thinking, was to bake his daily bread, make him desserts, entertain him at the piano, and serve as a hostess to his guests—and that was all. He saw nothing wrong with these filial demands, either in terms of their triviality or in terms of her time. Dickinson did. She must have felt the injustice in the fact that her father's efforts to win glory for himself in the marketplace were considered noble "sacrifices," while she was forced to use her time to contribute bread, pudding, and music, which were considered only her rightful duties—a conviction shared by everyone except herself, for she was convinced that she could be as great as her father to the world, or greater.

All this was not really Edward's fault; he had no reason to expect anything else from a daughter than "life's little duties," as she called them. His attitudes—male chauvinism in our day, cultural tradition in his—may have been taken for granted by anyone else than his daughter, but Dickinson had a conviction of her own potential that made her father's expectations hard to take—particularly since fulfilling Edward's expectations brought her no esteem in his eyes. Rather, her compliances only confirmed and reinforced his sense of her capabilities and worth as a woman. Although her rebellion was never overt—Edward never discovered the major mode of her rebellion, which was her poetry—their skirmishes, particularly those over modern literature, were only the slightest tip of the iceberg, and were charged with the massive bulk and weight of resentments that were kept supressed below the surface. How can she have a soulmate in a man society perceives as saving the world while she as the good daughter "diverts" him, as Whicher says, with puddings and music? Emily Dickinson's point of view has been ignored too long—her foolery is quite serious. She, more than anyone else, was aware of the absolute futility of the desire to emulate her father, an awareness that gives a self-mocking edge to her anger; and I think that this is the insight we must have when we analyze Emily Dickinson's relationship with her father.

If her father was unaware of her resentment, it is only greater evidence that they did not enjoy a close relationship. If he was aware, he would have been cruel to perpetuate these duties. Neither speaks well for a healthy, close father-daughter relationship. Never mind that Victorian families were not really "close;" the child's feelings and needs are the same whether society condones neglect or not. In any case, Dickinson was critical of her father's paternal failings. It seems he would have had to be blind not to notice Emily Dickinson's discomfort in the role of dutiful daughter, but perhaps it was more that Edward's blindness was a function of his being emotionally unprepared—hence unwilling—to recognize the degree to which his daughter could have matched his worldly success, as the following excerpt from a letter to his fiancee suggests:

> *I passed Tuesday evening, of this week, in company with Miss Sedgwick, the Authoress of 'Redwood' & 'New England Tale,' at a party. . . . She had an interesting countenance—an appearance of much thought, 'rather masculine features. And I feel happy at having an opportunity of seeing a female who had done so much to give our works of taste so pure and delicate a character—and a conscious pride that women of our own country & our own state, too, are emulating not only the females but the men of England & France & Germany & Italy in works of literature— 'we are warranted in presuming that, if they had opportunities equal to their talents, they would not be inferior to our own sex in improving the sciences. 'Tho I should be sorry to see another Mme. de Stael—especially if any one wishes to make a partner of her for life. Different qualities are more desirable in a female who enters into domestic relations—and you have already had my opinions on that subject—*[34]

"Different qualities," indeed. This letter outlines the problems any daughter is going to have growing up with such a father if she has literary aspirations, and it also sets out the specific terms of Dickinson's lifelong dilemma. Women who think and write could earn her father's respect, but they could never have his love. Dickinson was caught between her need for her father's recognition of her potential and her need for his approval of her as a daughter. Edward's attitudes also reinforced the notion that "woman writer" is a contradiction in terms, which could only aggravate Dickinson's feeling of being a "Kangaroo among the Beauty."

Emily Dickinson appears to have resolved her dilemma by outwardly conforming to the role of a dutiful daughter and concealing her "masculine" rebellious identity as a poet. She wrote poetry without her father's knowledge late at night when the rest of the house was sleeping and recorded the strain such deception placed on her. Essentially she gave up trying to convince her father of her worth, and instead, through her letters, went in search of other father figures who were more predisposed in favor of women literati. At the same time she took up her battle against her father's expectations of her to stay home and perform "life's little duties." In her letters she gave voice to her conflict with her father; but the real battle was fought between a woman poet and a patriarchal society that regrets the existence of its talented women. The world has them both wrong in assuming the father is a sturdy light, because no one recognizes *her* equal or greater abilities. She shares the self-image of the lonely person saving the world; *she* would like to be revered for sacrificing herself for holy causes, and in fact this is precisely the image she gives of herself. But the world does not see her like this, and neither does Edward, so she continues to make literary erosions upon his character and dignity.

An analysis of Dickinson's letters reveals that Dickinson's rebellion from her father assumes several forms: exaggerated obedience as a Dutiful Daughter (including her refusal to leave her "father's ground for any House or Town" through moving away, marriage, or career); her continual efforts to expose her father's true "at home" character; her poetry, and the fact that she keeps it secret from him; her refusal to abide by the expectations set for her by a patriarchal culture; and finally, her rejection of this patriarchal society itself. She scorns the world for its failure to properly value its women, and in the process, she rejects the masculine world and what it represents, just as she rejects the feminine.

We will see Dickinson in her letters to the world, then, dissociating herself from her father's life in precisely the same way as she does with her mother. But while she seems to reject her mother because her mother is not "great," she must reject what her father stands for as well because his possibilities are not available to her. Dickinson derides her father's value of fame and success because they are not within her reach—and what she cannot forgive is that he does not even realize the injustice of the situation. She can joke about her father and his fallibilities, but the fact that she does so in her letters and not to his face is not only a function of pragmatic cowardice, it seems to me, but a sign that her quarrel is not with her father personally so much as it is with a world which reveres her father at her expense. Therefore, to cut him down or otherwise satirize him in her letters is actually a way to attack a social structure which automatically confers on him (or any man) autonomy, power, and influence. Even as Emily Dickinson played along with her role as dutiful daughter, then, she was pointing out to her correspondents the terrible inappropriateness of this role for a person of her abilities.

But one other account of Dickinson's bias regarding her father must be set forth. Dickinson has a specific grudge against her father which John Cody has illuminated. Whicher had stated that the father must be "taken for granted beside her and in her," but this is manifestly not the case for Dickinson, who is resentful about her inability to take her father's presence for granted. She feels he has neglected her in favor of an "admiring bog": his voters, clients, colleagues, and cronies. As a man of the world, a lawyer and state and local politician, he moved in and out of his family's life with regularity. More often than not, he was absent from home, which profoundly affected his dependent wife and daughters. Lavinia's diary of 1858 (when Dickinson was already twenty-one) is revealing in this regard, if her response can be said to reflect the mood of the rest of the family, for her account of her life is largely the record of her father's comings and goings.[35] An entry covering several days may consist only of "Father's *gone!*" until we see, several days later, "Father's *home!*" Because his family was so dependent upon him, his vigorously practiced autonomy occasioned trauma and feelings of insecurity and rejection. Another reason

Edward Dickinson's absence is interpreted as rejection is his lack of demon-
strative affection. Dickinson's sister Lavinia writes, "He never kissed us good
night in his life—he would have died for us, but he would have died before he
let us know it!"[36] Her brother Austin reports kissing his father's forehead when
the father is a corpse: "There, father, I never dared to do that when you were
living."[37]

Dickinson's relationship with her father is painful to her, and if she rebels
against her father and what he represents, it could hardly have been "delightful"
to her. As her poems make clear, she took her rebellion against her father very
seriously indeed. Being witty may have been a socially acceptable way for her
to cope with the injustice of the world's disregard for her own capabilities. Her
frustration is being unknown, unseen by a world which is blind to her potential
because she is not a "son": *this* is the "cardinal fact" to her. If indeed she is
her father's daughter, she is the only one who knows it.

How this affected her decision to write poetry, the attitudes and philoso-
phies the poetry embodies, the kinds of poems she wrote, and her aesthetics,
should be our primary concern. We must examine why Dickinson portrayed her
father as she did: why she insisted her readers see she is both daunted and
undaunted by him; why she kept her mother out of her writing when her mother
was always there, and why she featured her father when he was never there.
Was it along the lines of her remedy for absence, "To fill a Gap/Insert the Thing
that caused it—" (546), or is her calling the reader's attention to her relationship
with her father part of her strategy to dissociate herself in her reader's mind
from the feminine world in order to raise her status? Or is Edward Dickinson a
victim of the "daughter construct" which Dickinson erects as a poetic strategy?
In answering these questions, I am arguing for a re-evaluation, if not a reinter-
pretation, of Edward Dickinson's role in his daughter's development as a poet
that has so far been "taken for granted" in our studies.

VERY WELL, FATHER: SPITE AND THE DUTIFUL DAUGHTER

An early recorded incident between father and daughter will serve as a
paradigm for the dynamics of their relationship to follow. Edward is generally
known to have been a singularly disapproving presence in his household, particular, querulous, and cranky. He had evidently been complaining about a
chipped plate which he felt was being placed repeatedly before him at the table.
On the afternoon on which the incident occurred, he found the chipped plate
before him once again, and must have made some dry or whining remark (he
was capable of either), because Emily Dickinson suddenly snatched up the
plate and ran out to the back garden, whereupon she proceeded to smash it to
pieces "so he would never be offended by the plate again."[38] This unexpectedly
rash, passionate act of overzealous or exaggerated duty has mockery and vio-

lence in it; it is illustrative of Dickinson's almost masochistic insistence throughout her life on pleasing her father to spite both of them. By obeying him to extremes, she seems to be showing the world the absurdity of his commands: she uses obedience as a mode of rebellion. In fact, she seems to have deliberately set herself out as a martyr to this troubled tyrant clown who "steps like Cromwell when he gets the kindlings" (*L.* II, p. 470), bending to his will even when it is against her own or his own wishes. This sense of willful perverseness is seen even in the legends during Dickinson's lifetime: "In the garden one evening Emily and a young man with her turned suddenly to see Emily's father standing over them with a lantern, ordering her back into the house. Emily is said to have replied, 'Very well, father, if you do not trust me out of your sight, I will never leave your garden again.' " As Genevieve Taggard notes, whether the incident ever occurred is not important: it is a "folk way of telling what the neighbors knew to be true" about the relationship in general.[39] Another case in point is the contemptuous attitude Dickinson expresses towards an "obedient daughter" who foolishly will not let herself visit her friends in Amherst because she "preferred to gratify her father" (*L.* I, p. 35). Here it is clear that being a dutiful daughter means pleasing one's father, and that pleasing one's father means being foolishly self-sacrificing. Yet two years later Dickinson describes herself in these same terms: "Father wishing to hear the piano, I like an obedient daughter, played & sang a few tunes, much to his apparent gratification" (*L.* I, p. 59). She stresses, however, that she is only "like" an obedient daughter; even though she has submitted to her father's wishes, she does not identify herself as an obedient daughter; rather, she impersonates one and mocks both of them in the process.

But if Dickinson mocks herself when she puts on the mask of duty, she is also careful to admit every time she is so "defeated." Every interaction with her father is put in terms of a battle of wills, and she always loses and ends up being dutiful: thus she is defeated when she is taken home to "headquarters" away from school against her will, or stays home and comforts "my parents by my presence," or submits to her father's administration of medicine which she describes as a form of torture he especially enjoys. When she thanks her cousin for a book, she describes herself in the romantic idiom of a captive in a "dungeon" dreaming in her solitude "of freedom—and the future" (*L.* I, pp. 75–77). But she does not show herself trying to escape. She stays home and endures being dominated. Her life is lived according to her father's whims. He always gets his way, whether it is to take her away from school or even to go to school: "Father wishes to have me at home a year, and then he will probably send me away again, where I know not." She knows that having to leave school at this time will "seal" her "fate," but there is nothing she can do.[40] Her father is not only a kind of tyrant, then, but he is also a very unapproachable person even when he means well. Dickinson tells Higginson that she could not tell time until she was fifteen: "My father thought he had taught me but I did not understand & I was afraid to say I did not & afraid to ask any one else lest he should know" (L. II, p. 475). Surely this is a tragicomic image when children try to protect a parent's feelings by not pointing out their incompetence in dealing with them. Dickinson tells her friends and other family members that her father is so unapproachable that she "dares not" ask him to read a letter or to have him fill a prescription for her (L. I, pp. 263, 274).

At the same time, Dickinson's mother tells us that Emily complains about her father's absences,[41] and we see Dickinson telling her friends that she cannot visit them for fear that her father might miss her (L. II, p. 337). Perhaps her scorn for the dutiful daughter is a pose. However, the majority of her early letters make it clear that while she is outwardly deferential to her father, her commitment to duty is only superficial. She might comply with his demands, but her heart and spirit rebel. What is important for us to know is that she presents herself in opposition to her father on the subject of literature. He only reads on Sunday, she proclaims, and those books are "*lonely* and *rigorous*" (L. II, p. 473). He wants the family to read only the Bible (L. II, p. 475), and legend has it that books had to be smuggled into the house by way of the piano bench or the bush by the front door. At one point, he discovers a copy of *Reveries of a Bachelor*, and denounces it as trash (L. I, pp. 238–39). On her part, Dickinson purports to be so influenced by this book that she wants to write her own version of the story: it involves a recluse-nursemaid daughter who renounces any adventure in the world to care for a sick father. At another time, she relates her father's reaction to Melville: "I got down before father this morning, and spent a few moments profitably with the South Sea Rose [*Typee*]. Father detecting me, advised wiser employment, and read at devotions the chapter of the gentleman with one talent. I think he thought my conscience would adjust the gender" (L. II, p. 427).[42] Emily Dickinson is almost thirty-four when she records this incident from their continual skirmishes, and her poetry has reached its peak. She can just imagine what her father would think of her writing poetry if he cannot abide her even reading Melville. Poetry itself represents to Edward all that is sinful, worldly, and trivial. It has no place in *their* life, but it does in *Dickinson's:* "We do not have much poetry, father having made up his mind that its pretty much all *real life*. Fathers real life and *mine* sometimes come into collision, but as yet, escape unhurt" (L. I, p. 161). Her father insists on "Prose," not the kind Melville writes, but the kind of serious attitude toward living which does not include art for pleasure's sake. Edward maintains a critical attitude toward any of Dickinson's achievements or ideas— at least, this is the impression she wants to create. For example, she tells her brother of an incident in which her father has forced her to make conversation with some unexpected (and unwanted) guests. Playing the role of the dutiful daughter, she endeavors to make safe conversation about the weather, but when she strays from the weather, she gets "such a look . . . from my rheumatic sire" that she tries to "shrink away into primeval nothingness' (L. I, p. 185–86). It was her father's victory just to have made her talk in the first place, for when she creeps into the sitting room "more dead than alive . . . Father looked round triumphantly." On another occasion, she tells Austin that she had planned to send him apples:

> *Father overheard some of my intentions and said they were 'rather small'—*
> *whether this remark was intended for the* apple *or for my noble self I did*
> *not think to ask him—I rather think he intended to give us* both *a cut—*
> *however—he may go!* [L. I, p. 127]

That Dickinson deliberately misinterprets his critical comment on the size of the apples is significant, particularly in the light that she is telling this to her brother. Dickinson makes a point of showing that she can shrug off her father's lack of esteem as well as his habit of criticism of her, but she also emphasizes how her father is protective of her brother: he wants his son sent *larger* apples. Dickinson's relationship with her brother transcends typical sibling rivalry because of her sensitivity to being her father's daughter, not his son. Austin has preference, and she must endure hearing him constantly praised and being protected *from her* (L. I, p. 237). In her letters to Austin, we see her obsession with the father-son relationship from which she is excluded. Dickinson stresses in her letters how their father cares for him: their father feels he has a "blessing in his son," as if, she says, "it was a blessing to have an only son" (L. I, pp. 231). She is in the peculiar position of having to reassure Austin of his father's regard. We wince when she insists, "I believe at this moment, Austin, that there's no body living for whom father has such respect as for you," knowing how hopeless Dickinson feels herself about gaining her father's respect and serious attention. Therefore, when her father tells her that her brother is a perceptive person, she reports the incident to Austin, telling him she answers her father like a dutiful daughter: "Of course I answered 'yes sir.' " But she stresses the strain of this role as go-between concerning father and son. She makes fun of herself, but she shows resentment towards both when she adds, "but what the thought conveyed I remained in happy ignorance." Significantly, she does not attempt to find out. Certainly she is jealous. As the son, Austin is educated and goes out into the world. In one letter, Dickinson is supposedly expressing pity for his plight. She generously and self-sacrificingly offers to change places with him: "I am so sorry for you. I do wish it was *me*, that you might be well and happy, for I have no profession, and have such a snug, warm home and *I* had as lief suffer some, a great deal rather than not, that by doing so, you were exempted from it. May I change places, Austin? *I* dont care how sharp the pain is, not if it dart like arrows, or pierce bone and bone . . . I should be twice, *thrice* happy to bear it in your place" (L. I, p. 162). It is hard to determine how facetious she is being here. However mockingly, she tries to raise the status of being at home and having no profession. She would quite likely jump at the chance of changing places with him, but she cannot: it is a totally futile, if safe, offer to make to Austin, because she does not have his educational opportunities, and never will, and they both know it. This is why she is half serious (at least) when she tells him how much she dislikes reading his letters aloud to the family, as her father insists, because her father is so enthusiastic about his son's talents and achievements. To make her read the letters only aggravates her resentment. Dickinson says, in what may be an understatement, "I dont love to read your letters all out loud to father" (L. I, p. 243). Her account of reading one of his letters to her father gives insight into the problem. Theoretically, she is censoring the letter as she reads in order to keep Austin out of trouble if he has said anything that will embarrass him if his father hears: "I reviewed the contents hastily—striking out all suspicious places, and then very *artlessly* and unconsciously began. My heart went 'pit a pat' till got safely by a remark concerning Martha, and my stout soul was *not*, till the manuscript was over" (L. I, p. 136). She implies that they are co-conspirators in league against the father. We note that the way in which she is able to fool her father for them is to exploit her femininity by acting "artless" and "unconscious." In other words, not showing her real intelligence is a strategy: she will use his ignorance of her capabilities to get away with small defiances. But at the same time she is forced to perpetuate a degrading pose which again only substantiates his perfunctory neglect of her real attributes and potential. In this way, being a dutiful daughter means being "artless" and "unconscious" (the opposite of what it takes to be a poet); and her hidden potential is only that she can be unexpectedly naughty. Her strategies work because she is a daughter and her father consequently does not expect anything else *than* duty from her. As Higgins has noted, Edward Dickinson assumed that his daughters, like his wife, "care more about puddings than poetry." Edward "expected a good deal of his children, especially Austin. . . ." but his high demands on Emily were that she greet his guests at his annual commencement reception.[43] That—and, of course, that she never leave home. Because of Edward's different expectations for son and daughter, the daughter can get away with harmless boondoggles, but at the same time she resents the fact that Austin is so important to her father that "he [her father] cant get along without you" (L. I, p. 269). He can't get along without her, either, but in the meantime Austin is making him proud. When Dickinson fails to respond enthusiastically to her father's praise of her brother, insult is added to injury—she is chastised. What is particularly revealing is that lack of respect for Austin is equated in her father's mind with her insubordinate taste for modern literature: "Father was very severe to me; he thought I'd been trifling with you, so he gave me quite a trimming about 'Uncle Tom' and 'Charles Dickens' and these 'modern Literati' who he says are *nothing*, compared to past generations, who flourished when *he was a boy*. . . . [She then goes on to relate his discovery of the Ilk Marvel book *Reveries of a Bachelor* which her father discovered her reading and found "ridiculous.] . . . so I'm quite in disgrace at present" (L. I, p. 237).

Even though she and Austin supposedly share similar values—books— and similar problems in dealing with their father—both are insecure about his esteem—Dickinson tries to make Austin see the difference in the nature of their two relationships because of the fact that she is a daughter and he is a son. Austin does not have to be "obedient." Interestingly, when Dickinson does an act which she feels is bold, wicked, or cunning, she says that she is "Austin" of whom "Emily and Vinnie" would disapprove. Thus the dutiful daughter in her disowns her "masculine" impulse to make a social transgression. Dickinson may want to enlist Austin as a witness to the unfair sexual discrimination she experiences, but although he is manifestly aware of his sister's potential—he could not help but be, for he is her favorite sounding board—he never feels it is a wrong that he, and not she, is asked to go out into the world. Austin was always too preoccupied to take his sister very seriously, even though his esteem was very important to Dickinson. When she died and Lavinia was trying to arouse support for getting the poems published, Austin was not interested; he was too busy to care whether she ever became famous or a public figure in her own right.

Given the fact that Emily Dickinson insists to Austin that she is not regarded by her father with the same esteem that he is, it is interesting that the identity she projects to the rest of the world is in terms of an almost unnaturally close relationship with her father and his need of her. At the age of twenty-eight, she writes that she does not go out at all "lest father will come and miss me, or miss some little act, which I might forget, should I run away" (*L.* II, pp. 298–99). At thirty-six, she tells Higginson that she cannot come to visit him in Boston because "father objects because he is in the habit of me;" and "I must omit Boston. Father prefers so. He likes me to travel with him but objects that I visit" (*L.* II, pp. 450, 453). Later, she offers no excuses: "I do not cross my Father's ground to any House or town" (*L.* II, p. 460). Perhaps these statements are not proof of Edward Dickinson's possessiveness, but represent a kind of fantasy on Dickinson's part that she is so indispensable to her father that he cannot let her go.

But Dickinson maintains a fiction at the same time that she does not have any parents at all: "I guess I have done wrong–I don't know certainly, but Austin tells me so, and he is older than I. . . . When Vinnie is here–I ask her; if she says I sin, I say, 'Father, I have sinned'–if she sanctions me, I am not afraid" (*L.* II, p. 348). So which is it? Either she wants her reader to believe that she does not have any parental guidance or direction, she has just enough, or else she has too much. This contradictory state of feeling that she lacks a father and is oppressed by too much father continues until her father's death. Dickinson's comments after her father's death, as in the case of her mother, reveal she is responsible for her ambivalence. Six months after she had told a friend she had no parents but her sister, she writes about her father's death, when she is forty-four: "I cannot recall myself;" her mind now "never comes home" (*L.* II, p. 526). She appears to be devastated. Thus identity, home, and sanity are a function of her father's presence: he was in fact a necessary part of her psychological landscape—at a distance. Dickinson recounted the last afternoon she spent with her father. She had expressed a desire to be with him that day, which surprised and pleased him, as she usually kept to herself. He told her as the afternoon wore on that he "would like it not to end," but Dickinson was apparently embarrassed at the intimacy and, seeing her brother approaching, suggested that father and son go off for a walk instead. Perhaps their encounter was too gratifying. She preferred to think of him in the way she described him to Higginson: "His heart was pure and terrible and I think no other like it exists" (*L*. II, p. 528).

It appears then that it was really Edward who was given a role to play in their relationship, one that was as difficult as her own. He was to be distant, disapproving, antagonistic to poetry, and chauvinistic, if she was to write poetry as his daughter; Dickinson could not leave him because he was instrumental in her motivation to write poetry. Edward's role in the poetry is shown in one of Dickinson's first poems (1858) that she encloses with an inscription in a letter to her sister-in-law:

> *Sleep is supposed to be*
> *By souls of sanity*
> *The shutting of the eye.*
> . . . .
> *Morn is supposed to be*
> *By people of degree*
> *The breaking of the Day.*
>
> *Morning has not occurred!*
>
> *That shall Aurora be—*
> *East of Eternity—*
> *One with the banner gay—*
> *One in the red array—*
> *That is the break of Day!*

[13]

Nothing is as it should be: the day has not broken for her and she will only be awakened at death. Dickinson then reveals that the cause of her predicament is her father: "To my Father—to whose untiring efforts in my behalf, I am indebted for my *morning hours*—viz—3. AM. to 12. PM. these grateful lines are inscribed by his aff Daughter." Because of her father's "efforts," Dickinson experiences no morning. He is the factor responsible for her lack of status, her insanity, and her inability to feel at one with and at home in the world. He does not let her sleep: she is not a person of "degree." She indirectly suggests that he is her motivation for her writing poetry, because it is in her night hours that she wrestles with her poems and the nightmares that produce them. While he is to blame for dominating her day, his failure to awaken her activates her need to rebel and write poetry—to distinguish herself and revenge herself on him at the same time. We should note that throughout her poetry, day and morning take on the symbolic meaning of the time in which the expectations on her as a dutiful daughter are the greatest and her destiny is most threatened. Thomas Johnson contends that Dickinson's inscription to her father only refers to the fact that he woke her up in the mornings, but Dickinson has written that she is the early riser (*L*. I, pp. 163, 276). Even if her father *did* wake her up, the implications of the poem and letter are that 1) she does not get up because she has not slept, and 2) when she does "wake" it is to a nightmare or death. Finally, it is important to note that she does not send the letter or the poem to her father, to whom, after all, it is inscribed, but to Susan Gilbert. Dickinson shows herself unable to communicate with her father. If she could communicate with him, she would not need to write the poem. Her poetry depends upon her father's distance and his failure to understand her true identity.

Therefore, it follows that after her father is dead, Dickinson finds herself, as she claims in her letters, no longer able to write. Edward is no longer there to make absent. But she asks Samuel Bowles to accept the customary "portrait":

> *As Summer into Autumn slips*
> *And yet we sooner say*
> *"The Summer" than "the Autumn," lest*
> *We turn the sun away,*
>
> *And almost count it an Affront*
> *The presence to concede*
> *Of one however lovely, not*
> *The one that we have loved—*
>
> *So we evade the charge of Years*
> *On one attempting shy*
> *The Circumvention of the Shaft*
> *Of Life's Declivity.*
>
> [1346]

This "portrait" is remarkably controlled in terms of emotion and technique for one who is supposedly too distraught by grief to write. The sonnet is a philosophically detached meditation not so much on death as it is on our attitudes toward mortality and old age. Dickinson makes gentle fun of our human tendency to feel all right about acknowledging "Summer," the fact that life rises to a peak of fulfillment, while we do not want the decay which is the natural result of such growth. To admit that "Autumn" is an inevitable part of our destiny risks bringing death that much closer (we will "turn the sun away"). We proceed to try to evade paying the price for having matured. Dickinson's choice of "Autumn" instead of winter to symbolize the inevitability of our "Declivity" is important, for she is emphasizing that maturity is a gradual downward slope into death: old age is emblematic of maturity as well as death.

If we did not know that the poem was intended to describe her father, we

would interpret it as a particularly passionless and aloof view of human nature.
The fact that we know that Dickinson wants her reader to think it is about her
father is important, for it implies that she wants Bowles to see how mature she
is in her attitude toward her father's vulnerability. I think that Dickinson
therefore is using this poem to indicate that now, at her father's death, she is
not intimidated by his power; she sees his weakness, and she almost patroniz-
ingly forgives him as she forgives humanity. The other side of her refusal to
acknowledge her father's supposed invulnerability is her joking about his resistance to life, even "Summer." When a relative sends a wreath commemorative of his death at Christmas, Dickinson writes back that she is sure the woman
knew he was dead or she would not have dared send him a Christmas gift, "for
you know how he frowned upon Santa Claus—and all such prowling gentlemen"
(L. II, p. 531). We must keep in mind these attitudes toward her father that she
expresses when we then see her romanticizing "those amazing years I had a
father," as she would later do with her mother, or being so melodramatic that
she sends her father's last present of books to Higginson because she cannot
face opening them (L. II, p. 543, 547). But however ambivalent she was about
her father, she internalized him, even the parts of him that she mocked. One of
her last statements in reference to him is that if she were to see her friend Mrs.
Holland again, she would begin every sentence with "I say unto you" (L. II, p.
537; III, pp. 849–50); her father's alienating way of expressing himself is to be
hers as well.

ALL MEN SAY WHAT TO ME

When Emily Dickinson's father died, she turned to other men for support,
notably Judge Otis Lord of Salem and Thomas Wentworth Higginson. But even
during her father's lifetime Dickinson established relationships with men that
were predicated on her need for a father. Analysis of these relationships reveals
much about Dickinson's relationship with her father, for we not only see her
acting as a daughter in reference to a father-figure, but we see that no relationship was formed out of the context of her own relationship (as she perceived it)
with her father.[44]

No matter what her age or their age, Dickinson approaches males—with
the exception of her brother Austin—as a little girl seeking approval, advice,
love, esteem, wisdom, sanction, forgiveness, and notice. She addresses them
with reverence, deference, and submission as well as occasional arch coyness,
even the ones who were more nearly her contemporaries (Samuel Bowles, for
example). Many of them were older (Judge Lord was more her father's age), and
all of them were in positions of worldly and spiritual power and authority. They
were men with whom Edward was directly associated in his law practice, his
involvement in state and local politics, in the running of Amherst College, and
so on. Thus her first "Master" was a principal of Amherst Academy; Benjamin

Newton, who tutored Dickinson, was a law student in Edward's office; Eldridge Bowdoin, the recipient of her Valentine poem, was her father's law partner; Judge Lord (whom she describes as "my father's closest friend") was her father's colleague by profession and politics. She also was in the habit of turning to older men for advice about spiritual matters. All of these relationships were based on her insistence that she needs the instruction and authority that her own father cannot provide her: "I had no Monarch in my life, and cannot rule myself;" "Father . . . too busy with his Briefs–to notice what we do;" "Will you help me improve?" (*L*. II, pp. 414, 404, 403, 415). It is curious, given her ambivalence to her father's dominant role, that each male is sought as a Master, Tutor, Preceptor, or Monarch. In each relationship, she promises to be both obedient and remarkable: her father's daughter. Perhaps her strategy is to find men like her father; she can then convince *them* of her worth. She cannot let her father see her real identity (or he has refused to see it), and consequently her father's only concern is that she not "disgrace" herself (*L*. I, p. 49).

But Dickinson's efforts to distinguish herself in the eyes of a series of fathers fail for the same reasons that she fails with her own father. In the process of acting both dutiful and worthy, she is misunderstood. As she complained to Higginson, "All men say 'What' to me but I thought it a fashion" (*L*. II, p. 415). Her letters, to me, do not so much clarify her identity as a worthy person deserving of notice as they perpetuate her martyrdom as the unrecognized and unidentified true "Son." In other words, Dickinson not only perpetuates her identity as "daughter" in her relationships to men, but she perpetuates the role of "father" as well: she deliberately approaches men so that they underestimate her as "artless" and "unconscious" and thereby never recognize her real identity. She will never step out of the role of the little girl acting in reference to a father.

Perhaps the most significant aspect of these surrogate father-daughter relationships is that they are specifically set in the context of her relationship with her father. The subject matter of the correspondence revolves around the extent to which Dickinson feels her father loves and esteems her and whether she is important to him or not. This may or may not have been her foremost concern in her life (certainly she does not take her "father's presence beside her or in her" for granted); but these are the terms in which she wants to be understood. Dickinson wants the world to identify her with her father, even if it is only an acknowledgment of his neglect and punishment of her. I see the daughter construct informing her relationships with men, then, in terms of 1) her choice of men who were close to her father in his worldly activities and who were like him in terms of power, prestige, and authority, if not occupation and age; 2) her effort to achieve a fatherly esteem and recognition; 3) her pose as the daughter as playful, teasing, pert, and humbly anxious ("Did it offend thee?"); 4) her insistence on being identified with her own father; and 5) her compulsive worry over her relationship with her *other* "Father." She cannot confront her father or Father to their respective faces, so she appears to be working out her ambivalent feelings as a daughter in relationships which she models on the one troubling her. Her letters to other men keep her in communication with her father.

It is especially illuminating to discuss Dickinson's relationship with two (or three) "Masters" in her life, Judge Lord, Higginson, and the as yet unidentified "Master" lover, to illustrate how she presents herself to a lover and to an editor (the two keys to fulfillment) as a daughter to a father. Judge Otis Lord, the man she describes as closest to her father (*L*. II, p. 567), is clearly a means for Dickinson to cope with her Oedipal fantasies. When her father died, she turned to Lord for a passionate love affair. There is no doubt in biographers' minds that her attraction to Lord was based on the association of Lord with her father. Richard Sewall gives a wryly forbidding account of Lord that makes it seem inexplicable that Dickinson could ever have loved him.[45] But Sewall makes it clear that both Edward and Austin admired Judge Lord intensely. He had the reputation of being one of the sternest, most authoritarian, awesome, and powerful men in the state. He was not Edward, but close. Sewall suggests that Dickinson even thought they were alike in their unrevealed natures as well as their public images, in that both were lonely and vulnerable. As she called her father a man who never played (*L*. II, p. 486), she wrote about Lord: "Abstinence from Melody was what made him die" (*L*. III, p. 861). In the letters she wrote him when she was in her fifties, she is a teasing, naughty little girl dreading punishment and hopeful of the attention being punished brings: "Will you punish me?" (*L*. II, p. 615). She feels unworthy of him because she has been wicked; if he pretends to tolerate her at all, it is only because he has been forgiving: "Our life together was long forgiveness on your part toward me" (*L*. III, p. 728). At the same time, she insists that she does not know what her "Crime" is: she only assumes that she has sinned because she experiences rejection. The "Penalty" is "rosy" because at least it is a kind of fatherly notice: she wants to be so much a part of him that she asks to be punished by being "incarcerated" in him. In other words, she wants to totally submit herself to him and obliterate her own identity, autonomy, and freedom, just so that he will "forgive" her.

Similarly, in the "Master" letters, Dickinson maintains a submissive status in relation to the man. She craves male authority and domination, and stresses her small size, dependence, willingness to submit, and her gratefulness for attention. She even professes a reverence for the name "fathers," which is so sacred it is not to be spoken (*L*. II, p. 374). In these ways, she seems to be playing up to her reader's masculinity: "I dont know what you can do for it—thank you—Master—but if I had the Beard on my cheek—like you—and you—had Daisy's petals—and you cared so for me—what would become of you?" "A love so big it scares her, rushing among her small heart . . . who would have sheltered him in her childish bosom—only it wasn't big enough for a Guest so large—this Daisy—grieves her Lord—" (*L*. II, pp. 391–92). We see the reference to "Master," the deferential "thank you" inserted midstream, the appeals to his largess and pity for her humbled dependence which she shows is a function of her femininity (absence of a beard). "Daisy" is afraid of offending her master and bends her "smaller life," as she calls it, to his. She stresses that she is better than meek: she is "meeker," for she wants her master to be "glad," and that is her only want. She stresses that he is "so large" and she is "small . . . childish," not "big enough," and blundering. She asks to be taught grace and majesty (even the wren knows more than she does). She implores him to punish but not banish her, imprison her but only forgive her before she dies, to incarcerate her in himself. She closes her letters with the promise of a little girl: "I will never be noisy when you want to be still. I will be (glad) your best little girl–."

It is ironic that Dickinson presents herself to a lover—small, obedient, quiet, meek, modest, unassuming, dependent, submissive—in the same degrading terms as she did earlier to her brother when she said, "I'll be a little ninny. . . ." In both anger and play, she feels that in order to be loved by a man she must assume the posture of the naughty yet yearning daughter to her father, whether this man be brother, editor, lover, or god.

But Dickinson claims that she feels "yearning and replyless" in spite of her best efforts to be this loved dutiful daughter, or so she tells Lord. That is, she is still emotionally hungry and unsatisfied. She has prayed, "but Prayer has not yet an answer and yet how many pray!" Therefore she does not pray but goes to Judge Lord himself for a "church." Writing to him is her way of praying: thus in her mind, God, Lord, and her own father are equated. Her remarks to Maria Whitney—"You are like God. We pray to him, and He answers "No" (*L*. III, p. 780)—are illuminated in this context in which her feelings about her rejecting father are transferred to her lover and God. But most revealingly, when Lord does succumb to Dickinson's strategy of posing as an obedient daughter and offers to marry her, Dickinson refuses (*L*. II, p. 617). Even though her letters profess her yearning need and her sense of rejection, and claim that she only wants to be incarcerated in him, when it comes right down to it, she realizes that her own withholding increases his appetite; and besides, she does not want to be so gratified. Apparently, she has her "Lord" and father as close as she needs him to be.

THOMAS WENTWORTH HIGGINSON

What we have seen so far are two "daughterly" attitudes on the part of Dickinson toward her correspondents. As a rebellious daughter seeking autonomy and proclaiming her refusal to be "common," she insists that she will not submit to any authority which she equates with a patriarchal world. But she also uses the pose of the dutiful daughter in which she downgrades her capabilities in order to gain love. In both cases she is operating in reference to society's ideas about women's destinies. Examining her letters to Thomas Higginson reveals that both the dutiful and rebellious daughter are fused into her identity as a poet. The letters to Higginson are invaluable because they provide us with the opportunity to analyze how Dickinson uses the word to establish her identity. Dickinson's other correspondence is more or less commemorative of relationships already established in person, and the letters serve to continue the friendship. But Dickinson initiated her relationship with Higginson (15 April, 1862), and they corresponded for eight years before they met when he came to visit her on 16 August 1870. Therefore we see her go through the process of introducing herself and defining her identity out of the context of any personal interaction or prior knowledge on his part about her or her family. Through her words, Dickinson can present herself exactly as she wishes herself to be seen. The way she presents herself, then, is significant in our study of how she wants to be perceived. The self she unveils to Higginson is especially important because she was at the apex of her creative effort. Here is her opportunity for once to be identified as a serious poet: but she presents herself as a daughter.

That Emily Dickinson approaches Higginson as a little girl in search of a father-master-tutor-preceptor shows that while her identity as a daughter may be impelled by psychological needs, as I have tried to suggest, her identity as a daughter is also conceived by her as a strategy to further her poetic career. After all, she is responding to Higginson's lead article in the *Atlantic Monthly* in which his "Letter to a Young Contributor" gave encouragement and advice to unknowns pursuing a career.[46] He is the authority she needs who can tell her if her Verse is "alive," and she has "none else to ask" (*L*. II, p. 403). The premise of their relationship is that she is for all practical purposes a fatherless orphan whom he, in the goodness of his heart, cannot turn away. In her first letter, she makes her identity an issue: she comes to Higginson to identify her because her father has not. We see that she relates her father's inability to recognize her as a "son"—i.e., her potential to be "great"—to her chronic suffering from being unidentified. Therefore she does not sign her name to her letter, but "encloses" it in a card within its own envelope, which emphasizes the particular significance she gives to her name or identity: it is too sacred for conventional consumption, and must be treated with care; possibly it is fragile and cannot be mishandled; it is too trifling to call attention to. Finally, the enclosure of her identity—her name—which she wants him to open and discover, symbolizes both her private female sexuality as well as her secret poetic self. From the world's viewpoint, Dickinson feels unesteemed as a woman, and thus devalues her own identity by trying to hide it: but she also gives this editor the thrill of "knowing" her. Her question, "I enclose my name–asking you, if you please– Sir–to tell me what is true?" is deliberately ambiguous. The dashes make it unclear whether she wants him to answer her previous question about what is true about her identity (is she a poet?). It is, of course, the same question. Can a woman be a poet? In the "identity poems" we see that the persona feels she has no identity and consequently doubts if she is alive: writing poetry makes her into a neuter, and she does not even know if she is a poet. Higginson can confirm that her poetry *is* poetry (and therefore does live), and this would affirm her identity or life as a poet. But Dickinson insures that Higginson identify her as a daughter by addressing him with the reverence due a father: "If you please–Sir–." Presumably if her father had properly identified her in the first place, as a poet as well as a woman, she would not need to make a father out of Higginson for this purpose. Years later, Dickinson writes Higginson that "I would like to be what you deem me . . ." (*L*. II, p. 453). In order to be taken seriously, she has to convince him she is worth taking seriously. He has no basis on which to deem her except that which she tells him. In effect, then, she is giving herself an identity by which she can be taken seriously by a father figure.

Emily Dickinson's reply to Higginson's first letter is especially revealing of her pose as daughter, for his questions about her family allow her to give her version of her life, to redefine herself as she would be understood. Because she initially presented herself as a child, he must have asked her age; but Dickinson transformed the question: "You asked how old I was? I made no verse–but one or two–until this winter–Sir–." We note the deference ("Sir") as we notice the lie: she had written at least 500 poems by the time she wrote this letter. But this is not the point: he asked her for her age, in terms of years, and she answers him in terms of her poetic development. It is not just that she scorns defining herself in conventional terms, but that she subtly informs him that his interest should be in her poetic achievement and not in her biography. She is a poet, not a woman: she knows one cannot be both. Therefore, she answers the question that she feels he should have asked and that no one *but him* could ask. Everyone she knows takes her identity as a woman for granted, and it does not occur to them to ask her how "old" she is: they think they know. But why does Dickinson mislead Higginson when she answers? Perhaps she wants him to think that she is a "young" voice (the column was addressed to "young contributors") because he will not expect so much from her. Perhaps she feels that it is a bold act to admit her poetic aspirations to a judge-figure in order to be identified—or sentenced. But the irony of her relationship with Higginson is that she feels that she cannot divulge her real identity: just as she uses her "artless" mask with her father so that he will not reject her, she uses the same dutiful daughter mask to Higginson so that he will not turn her away either. Convinced that Higginson would be repulsed if she revealed her true ambition and aggressive drive, she is submissive and reverent: the "Sir" at the end of the sentence seems to function as a kind of feint asking his leave.

In continuing her portrayal of herself, she presents herself to Higginson as an orphan in search of a master, chronicling her ill luck with master figures ("He was not contented I be his scholar—so he left the Land"). As she recites her story, we see her engaged in artifice, formulating a legend or mythology about her life. Although biographers have dismissed her remaking of her history, excusing her white lies as a "pose," the matter of veracity is irrelevant, and the fact that it *is* a pose is crucial.[47] What is important is that Dickinson chose to present herself as essentially alone, isolated and alienated. She de-

scribes herself as being *intellectually* orphaned: her mother does not care for
thought, and her father is too busy with his own life to help her out. Besides,
he is ambivalent about wanting to help her; for example, he buys her books but
"begs" her not to read them "because he fears they joggle the Mind" (*L*. II,
p. 404). Thus he is shown to be a kind of benevolent fool at cross-purposes with
himself and his desires concerning his daughter: perhaps Dickinson makes her
father out to be a fool so that Higginson will be warned not to be similarly
foolish in his dealings with her. And if she gives the impression in later letters
to him that her life is dominated by her father, it is to show herself being
tyrannized by a clown the world takes seriously. She debunks her father's
dignity. When he feels especially important and noted by the public, she says,
"We young ones laugh in our sleeves, and think he is rather crazy." She makes
fun of his inability to enjoy himself at a concert—he looks "*mad*, and *silly*"
(*L*. I, pp. 119, 121). On a similar note, she refuses to take religion seriously,
saying that she does not accept the "Eclipse" they address every morning as
their "Father." Dickinson introduces herself to Higginson as the "only child" of
a neglectful, odd father and inconsequential mother, at odds with society because she cannot accept their notion of—or their reverence for—a "Father."
Perhaps she is only trying to make herself appear singular; but she casts herself
in the role of dutiful/rebellious daughter to a patriarchal order.

Similarly, when Higginson asks her for a picture, she does not want to be
taken at face value. "Could you believe me—without? I had no portrait, but am
small, like the wren, and my hair is bold, like the chestnut" (*L*. II, p. 411). She
gives him a portrait in words, and we note that she only refers to what were
taken to be her "best" features, her hair and her eyes. Her analogies are
revealing about her self image and, again, are designed to express a poetic
sensibility. Her eyes are like the sherry that the guest leaves in the glass. If she
had said only "like sherry," one would merely imagine a color, but the implication here is that her eyes have been drunk by people who have then left her;
there is more of her that they leave untouched. Her description also suggests
that there is a quality of absence in her eyes which records loss: something is
missing that had been there. These are not traits a camera would pick up.
Dickinson wants Higginson to see her through her own eyes. Emily Dickinson's
description of herself and her family show us what she thinks a poet's background and appearance should be. We can profitably contrast this image with
the description she gives of herself, written about the same time, to a girlfriend
she had just met (Catherine Scott Turner), for it shows how differently Dickinson
relates to men—older or not (*L*. II, p. 349). In asking Kate if they should be
friends, Dickinson defines herself once again as she wants to be judged: "Dare
you dwell in the *East* where we dwell? Are you afraid of the Sun?—When you
hear the new violet sucking her way among the sods, shall you be *resolute?* All
we are *strangers*—dear—The world is not acquainted with us, because we are not
acquainted with her. And Pilgrims!—Do you hesitate? and *Soldiers* oft—some of
us victors, but those I do not *see* tonight owing to the smoke. —We are hungry,

and thirsty, sometimes–We are barefoot–and cold–. . . ." Her symbolic abbreviations can be translated: she is afraid of masculine power (the sun); she is familiar with resurrection (the dawn); she is shaken by spring; she is alienated from society on her own terms as a woman; she is a defeated warrior, malnourished and not taken care of. She is a daughter, writing another indictment against her parents, but her tone is different from her presentation of these same essential facts that she gives to Higginson. She wants him to be a parent; she wants Kate to be a fellow conspirator against the parent world. It is clearly an "us" versus "them" dialectic. And she is imploring to Higginson in manner, while she is aloof and holds herself out as a member of the select, alienated "elect" to a girlfriend, sure of herself and her career to the point of arrogance. Most important of all, Dickinson defines herself as a poet: sensitive, and familiar with creation. Dickinson's letter to Higginson gives us insight into the pose she felt she must assume in order to convince Higginson as an editor and member of the worldly "elect" to help her "grow" as a poet. She must be the daughter: "Could you tell me how to grow," she asks, "or is it unconveyed— like Melody—or Witchcraft?" (*L.* II, p. 404).

In the conventional sense of the word, "growth" cannot be taught. An apple can grow to a certain size: without water, it might not reach this size, perhaps, and with more nourishment, it might be especially large but for all practical purposes, its size is predetermined. A human being's physical growth is similarly limited by heredity and is therefore essentially out of one's control. Dickinson wants to know if Higginson can help her to enlarge herself; as an editor he has god-like powers ("Are you perfectly powerful?" [*L.* II, p. 412]). She suggests that she might have the innate potential to increase her abilities if she is properly nurtured. She does not accept that her female sexuality in itself is a fate which precludes becoming larger. She wants to control her destiny, and not leave her realization of her potential to chance. Presumably she refers to her stature as a poet, because Higginson has just proclaimed himself an authority on how aspiring writers should go about interesting editors and getting published. Her question is: can he advise her? Significantly, she does not ask him to nurture her, only to tell her how to help herself. But she builds into her question an excuse for Higginson. He can tell her that one cannot help a poet: the poet either has the potential or not. However, the examples she gives indicate that Dickinson does not believe she cannot be taught to grow, because melody and witchcraft can each be "conveyed." She only wants help to reach her full size, not to be changed into anything she is not. The issue is size, not evolution: "I could not weigh myself–Myself–My size felt small–to me." The problem is that her "size" depends not on her innate abilities, but on the judgment and perception of a male authority figure. *She* obviously does not want to think that she is small. She wants to "grow" and she writes to have him tell her that she can. Most important, she hopes that he will see her in terms of potential. Then he will be glad to father her into being (perhaps) a "son." In this regard, she not only appeals to his paternal sensibility, but also resorts to subtle feminine flattery designed to raise his competitive masculine instincts by telling him that two nameless "Editors" (intimate friends of her father and herself) implore her for her "mind." In other words, they want to publish her. Higginson is thus offered the chance to be a father to a desirable poetic daughter: Dickinson shrewdly implies that others might like the honor of leading her to maturity. Although she asks him to be the "friend" she needs (given that he thinks her poetry is "spasmodic" and uncontrolled [L. II, p. 409]), this "friend" is a father. Thus, like a daughter, she promises loyalty, and hopes that her fidelity as his "Scholar" will make him merciful in his punishing role: "You will excuse each that I say, because no other taught me" (L. II, p. 460).

Apparently Higginson cannot pass up this responsibility in the terms in which Dickinson presents it. He will tell Dickinson that her size *is* small and that she should *not* publish. Even though he has failed to identify her as she wishes, Dickinson keeps up the fiction that she is his "Scholar" and that he is in control of her poetic growth and destiny. Higginson responds in kind. Higginson took his responsibilities as her teacher exceptionally seriously and never gave up hoping that she *could* be taught. Seven years after they began corresponding, Higginson was still convinced by her artifices that ". . . if I could once take you by the hand I might be something to you" (L. II, p. 461). If only she would learn what he could teach her. He shows a real sensitivity and concern lest he violate her trust in his position as a "perfectly powerful" father. His role as preceptor weighed upon his conscience: "I hope you will not cease to trust me and to turn to me; and I will try to speak the truth to you, and with love." People have wondered why Emily Dickinson chose Higginson to be her "Master," since his tastes were admittedly conventional. It appears that she chose wisely and well, for she was looking for a father who would treat her with respect, if not understanding. Critics have also pointed out that Dickinson never took Higginson's advice and therefore wonder why she kept up the pretense of being his Scholar. It is as if she was trying to go through authorized channels in her quest for glory and her effort to enlarge herself to her full potential, in order to remain a dutiful (loved, if not esteemed) daughter at the same time. By affecting an obedient, submissive, humble pose, she keeps Higginson relatively faithful while she freely rebels against his precepts and frolics as a naughty "witch" poet with impunity. Perhaps she does not want him to see her as autonomous and self-reliant. She would rather he see her as a harmless little girl or even as eccentric, for these are safe images for women. Thus she tries to sell him on her image as shy and harmless: she is so "small" her "little shape" will not take up room on his desk. She only wants his advice: " 'twould be control, to me." *Would* he be her preceptor? (L. II, p. 409). She promises in return the quality she is convinced is effective in dealing with fathers:

Obedience—the Blossom from my Garden and every gratitude I know. Perhaps you smile at me. I could not stop for that—My Business is Circumference—An ignorance, not of Customs, but if caught with the Dawn—or the Sunset see me–Myself the only Kangaroo among the Beauty, Sir, if you please, it afflicts me, and I thought that instruction would take it away. [*L*. II, p. 412; see also p. 480]

Dickinson gives the reasons why she wants him to agree to be her preceptor, if only in name. First, she wants to write poetry ("My Business is Circumference"), even though she knows "Customs"–that women do not write great poetry. She is afraid that if people recognize her as a powerful poet ("caught with the Dawn") she will be punished, solely because she does not fit in with the male literary community: she is the only "Kangaroo among the Beauty." It is not only that she is a woman, but that she writes with conscious singularity. She can write according to "Customs"—like men—but she disregards them, and this is precisely *why* she is able to capture the "Dawn." She thinks that "instruction" will take away the possibility of her being punished for her bold heresies. Higginson can sanction her efforts. If he cannot substantively change what she is doing, at least Dickinson has let the world know that she is under guidance. Just having Higginson as her "preceptor" allays Dickinson's guilty conscience.

Perhaps because Dickinson acknowledges to herself that her obedience to Higginson is only a strategic pose, she represents herself as insecure. When she does not hear from Higginson, she interprets it as a rejection for *disobedience*, and asks if she has "displeased" him (*L*. II, p. 417). We see a familiar pattern. In her second letter, she had told Higginson, "And if at any time–you regret you received me, or I prove a different fabric to that you supposed–you must banish me." She is terrified he will find her unworthy and banish her. Therefore she assures him that she has not been disobedient when he has not written: "Speak, if but to blame your *obedient* [ital. mine] child." She repeats the plea she made to her master: that he punish but not banish her. As long as she is not banished by him, she is recognized as existing (*L*. II, p. 412). Higginson's importance to Dickinson is that he provides her with a particular identity: "I know not what to deem myself–Yesterday 'Your Scholar' " (*L*. II, p. 425), that is, the one who studies to be a poet. She continually entreats him to acknowledge her, just as she wants her father, and brother, and Master to do, and when he is silent, it is an absence to her which makes her insecure in terms of her identity. Twice she told Higginson that he had saved her life (*L*. II, pp. 460, 649). Presumably, what she is referring to as being "saved" is her identity as at least an aspiring poet. For our understanding of Dickinson and the dynamics involved in producing her art, it is important to emphasize that Higginson "saves" her in his role as a father. Her identity as a poet depends upon recognition from an older man with power, even if this older man is blind to her real capability and helpless either to impede or to augment her real growth. But perhaps, as I have suggested, Higginson's fatherlike obtuseness about her poetic skills is a function of Dickinson's sham as dutiful daughter. Even if this is so, however, we must understand that Dickinson felt that she needed the fiction of a "Monarch" in her life, but not just because she was helpless without one ("I . . . cannot rule myself, and when I try to organize—my little Force explodes . . ." [*L.* II, p. 414]). If she sins, it is her "Preceptor's charge" (*L.* II, p. 415).[48] She was able to simultaneously follow the path of duty (by way of his "instructions") and to rebel because as her poems will reveal, she was convinced that she had taught herself both melody and witchcraft. Therefore, she had taught herself "how to grow," and she did not antagonize any of her fathers in the process. This is not to say that having all men say "What" to her and being unknown and misunderstood by her fathers did not deeply affect her. She was protecting herself by making her fathers ignorant of her real identity and assurance as a poet, but this lack of recognition, as the identity poems show, causes her identity crisis. Her insistence on finding fathers for herself, then, only aggravates and perpetuates her identity crisis. But she has to have a father in order to rebel against a social and cultural norm in which daughters who succeed are kangaroos or Mme. de Stael's.

FATHERS AND THE FATHER'S DAUGHTER

What emerges from an analysis of Dickinson's relationship with men is a pattern of behavior that is modeled on her experience as her father's daughter, which results in an attitude toward men that Clark Griffith defines as "compounded of awe and bitterness, of reverence and fear, all struggling together in one uneasy emotional amalgam."[49] Dickinson projects this ambivalent attitude onto all concepts which she interprets as authoritarian and which try to exercise power over her. Whenever she feels powerless and dependent, she conceptualizes the situation as an encounter between father and daughter: thus she takes secret pot-shots and irreverent jabs at dignified, sacred precepts, principles, and personages, including the seasons, time, God, and her country, all of which are seen trying to restrict her as a daughter and keep her from being "great." Thus time is an "Old Father" who is "more stern than ever." She describes herself as "so vexed with him . . . that I ran after him and made out to get near enough to put some salt on his tail, when he fled" (*L.* I, pp. 13, 16). In another reference, she satirizes Time as this father and is fully aware of the implications of her satire:

> *But I will not expatiate upon him any longer, for I know it is wicked
> to trifle with so reverend a personage, and I fear he will make a call on
> me in person to inquire as to the remarks which I have made concerning
> him. Therefore I will let him alone for the present.* [*L.* I, p. 20]

In the same vein, she wants to cheat "Jack Frost," "Old Winter," and the seasons, which should be "improved" (*L.* I, pp. 21, 24, 37; I, p. 356).

Dickinson's specific references to God as a Father are willful and critical.

As we saw with her treatment of Edward Dickinson, she seems to be attacking the reverence with which God is treated by society. In her letters, he is a "good man" who "*also*" writes about Paradise (*L.* II, p. 329). On the other hand, she deplores his failure as a parent: "How many barefoot shiver I trust their father knows who saw not fit to give them shoes" (*L.* II, p. 353); or "God is rather stern with his 'little ones' " (*L.* III, p. 678). If she impugns His character, it is to revenge herself on His emissaries who misrepresent Him as a good Father and who in their complacency are themselves misled. For example, she says that when others think they are worshipping "God" in church, He is actually not there at all. He is visiting *her* and, she adds, looking "very gloriously" (*L.* I, p. 86)—suggesting that she is the one who is being adored by *him*. Therefore, her rebellion against God is a rebellion against society, and we see Dickinson exposing both God's inadequacies and society's deception. Like her father, God is stern and absent and withholding and undeserving of love or respect. He is "penurious" with her, even stingy with the bird music—and when she prays, He answers, "No": "Then we pray for Him to rescind the "no," and He dont answer at all, yet 'seek and ye shall find' is the boon of faith" (*L.* III, p. 780). She is the daughter: "We do not know that he is God–and *will* try to be still– tho' we had really rather complain" (*L.* I, pp. 84). It is significant that her next sentence relates her satire about The Sewing Society which she does not attend. Being obedient means being "still", acknowledging God, and attending sewing society, a lady's proper activity; all are one to her, and she would rather "complain" and be damned. Thus we see bold irreverence. Even God's divine plan is suspect: "God is not so wary as we, else he would give us no friends, lest we forget him! The Charms of The Heaven in the bush are superceded I fear, by the Heaven in the hand, occasionally" (*L.* II, pp. 338–39). By giving her friends and then taking them away, God insures her need of Him to pray to for consolation. Thus when she feels particularly stricken, she says that God is "more 'Our Father' "–that is, He is withholding: more father means less love (*L.* I, p. 94).[50]

Emily Dickinson's major problem with God is that she simply cannot imagine God in terms other than her own father: "When Jesus tells us about his Father, we distrust him. When he shows us his Home, we turn away, but when he confides to us that he is 'acquainted with Grief,' we listen, for that also is an Acquaintance of our own" (*L.* III, p. 837). In other words, God and religion cannot be accepted unless one has been able to trust a father and experience the security of a home: "When it becomes necessary for us to stake all upon the belief of another, as in for instance Eternity, we find it impossible to make the transfer–" (*L.* III, p. 920). Because of her experience with her own father, she claims she cannot accept religion, and the reader is not to blame her if she is consequently wicked. She can satirize society with impunity, and say that "the morning exercises were perfectly ridiculous, and we spent the intermission in mimicking the Preacher," or she can hope for a Goliath or Samson "to pull the whole church down" (*L.* I, pp. 251, 284). She cannot trust what "the Clergy say" because they have lied to her by telling her God will answer her prayers, and she resents their efforts to make her feel small. If they call her a "Vain–Sinful Worm," a description which Dickinson finds particularly offensive, she will refuse to take their word on other matters: "Do you think we shall 'see God?' " (*L*. II, p. 339). Why should she believe them when they discuss Judgment Day and Heaven, if by believing what they say she will only be forced to acknowledge her dependence, her lack of power and control, and her status as a "worm"? In a very interesting juxtaposition of ideas, Dickinson writes, "I haven't any paper, dear, but faith continues firm–Presume if I met with my 'deserts' I should receive nothing. Was informed to that effect today by a 'dear Pastor.' What a privilege to be so insignificant!" Her lack of paper is a sign of God's disfavor, perhaps because she sins by writing poetry. Even so, she has "faith" because as she understands it, faith and the whole religious structure are premised on a sense of loss: "If every prayer was answered, there would be nothing left to pray for–we *must* 'suffer' . . ." (*L*. I, p. 84). What Dickinson seems to hold against religion is that it enforces her sense of helplessness and rejection. When "Mr. S." preaches on "predestination," Dickinson rejects what he says because "I do not respect 'doctrines,' and did not like to listen to him."

It is noteworthy that Dickinson discusses her decision to reject doctrine and God in reference to her experience as a child. In the following sentences, the first written when she was forty-four, the second when she was fifty-four, she is still rehashing why she has not accepted Christ. She recounts scenes in which she refuses to cooperate with the clergy in accepting Jesus Christ: "When a Child and fleeing from Sacrament I could hear the Clergyman saying 'All who loved the Lord Jesus Christ–were asked to remain–' My flight kept time to the Words" (*L*. II, pp. 524–25). "The cordiality of the Sacrament extremely interested me when a Child, and when the Clergyman invited 'all who loved the Lord Jesus Christ to remain,' I could scarcely refrain from rising and thanking him for the to me unexpected courtesy, though I now think had it been to all who loved Santa Claus, my transports would have been even more untimely" (*L*. III, p. 835). She wants to foster in her reader's mind the image of herself as a child—a rebellious child—who is not to be taken in by the embarrassingly "boyish" way in which religion is presented (*L*. III, p. 815). She refuses to degrade herself. Also, as a child she has been unable to "trust," and she directly associates her inability to feel that she belongs to society and to the church with her experience as a child.

Therefore, she will distance herself from this culture in her letters by insisting that she is a pagan and that as far as literature is concerned, she likes "poison very well," that she does not have "the *slightest* respect" for the man who makes paper, that she wishes the " 'faith of the fathers' didn't wear brogans [traditional wooden Pilgrim shoes], and carry blue umbrellas" (*L*. II, p. 358; I, p. 184; II, p. 359). She mocks the social fervor which builds Almshouses and "transcendental Stateprisons," and which blows out the sun, and encourages invention (*L*. I, p. 92). Even as regards her spelling, Dickinson rebels against convention in her "lone Orthography," because to spell words as society teaches her they are spelled is to submit to a higher authority. "Should I spell all the things as they sounded to me, and say all the facts as I saw them, it would send consternation among more than the 'Fee Bees!' " (*L*. III, p. 774). She saw "no need to improve" on her childhood spelling. In other words, she questions everything she is taught: she does not trust. In all these accounts of her modes of rebelling, Dickinson presents herself as willfully estranged.

Thus Emily Dickinson will scorn even writers the world esteems: "Longfellow's 'golden Legend' has come to town I hear–and may be seen *in state* on Mr. Adam's bookshelves. . . ." She half expects to hear that the authors have "flown some morning and in their native ether revel all the day." She makes the reasons for her contempt explicit: it is because *she* wants the opportunity to be venerated. "For our sakes," she writes, "who please ourselves with the fancy that we are the only poets, and everyone else is *prose*, let us hope that they will yet be willing to share our humble world and feed upon such aliment as *we* consent to do!" (*L*. I, p. 144). She is forced to live in a world which humbles her and she consents to live in it, temporarily, but she does not let her reader forget that she is a kangaroo who does not fit in.

In her desire to get people to see through her mask as a dutiful daughter, Dickinson resorts to what appears to be antifeminism. We see her scorning "a little *daughter*": "Very promising *Children* I understand. I dont doubt if they live they will be ornaments to society" (*L*. I, p. 17). Being an ornament to society, a dispensable trimming, is not Dickinson's idea of a "promising" destiny. Neither is society's idea of a woman's utility: "I think they [the two daughters who have just been born] are both to be considered as Embryos of future usefullness . . ." (*L*. I, p. 200). Dickinson shows herself to be very bitter about a daughter's lack of possibility: "the girls are pretty girls, very simple hearted and happy and would be interesting if they had anybody to teach them." That is why she is so determined to find a Master/Preceptor/Tutor/Father figure who will "instruct" her and in so doing, make her "interesting."

Dickinson's frustration with the possibilities of her destiny as a daughter is explicitly expressed. She wants to know, when her father is a delegate to the national Whig Convention, "Why can't *I* be a delegate to the great Whig Convention?–don't I know all about Daniel Webster, and the Tariff, and the Law?" (*L*. I, p. 212). But she acknowledges the futility of her wish to be included in politics. When her father is considered for a slate on the Constitutional-Union Party for Lt. Governor, she says, "I hear they wish to make me Lieutenant-Governor's daughter" (*L*. II, p. 368). Admitting the hopelessness of any political ambitions given her culture, ambitions which her father can achieve, she rejects the political system itself which fosters this sexual injustice: "George Washington was the Father of his Country–'George Who?' That sums all Politics to me–" (*L*. III, p. 849). Even history is interpreted and rejected in terms of our reverence for fathers. Dickinson concludes, "I dont like this country at all, and I shant stay here any longer! 'Delenda est' America, Massachusetts and all!"

(*L*. I, p. 212) No, she will abandon it all for her own private world ("My country is Truth,"[51]) and patriotism will be defined in terms of the "intellect" to one's "native land," the mind (*L*. II, p. 525). Fealty to country and fatherland will be abrogated as part of her challenge to a culture so undemocratic toward its women citizens that she labels the new president "a new Czar" (*L*. III, p. 849). Similarly, Emily Dickinson's criteria for great literature becomes that which has more than "pure little lives, loving God and their parents, and obeying the laws of the land" (*L*. I, p. 195). In her letters, then, she tries to give an image of herself as a rebel who scorns the *pure* and *little* life as a dutiful daughter she is supposedly leading. Her "great" literature follows.

PART THREE

Daughter at Work: The Poems

"I dwell in Possibility"

4

Occupation—"At Home":
The Daughter Nobody Knows

I dwell in Possibility—
A fairer House than Prose—
More numerous of Windows—
Superior—for Doors—

Of Chambers as the Cedars—
Impregnable of Eye—
And for an Everlasting Roof
The Gambrels of the Sky—

Of Visitors—the fairest—
For Occupation—This—
The spreading wide my narrow Hands
To gather Paradise—[1]

[657]

Emily Dickinson's letters show her using the written word throughout her life to meet her conflicting needs as a daughter for love and esteem. Even after the deaths of her parents (she was forty-four when her father died and fifty-one when her mother died), she maintained the sensibility and conscious imagination of the Daughter, ambivalent about maternal nurture and seeking paternal esteem. While it would seem that her obscure life as a conventional daughter confined to her father's ground would restrict her art to similarly conventional "Prose," Emily Dickinson's poem "I dwell in Possibility" suggests that the opposite is true. Keeping herself outwardly immersed in the feminine orthodoxies of living at home; transforming all men into Edward Dickinson whose notice she seeks and whose power she both emulates and resents; maintaining

99

a self-image as a daughter in relationships; in short, being a daughter: this is "possibility," where Poetry thrives. As long as she remains a daughter, Emily Dickinson keeps at bay the common fate of Prose that her mother represents.

Thus we see that when Emily Dickinson, Dutiful Daughter, takes off her apron at the end of the day of household cares and reaches for her pen, she takes up in the poetry where she left off in her letters. There is the same cast, same plot: the father is an inept Eclipse; she "never had a mother;" and no one identifies the daughter as a poet or even poet-to-be. The parents we see in streetclothes speaking Prose in the letters come to the poetry dressed in costumes and masks. The poetry's lighting is darkened (only a few spotlights eerily beam). Emily Dickinson transforms her staid Puritan New England town into a gothic landscape of dungeons, abbeys, villains, ghosts: the daughter has gone abroad to romanticize her life into a suitable background for a poet to rival Elizabeth Barrett Browning and the Brontës. Her identity as a daughter is her key to poetic immortality. These poems not only manifest the daughter sensibility, but are the strategies of a poet who needs the daughter construct to create.

Therefore, while we see that Dickinson's primary, conflicting needs as a daughter for love and esteem find expression in the poetry, so that it is informed by and mirrors her experience as daughter in her father's house, her complaints, pleas, and defiances are given new emphasis by the poet. We may get the feeling in the letters that Dickinson is somehow not really serious when she complains of her mother being a burden, her father being a dictator, and herself being persecuted and neglected. And in the poetry we see the familiar defiance toward any manifestation of authority, be it father, God, clergy, Bible, rules of grammar, literary convention, social tradition, government, doctrine, technology, or society. But in the poetry the mood attached to the defiance is serious, tragic, intense. Joking gives way to criticism; wit turned upon itself as self-mockery in the letters twists outward in bitter accusation. Dickinson is her ambivalent self in the poetry, but her sense of conflict over her identity as a "kangaroo," a woman artist, reaches a shrill pitch; she still dissociates herself from the world of "Prose" with sublime scorn, but she shows the terrifying consequences of the ensuing identity conflict. The dutiful/rebellious daughter dialectic in the letters is reformulated in the poems as the tension between opposing self-images: martyr/witch, good girl/wicked girl, poet with breast/poet with beard, elect/damned. This is a daughter nobody knows: arrogant, hungry, angry, sneering, hostile, crazy, humble, incredibly and inexplicably self-confident, calm, ecstatic.

Emily Dickinson's never having been homeless, hungry, or poor does not mean the poems are not a psychological self-portrait chronicling the efforts of an archetypal daughter in her struggle to "grow" as a poet. Emily Dickinson's feelings about her daily life as a daughter which we witness in the letters are symbolically translated in the poetry to represent the repression and rejection necessary for Dickinson to write poetry. The childhood she describes is a climate of poetic "Possibility," a breeding ground for Poetry. Dickinson keeps operant her attitudes and needs as a daughter in order to exploit the child's specific use of language. If the images we get of Dickinson's parents and her life with them in the letters seem in retrospect almost documentary compared to the treatment the parents receive at her hands in the poetry, it is only because in the poetry Dickinson is distorting her experience as an aesthetic strategy.

We might wonder why, when Dickinson's mother was always home, there is no mother in any of the poems except a reference here and there to an abstract "mother nature," and perhaps a case can be made for two poems which I feel are expressly about a daughter's consciousness of her mother.[2] And while the father and society are accused of neglect and persecution, the mother is never held directly responsible for anything that happens to the persona. The mother's absence is consistent with the daughter's attempts to dissociate herself from her mother and the woman's world. By making her mother absent in the poetry, Dickinson symbolically erases the threat of her mother's destiny and all that her mother represents.

But while the mother can be seen to be absent from the poetry as a *mother*, she may be present in the ubiquitous form of her daughter's psychology. The daughter so closely identifies with the mother that she has internalized the mother/woman part of herself into her own persona. In fact, the persona is often characterized in terms of Mrs. Dickinson's traits. She is a martyr to duty, timid, submissive to male authority, humble, pious, devout, self-sacrificing, anxious, meek, plaintive, fluttering, dependent: the very words used to describe the elder Emily Dickinson. Thus what I call the "dutiful daughter" aspect of Dickinson's literary personality is a manifestation of Dickinson's mother's influence. In the poems, when the feminine is shown interacting with the masculine, Emily Dickinson and her mother formulate a precarious "I" or "we" who confront a father/husband. We saw in the identity poems that the consciousness of the woman poet is split into warring factions. Part of that war is this uneasy alliance between mother and daughter, duty and rebellion. When Dickinson says "Me from Myself—to banish/Had I Art" (642), she is describing the plight of a woman who recognizes the futility of rejecting the pregnable woman in her. The daughter realizes that, try as she does to banish her feminine identity, it is impossible to do so without "subjugating Consciousness." Therefore "Myself—assault Me" in endless strife and alienation.[3] The civil war of the daughter's consciousness is fought by three camps in the poetry: a dutiful daughter/mother configuration; a rebellious daughter poet; and a punishing and neglecting father/husband. Often, we see the mother and father camp form a temporary truce in the representation of society, and the daughter finds herself outnumbered: hence, the poems about the defeat of the identity and her ego.

The general meaning of the poetry can be more clearly understood if we perceive that Dickinson has internalized both of her parents. The father surfaces in the poetry as a dramatized "superego" as well as a character in his own right and in the persona's lawyer personality, bringing suits, arguing cases, making appeals, employing legal logic and legal terminology; and the mother appears

as absence, totally eclipsed, and in the representations of the dutiful daughter.
Our clues that she is there occur when Dickinson expresses identity conflict in
being a woman who wants to be "great," and when she is timorous, "little . . .
little . . . little." A way to understand this perhaps is that in order to avoid the
curse of becoming like her mother, Dickinson swallows her whole, just as Zeus
swallowed Thespis whole in order to ward off the fate of having a child by her
and having that male son kill him. The result was that his head split open and
Athena was born, goddess of wisdom and war. Dickinson's poems pop out of
her head motherless as well, armed and crowing to a father who is both father
and mother. But it is because she has completely internalized her mother so
that her mother *is* herself in conflict. In these ways, then, the poetry does mirror
and illuminate the daughter's experience in her father's house, and perpetuates
her identity as daughter.

The poetry of Emily Dickinson is best read as an "interdependent whole"
spoken in the voice of the daughter. To give a reading of these poems I have
selected representative groups that identify the daughter at work. Each group
illustrates an aspect of Dickinson's persona operating in the daughter construct:
1) poems dealing overtly with a daughter in relation to parents or figures who
function in roles Dickinson perceives as parental (society, God, and lovers);
2) the deprivation poems in which the parents are implicitly present by meton-
ymy (for example, to say that jail is a metaphor of childhood implies that the
child has a jailer); 3) poems of oral privation (which illustrate the basis of the
daughter construct). In later chapters, I shall focus on poems that renounce the
daughter identity, but in which the poet still remains a child for reasons of
poetic strategy; and poems which reveal the daughter most dramatically: those
in which being an orphan is deemed essential to her identity as a poet. All
these poems are informed by Emily Dickinson's domestic "feminine" experience as a daughter in her father's house. These distinctions will overlap somewhat in the poems, but as categories they emphasize the different ways in which
the poetry serves to perpetuate the strategy of the poet to remain a "daughter."
Tracing the daughter archetype in the poems as an interdependent whole will
facilitate a structural analysis based on the systematic development and relationship between the "Me" and the "Not Me" in its various modes as the child/
parent dialectic, yesterday/today dialectic, and the other dualities inherent in
the daughter construct. The organizing principle of my approach to the poetry
is the recurring archetypal pattern of rebellion, duty, and quest: there is a
ceaseless moving away from and toward a daughter's needs for love and autonomy, and a constant effort to resolve the tensions caused by these opposing
needs. In all the poems, the voice is that of the daughter in conflict between
her need to be loved and her need to be "great."

5

The Voice of the Dutiful Daughter

Because the poetic use of language was perceived by Emily Dickinson as a rebellious act, even her poems manifesting the sensibility of the "dutiful daughter" are rebellious in act, format, and style. But in one poem Dickinson purports to speak in the voice of the dutiful daughter. Poem 1 is dismissed as too trivial and weak to merit serious scholarly attention; as her first-known poetic effort, the poem is seen as an apprentice piece. The best that has been said about it is that it is atypical.[4] But the primary value of the poem is that it speaks in the traditional cadences of her contemporaries. As a "conventional" poem, it shows precisely in what terms Emily Dickinson conceived her poetry to be a rebellion from feminine duty. Because the poem speaks as one of "them," it reveals her sense of who "they" are and what "they" want from her as a woman poet—her sense of society's voice, conventions, standards, and attitudes. More important, the poem demonstrates her ability to reproduce this voice—if she so inclines. She is not, as she told Thomas Wentworth Higginson, "ignorant of Customs." Duty talks here with a youthful exuberance edging on parody; at age twenty-eight Emily Dickinson establishes herself as a virtuoso of "Customs," employing masculine literary conventions from the traditional opening appeal to the classic nine muses to the iambic hexameter couplets with which the poem proceeds:

Awake ye muses nine, sing me a strain divine,
Unwind the solemn twine, and tie my Valentine!

Oh the Earth was made for lovers, for damsel, and hopeless swain,
For sighing, and gentle whispering, and unity made of twain.
All things do go a courting, in earth, or sea, or air,
God hath made nothing single but thee in His world so fair!
The bride, and then the bridegroom, the two, and then the one,

Adam, and Eve, his consort, the moon, and then the sun;
The life doth prove the precept, who obey shall happy be,
Who will not serve the sovereign, be hanged on fatal tree.
The high do seek the lowly, the great do seek the small,
None cannot find who seeketh, *on this terrestrial ball;*
The bee doth court the flower, the flower his suit receives,
And they make merry wedding, whose guests are hundred leaves;
The wind doth woo the branches, the branches they are won,
And the father fond demandeth the maiden for his son.
The storm doth walk the seashore humming a mournful tune,
The wave with eye so pensive, looketh to see the moon,
Their spirits meet together, they make them solemn vows,
No more he singeth mournful, her sadness she doth lose.
The worm *doth woo the* mortal, *death claims a living bride,*
Night unto day is married, morn unto eventide;
Earth is a merry damsel, and heaven a knight so true,
And Earth is quite coquettish, and beseemeth in vain to sue.
Now to the application, to the reading of the roll,
To bringing thee to justice, and marshalling thy soul:
Thou art a human solo, a being cold, and lone,
Wilt have no kind companion, thou reap'st what thou has sown.
Hast never silent hours, and minutes all too long,
And a deal of sad reflection, and wailing instead of song?
There's Sarah, and Eliza, and Emeline so fair,
And Harriet, and Susan, and she with curling hair!
Thine eyes are sadly blinded, but yet thou mayest see
Six true, and comely maidens sitting upon the tree;
Approach that tree with caution, then up it boldly climb,
And seize the one thou lovest, nor care for space, or time!
Then bear her to the greenwood, and build for her a bower,
And give her what she asketh, jewel, or bird, or flower—
And bring the fife, and trumpet, and beat upon the drum—
And bid the world Goodmorrow, and go to glory home!

The "valentine" is a parody of a sermon, complete with "text" and "application," exhorting God's faithful to mate in accordance with natural, social, and spiritual laws. All spheres of the universe are shown to be in cooing accord, with the exception of one lone sinner whose wariness about entering into the mating mayhem threatens to disrupt the cosmic harmony. What Emily Dickinson has done is to impose the daughter construct upon the courting ritual itself so that mating, designed as it is to facilitate the child's entrance into the social structure, is presented in terms of obedience and rebellion. In spiritual terms, not to marry is to "disobey," to deliberately antagonize "the Sovereign." Dickinson utilizes biblical language to underscore her warning about the consequences of refusing to mate. One will be "hanged on fatal tree"—crucified like Christ—and will "reap" what one "sows." This punishment will be incurred because one has disdained, like Lucifer, to "obey" and "serve" God. Mating is presented as an act of social and religious duty, a submission to a patriarchal authority. Socially, one will not be "happy" if one is single. In a world "made for lovers," being single is not only a crime but it naturally puts one at odds with society. For Emily Dickinson, who remained single all her life, a universe in which everything has gone "a courting" whether in the sky, on land, on sea, or even in the grave, is bound to be a depressing place; certainly her images of a couple-happy world engaged in mindless hyperactive mating imply an absurd universe.

But what we must remember is that in this poem at least, Dickinson purports to advocate such dutiful adherence to social and spiritual doctrine. Thus she addressed her valentine sermon to a man in order to pressure him to pluck the nearest woman off a tree, where a bevy of candidates sit waiting and ripe for just such a moment, including herself (the one with the "curling hair"). We note that the decision to mate is male; the female persona cannot take the initiative to escape long silent hours full of reflection. That six women vie for one man to save them—rescue them, as it were, from the tree—may reflect the social reality of New England during this time, but it is time to herself that Dickinson the poet cherishes. To mate would make her lose her individuality ("two" become "one"); she would be like all the rest. Her renunciation of marriage in her own life puts her in the same category as a man with freedom to choose. Traditionally, women only can say "yes" or "no." Saying "no" before she is asked gives the woman a measure of autonomy. The poem shows being single as defying the universe in "fatal disobedience," and in the process, implying a man's privilege. Dickinson wards off such heresy for herself as a single woman by portraying herself pleading with a man to literally "come and get" her. What can she do if no man will climb a tree and claim a living bride? No one can say she is not an enthusiastic cheerleader urging him on.

The poem is a tour de force. What emerges from the poem is not a conventional valentine message so much as a criticism of the romantic rituals prescribed by church and state, accomplished through the use of poetic as well as thematic convention. The poem is a good example in poetics of the poet as Daughter being dutiful with a vengeance—the kind of exaggerated obedience she displayed in breaking the chipped plate in her father's garden so it will "never offend him again." We see a rigid conformity to common poetic practice in her use of language, rhythm, form, diction, rhyme, and syntax; the poem's conformity in style and form is echoed in her theme, so that the valentine itself symbolized the tyranny of social pressure to conform to social behavior. A valentine *is* "Customs:" a stylized way of sending a prescribed message at a particular time as part of a prescribed ritual designed to result in a prescribed social convention, courtship and marriage. The theme is behavioral doctrine: everyone and everything lives to mate. Each atypical use of convention (length, technique, language, theme) embodies Dickinson's criticism of that "Custom." The poem is uncharacteristically long for Dickinson, roughly ten times longer than her average, while it is relatively short compared to the poetry published by her peers—even so, it seems to go on and on in endless "application," just like a sermon. The iambic hexameter couplets enforce a rigid and unimaginative rhyme scheme (be-tree, flower-bower, long-song) which compares unfavorably with her typical if idiosyncratic use of half, near, and slant rhymes, or no rhyme at all, and with her so-called "spasmodic gait" which critics today agree is one reason for Dickinson's poetic greatness. The poem is remarkable in that it employs no figurative language, instead relying upon the bald clichés of romance and the pulpit, when in the rest of her poetry Dickinson makes metaphor and simile, which she loved, work to their maximum yield (if not beyond). The sentiments it expresses are conventional (for example, the notion that the earth is made for lovers, or that being single is dreary, or that we live to mate), each of which Dickinson disputes in her own life and satirizes in her poetry. Emily Dickinson did nothing that was conventional or which undermined her individual autonomy: I have already discussed how she refused to read a letter which was addressed to both herself and her sister, explaining "A mutual plum is not a plum." She rejected Judge Lord's marriage offer in her late years, explaining that she could not part with even her "crust" (*L*. II, p. 617). *Her* world owns no damsels or knights, and love speaks not in whispers but in condescending silence. The world she pictures in *this* poem is trivial; the Earth itself is embarrassingly "coquettish."

Fairly sagging with exempla of obedience—there are at least thirteen different matings described, each of dubious ends—the poem represents a response to society's monotonous, singsong rhythm urging headlong and mindless submission to society and the Church. People who mate are like poets who write in rigid couplets: both have a singsong sensibility, and do what they are told. That Emily Dickinson has absolutely no intention of conforming to poetic and social practice is evidenced by the fact that she never speaks again as she does in this poem. The remaining 1775 poems are singular in spirit, style, and theme. Emily Dickinson knows "Customs," but she wants no part of them, and in the following poems she tells us why. That her valentine poem is ignored today as uninteresting and weak is evidence in itself that Dickinson's cultivation of the voice of the "rebellious daughter" was informed by a shrewd and even courageous faith in her judgment about duty. I have discussed Dickinson's attitude toward duty ("Duty is ever ugly to me"). Her achievement in this valentine sermon is that she is able to impart what is "ugly" about duty in social and poetic practice without having crafted an "ugly" poem in the process. The rebellious daughter poet shines through even these classic and traditionally inspired lines.

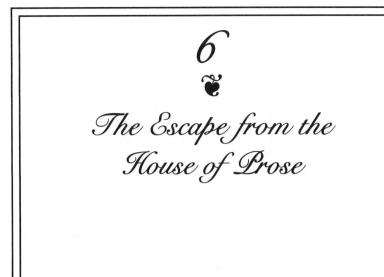

6

The Escape from the House of Prose

While in the letters there is no stated rationale for the daughter's corrective portraits of her father and other authorities as tyrant buffoons she rather perversely prefers to humor, the poetry of Emily Dickinson reveals that behind her exposés of parental malfunction is her beleaguered identity as a woman artist. No poem shows more clearly her sense of the relation between the rebellious daughter in her father's house and the poet in the House of Prose than the following allegory of poetic growth voiced by the woman poet looking back on her career:

> *They shut me up in Prose—*
> *As when a little Girl*
> *They put me in the Closet—*
> *Because they liked me "still"—*
>
> *Still! Could themself have peeped—*
> *And seen my Brain—go round—*
> *They might as wise have lodged a Bird*
> *For Treason—in the Pound—*
>
> *Himself has but to will*
> *And easy as a Star*
> *Abolish his Captivity—*
> *And laugh—No more have I—*

[613]

Dickinson draws an analogy between the consequences of trying to express herself as a little girl in her own father's house and trying to express her voice in poetry when she is an adult in a world still governed by a patriarchy telling its women how to behave. In both cases "they" try to make her "shut up."

Dickinson will play with the slang connotations and literal meaning of the phrase: as a little girl she was "shut up" in a closet, presumably because she did not "shut up" and be "still."[5]

In retrospect, the poet equates the punishment and repression symbolized by the closet with the "prose" she is expected to live and write as an obedient adult "little girl." As we saw in her letters, Dickinson conceives poetry to be the opposite of "prose." "Prose" is the singsong conventional mentality we witness in the Valentine Sermon. "Prose" is also illuminated as a concept when Dickinson dissociates herself from her family by virtue of her poetic sensibility. She exposes her father as a muted intellect by telling her correspondents that her father disdains poetry in favor of the Bible, "real life," and "Prose." She describes their clash, and extends this separation of lifestyles of father and daughter to society and women when she writes on another occasion that she and Susan Gilbert are the "only poets" in a world where everyone else is "prose." "Prose" becomes Dickinson's term for society's value and repressive enforcement of conformity; poetry, on the other hand, is that which is free from the limiting rules and restrictions of conventional behavior—conceptually the same type of rules she breaks when she speaks her mind and therein defies conventional notions of good behavior for little girls and poetesses. "Poetry" is not only *what* she says, then, and the *way* she says it, but the *fact* that she says it. Virtuous women, as we learn from nineteenth-century texts on behavior, are quiet, passive, and timid; dutiful women are "still." The ultimate still behavior, of course, is practiced by the corpse: the ideal for women, children, and female poets is little more than a total negation of vitality and potential. Dickinson's analogy between the little girl who misbehaves by violating expectations of "still" behavior—speaking up or out—and the women who by writing poetry are not ladylike, shows that she considers society's punitive attitude toward her poetry to be a function of her identity in society's eyes as a little girl. The self-image of the mature poet (when she wrote this poem, she was thirty-two years old and had written over 600 poems) is the rebellious daughter refusing to silence herself, struggling for a "voice," even though by writing in secret she lives out the metaphor of being a "closet poet" who is published posthumously. For of course the parental authoritarianism is futile: the mind of the daughter/poet is only stimulated by repression. Her brain still goes "round" even if in society's eyes she is still in the closet of prose as a dutiful daughter in her father's house. Dickinson's reference to "brain" rather than "mouth" also tells us that she understands society's command to silence herself as a rebuke for her *intellectual* activity: in short, for thinking. Her thoughts are anathema to society.

Emily Dickinson's chronicle of being "shut up in prose" has a more specific meaning in regard to her career. This poem was written in 1862, the same year she wrote for the first time to Thomas Wentworth Higginson asking him for his opinion of her poetic potential. At the peak of her career then, she approached him in the voice of the "little girl." When Higginson could not be enthusiastic about her poetic prospects, Dickinson was then in a position to interpret his response as a critical father to a naughty daughter, and could beg to be given a chance to win his approval by future "obedience." But in her poetry, and in this poem in particular, which remained private, Dickinson implied that following his advice would in effect "shut her up in prose" because he asked for a "still" form of poetry that employed the conventional use of words, rhyme, and rhythm, contrary to his advertisement for poetry that "breathed." As a biographical allegory, "They shut me up in Prose" could refer to the enforced suppression of Dickinson's literary ambition represented by Higginson's refusal to publish her. In their correspondence as well as in this poem she revealed her hypersensitivity to correction or admonishments from those who demanded "still" behavior from her. No doubt even Higginson's mild and courteous advice was experienced as the daughter being reproved by her parents for too lively behavior.[6] "They," the publishing world, wanted her to be dutiful, to follow conventions for meter, spelling, syntax. If she were to express herself as a dutiful daughter as she had in her Valentine Sermon using traditional male-sanctioned practices, however, she would effectively be stifling her art; if she behaved like a dutiful daughter following traditional female (and male-sanctioned) practices in social behavior, she would be "shut up" because she would be regarded as having nothing to say. The only was she could free her voice from her feminine identity and destiny—a closet of Prose in itself—was to write poetry. Therefore this poem delineates Dickinson's aesthetics of rebellion. The poem is defiant and scornful (notice, for example, the metrical emphasis on "Still!" which begins the second stanza with a forceful mockery of society's futile efforts to control her), a manifesto of rebellion, not the work of a daughter feigning "submission" to her father-editor. Her poetry constitutes a disobedience to a patriarchal tradition which cannot enforce its own precepts.

Emily Dickinson's only problem is that "they liked me 'still'." She wants to be loved, but if she is obedient and pleases "them," she will end up in Prose or "still." If she defies their expectations, she can never be loved nor attain poetic recognition: but her mind has escaped. Ironically, Dickinson's "escape" takes her straight back to her "Closet" where she writes in secrecy and seclusion. The effect of this continual effort to escape is seen in the poetry, where her voice is characterized by silences and stutters; and thematically, the poetry manifests a "stilled" consciousness which is weary of identity conflict and at times is actually a corpse.

THE REBELLION OF THE LITTLE HAND

The predicament this poem describes repeatedly occupies Emily Dickinson's imagination. Variations of the theme of "They shut me up in Prose—" can be discovered in numerous poems. In an earlier poem, Dickinson again makes

an analogy between her identity as a daughter and her role as a poet. She sees
herself as a rebellious daughter being punished by "them":

> Why–do they shut Me out of Heaven?
> Did I sing–too loud?
> But–I can say a little "Minor"
> Timid as a Bird!
>
> Wouldn't the Angels try me–
> Just–once–more–
> Just–see–if I troubled them–
> But don't–shut the door!
>
> Oh, if I–were the Gentleman
> In the "White Robe"–
> And they–were the little Hand–that knocked–
> Could I–forbid?
>
> [248]

She has disobeyed her spiritual Father's precepts by not shutting up, by being
"too loud." Her punishment is that she is shut *out*, not shut up. She is kept out
of heaven, which serves as a metaphor both for the poetic achievement of
immortality and the "perfect peace" enjoyed by the dutiful. Although she does
not know why she is shut out, she assumes it has something to do with the fact
that she writes poetry, displeasing those who want "prose" and like her "still."
Little girl and poet are again equated. The first thought that occurs to the
persona is "Did I sing–too loud?" In her attempt to express her voice through
poetry, she transgresses ladylike behavior. Her voice being "too loud" is a way
of saying that by writing poetry, she knows she is being too bold, assertive, and
aggressive. Her sense that "they" like daughters "still" is reinforced by her next
lines in which she assures her reader that she *can* be "timid," presumably the
quality "they" desire. The persona's apparent eagerness to please by offering to
adopt those traits of timidity and restraint that constitute the feminine code
resembles Dickinson's response to her brother Austin when he rebuked her for
her extravagant metaphoric style in which she had been "too loud" for his
tastes. But offering to be timid implies that such behavior is not natural to *her*.
Letting her reader know that any obedience she demonstrates is only a skillful
and cooperative *pose* is a subtle way to assert her individuality and rebellion.
She gives society what it demands, but robs it of any satisfaction in gaining
control over the writer/daughter. This is Dickinson's tactic in her relationship
with her father: pleasing him but spiting him in the process.

What is important about "Why–do they shut Me out of Heaven?" is that
Dickinson states that timidity and being "little" are society's requisites for
women. The word "minor," along with the diminutive "little" is significant, for
beyond "Minor's" musical connotation relating to singing, it suggests that what

society wants from her is nothing "major" or significant. If she sings more dutifully (i.e., timidly) she will be degrading herself into Prose, the kind of piece like "Awake ye muses nine." Therefore, her dilemma is whether to be "still" and "timid" and get into heaven with Prose, or to write real poetry and suffer the alienation of the outcast, ostracized and exiled for disobedient boldness as a woman and as a poet. Again, the daughter poet is rejected for not knowing her proper place.

Even though the persona in "Why–do they shut Me out of Heaven?" is more subdued than in "They shut me up in Prose–," she is not less rebellious. She questions the wisdom of God in keeping her out of heaven, just as she questions the authority and wisdom of those who shut her in the closet in their futile effort to stop her from "poetry." She distinguishes between God and the angels in the poem, although at the end of the poem she shows that they are the same, perhaps because the public as well as the omnipotent editor decide a poet's fate. It is finally the "Gentleman"—a secular God who controls poetic immortality—who rejects the knocking "Little Hand." The image of the "little hand" is important, for Dickinson gives us a diminutive reference to the self in specific relation to the hand which is the poet's tool: is her hand perhaps too little for God? Her poetry not "large" enough? Is being a little girl in itself a reason for being rejected by a social and spiritual alliance of fathers?

To Be Still, Timid and Minor

In "Why–do they shut Me out of Heaven?" Emily Dickinson portrays the dilemma she experiences as a woman writer where being dutiful is being timid and still and "little," particularly acceptable attributes for a well-received woman or loved daughter—or published female poet. But the poet refuses to be "shut up," at least privately. In "I shall keep singing!" (250) she continues her bird/ song analogy to herself as a poet, replying in her defiant, willful stance of the rebellious daughter to those who have apparently told her to be "still." It is unclear whether the authority who is being thus defied is her father, society, or God: but to the daughter poet, any authority figure who tries to repress her career is impotent: he cannot control her voice.

That the poet is the rebellious daughter in reference to a secular-spiritual world of prose fathers who try in vain to "shut her up" is illustrated in another relatively early poem which begins with a familiar childhood question: "What if?"

> *What if I say I shall not wait!*
> *What if I burst the fleshly Gate–*
> *And pass escaped–to thee!*
>
> *What if I file this Mortal–off–*
> *See where it hurt me–That's enough–*
> *And wade in Liberty!*

They cannot take me–any more!
Dungeons can call–and Guns implore
Unmeaning–now–to me–

As laughter–was–an hour ago–
Or Laces–or a Traveling Show–
Or who died–yesterday!

[277]

What is most important about these examples of the little girl or daughter triumphing over a punitive society which seeks to quell her voice—Dickinson's self-image as a poet—is how the little girl for Dickinson functions as both a metaphor for repression (the vulnerable, dominated, restricted existence led by women), and a representation of her own experience and identity as a little girl. In "They shut me up in Prose" and "Why–do they shut Me–out of Heaven?" the persona is locked up or ostracized for breaking taboos regarding little girls and poetesses. In "What if I say I shall not wait!" the little girl persona acquires a more complex meaning of repression. Society's regulations for little girls are enforced more tyrannically. Punishment is not administered in the world of house or heaven, but in the realm of civil and military authority (dungeons and guns). The restrictions placed upon the little girls are not externally imposed, taking the form of closet or gate; rather, they take the shape of her female body. The prison to which the persona is condemned is her own flesh. Such an extension of the original metaphor would not make sense unless the reader sees that it is society, represented by dungeons and guns, which makes the woman feel that her body is a prison. Society effectively incarcerates her by imposing restrictive behavior upon her. This is why Dickinson writes that the persona's flesh can be "filed" off: she is implying through her use of imagery that the female body is a chain or shackle, because it is chained and shackled by convention, Prose, expectations to be "still," "timid," and "minor." The persona's childish and even exuberant teasing becomes sinister and tragic when she projects victory over society's sexism by killing herself, filing off the offended, offensive flesh. The transcendent tone at the end of the poem is made ironic with the image of a woman celebrating her potential to escape the House— or closet—or chains—of Prose by committing suicide and thus ridding herself of her female sexuality.

Grim as the above poem may be, Emily Dickinson shows a persona at war with society because of her refusal to mind her manners and confine her voice. In these poems, conventions can be escaped, and restriction, dominations, repression, and vulnerability—the aspects of being a "little girl"—are converted through the use of the voice of freedom, power, invulnerability, and triumph: "For the Disobedience' Sake" (1201).

7

ଔ

The Daughter and the Awful Father of Love

The saga of the mistreated but unvanquished little girl continues in Emily Dickinson's poems about her spiritual life. The theme of impotent authority, which shapes both the poems about society's futile efforts to silence her and the poems about God's ineffectiveness as a father, was first heard in Dickinson's letters about her father. An analysis of the representation of the Deity in Dickinson's poems confirms the parental archetype: rejecting, absent, absent-minded, careless, businesslike, incompetent, contradictory, and pernicious. Edward Dickinson came first; God is simply a blown-up version, a ballooned Edward Dickinson on a string whom the daughter addresses as "Father in Heaven." God, no more than a superfather, differs from Edward only in degree; both are spectacular failures as fathers, but God fails on a cosmic scale. Because Dickinson's interpretation of God is bound to her conception of her father, Dickinson's God is the object of her plaintive quest for paternal love and protection, recognition, and forgiveness. The daughter simply transports her "father's house," by means of the metaphor the church has so conveniently supplied her, into "Heaven," so that in the poems Heaven is indistinguishable from the house in which she grew up as child. Accordingly, the little girl in "Heaven" acts the way Emily Dickinson describes herself in the letters to and about father figures. Alternately angry and imploring, she shoulders God's rebuffs, flings herself on his mercy, complains, jeers, sulks, defies his will, and feigns dutiful remorse. God is the "Awful Father" to the poet's dutiful/rebellious daughter.

An early poem (49, written circa 1858) reveals the extent to which the poet's relationship with the "Awful Father of Love" (1204) reflects the earthbound Emily-Edward relationship:

> I never lost as much but twice,
> And that was in the sod.
> Twice have I stood a beggar
> Before the door of God!

113

> *Angels—twice descending*
> *Reimbursed my store—*
> *Burglar! Banker—Father!*
> *I am poor once more!*
>
> [49]

At first glance this is a dutiful daughter poem. The speaker is submissive toward patriarchal authority; humbled by loss, she appears as a beggar at God's door, dependent on his mercy. But instead of regarding God as the rightful owner whose authority and judgment in matters of life and death must be accepted on faith, Dickinson purports to consider God a "Burglar" who unlawfully robs her when he takes the life of someone she loves. Thus she challenges the legitimacy of his power, for the image of God as a burglar denies the Christian notion that human life is only on a kind of lease which expires at God's discretion.

It is typical of Dickinson's crafty intellect that she should use the ideological mechanisms of orthodox Christianity to undermine God's authority. No member of her family's church would quarrel with her attributing to God any loss she experiences, whether through death or any other means, or calling God "Father," or her conception of God as a Trinity; but Dickinson uses these conventional interpretations as the foundation of her criticism when she translates the Trinity into a business partnership consisting of father, banker, and burglar. Unlawful as she feels God to be, she has no recourse after his third robbery except to turn, not to the police as one might expect, but to the local banker whose business operations evidently depend upon such burglaries to bring in needy customers who are "poor once more." That the speaker should be shown appealing to a burglar-banker combination instead of a civil authority shows that she does not expect nor desire justice. It is not just the burglar's connections which make persecution impossible; Dickinson's concern is to get her "property" back, and putting away the burglar also puts away the man who has the ability to restore her losses. The persona therefore represents herself in the rather humiliating position of begging her robber to return what he has stolen, relying on his shrewd mercy and businesslike pity. Humbled in this way by her need of a Father's mercy, she is forced to repress her pride or resentment in the acknowledgment of her helplessness to control the transactions of her "store."

Such an interpretation of loss as this poem represents shows that any loss she experiences only aggravates Dickinson's predisposed sensitivity as a daughter. God is seen as systematically engaged in reducing the adult to a state of childhood dependence and impotence. The poem has been previously understood as a clue to Dickinson's biography; critics try to determine who or what it was that Dickinson had lost (in the sod or out) at the time she wrote the poem.[7] But the poem does not concern itself with any person or event; what it does reveal is the correlation in Dickinson's mind between her own and her heavenly "father." The notion on which the poem pivots—of God's giving and taking away—is a Biblical convention, but Dickinson's casting the process as a trans-action in terms of business and finance is unique: it certainly is informed by her sense of her lawyer father's pecuniary interest in investment, loans, and money matters. And like her own father, God is seen to be creating her depen-dence upon him at the same time that he sadistically refuses to satisfy her needs. Dickinson suggests that it is in God's interest, just as it is in a banker's, to keep her "poor." It is as if, in Jobian terms, God robs her so that she sees his absolute supremacy and her absolute dependence: or, in the commercial terminology Dickinson has chosen for the poem, God wants to keep her begging loans, in perpetual mortgage to him.

The daughter emerges dependent, impotent, humbled, and imploring from her encounter with her heavenly father. But her interpretation of God's dealings as a two-faced member of the business community, a respectable banker who moonlights as a burglar and serves as his own fence, is disrespectful and ultimately critical—if not heretical as well—and serves to undermine God's dignity and awful power. The world of stores, burglars, bankers, begging, reimbursing, and losses is the antithesis of the spiritual realm; Dickinson's stress on the material or profane, as opposed to the spiritual, bespeaks a God who traffics in the world of trade—a common, worldly, secular God. Just as she does in the letters, Dickinson manages to rebel against her father in the process of recording her defeat at his hands.

We see a similar critical interpretation of God in "Victory comes late:"

> Victory comes late–
> And is held low to freezing lips–
> Too rapt with frost
> To take it–
> How sweet it would have tasted–
> Just a Drop–
> Was God so economical?
> His Table's spread too high for Us–
> Unless We dine on tiptoe–
> Crumbs–fit such little mouths–
> Cherries–suit Robins–
> The Eagle's Golden Breakfast strangles–Them–
> God keep His Oath to Sparrows–
> Who of little Love–know how to starve–
>
> [690]

Dickinson's poems about God seem to be a function of her desire to expose the wrongs of a father figure; when God is a "father," humanity is reduced to a childish state of dependence, humility, smallness, impotence, and frustration.

As in "I never lost as much but twice," there is no question of God's power, but Dickinson's purpose is to challenge the moral legitimacy of this power. She does not give God a reprehensible secular occupation (such as burglar or banker), but she portrays God as a bungler whose careless incompetence is destructive and constitutes an abuse of power, a violation of trust. It would not be so bad if God made people his children and then functioned as a responsible parent figure. But God creates dependence and then exercises his responsibilities with a perverse, even sadistic lack of concern: he confers victory, but too late to console a soldier who died for the cause; he feeds his children, but sets the table "too high" for them to eat. He does not make the food unreachable; he just makes them dine "on tiptoe" in order to get it. The God who makes you beg at his door after he has robbed you seems to be the same God who deprives you of nourishment and then has you dine on tiptoe. In both cases the persona being dealt with by God is represented as abused and humiliated, humbled by a sense of being small and powerless. Dickinson's God in "Victory comes late" destroys self-esteem, so that people are glad to settle for less (crumbs and the cherries that the birds eat—the birds who are accustomed to starving on "little love"), just as the speaker in "I never lost as much but twice" asks not revenge but only to have her property returned. In this latter poem, Dickinson suggests that it is in God's "economic" interest to rob her; if she is poor she will come begging. So it is with "Victory comes late," where Dickinson ascribes to God a motive for his cruelty. It may not only be his carelessness which deprives people, but his being "so economical." In other words, the speaker again sees God as a businessman like Dickinson's father who values material gain over human life or happiness. Such a critical interpretation of God comes directly out of the daughter's resentment about her own father's business concerns that make him "too busy–to notice what we do" and take him away from home. Emily Dickinson felt neglected by her father; what is interesting in this poem about God's neglect is that God is given the maternal role of nurturing. But God fails as a mother because he has her father's traits: he is stingy, careless, neglectful, powerful, and sadistic.

Through such poetry, Emily Dickinson can express her ambivalence to her own father and can rebel against the patriarchal religious and social super-structure in which she finds herself as a daughter, without incurring punishment or society's condemnation. But the poetry about an "economical" God also provides its own rationale. Although she claims to suffer from God's treatment of her in his role as a father, his alleged spurious perversity and ineffectualness in the situations Dickinson has constructed constitute a justification for the speaker's audacious, privileged attitude of casual disrespect. By the logic of the poems, she can disparage God's wisdom and justice, because according to her poetry, he deserves it. Thus Dickinson implies a familiarity with God, born of her encounters with him. He is a "docile Gentleman" (1487); "our Old Neighbor," a clear second choice in her search for company (623); a "jealous" playmate who takes his revenge on people who would rather play with each other than him (1719): it is as a pouting, petty child that he makes people die. Similarly, his treatment of Moses, according to Dickinson, bespeaks a childish cruelty. He tantalizes Moses by letting him see Canaan "As Boy–should deal with lesser Boy–To prove ability" (597). God's making his table too high, or robbing her and then restoring her losses is a similar kind of flexing of the spiritual biceps, beating the divine chest. Dickinson can only scorn such a bully. God should be larger, more heroic than to be constantly reminding people that they are littler than he. It is as if the daughter has found God out, and offers the poems as proof. What we must remember in all these poems is that it is in *her* "interest" as a revengeful, dependent daughter to reduce God to a human level on which he can be criticized and in the process, defanged, made tame.

Just as in her early letters Dickinson will present her father as a tyrant buffoon who is not to be taken too seriously, then, Dickinson describes herself being able to consider without qualm God's response to her imagined transgressions:

> *Over the fence–*
> *Strawberries–grow–*
> *Over the fence–*
> *I could climb–if I tried, I know–*
> *Berries are nice!*
>
> *But–if I stained my Apron–*
> *God would certainly scold!*
> *Oh, dear,–I guess if He were a Boy–*
> *He'd–climb–if He could!*
>
> [251]

On a scale of God's ability to punish, scolding ranks somewhere along with sending society to bed without its dinner. The image of a scolding God turns God once again into a parent who cannot cope, and humanity into a child whose needs constantly defeat the parent. Only children or errant husbands are ever scolded. (Rip Van Winkle comes to mind.) There is a finger-wagging aspect associated with the act which reduces the scolder to a thwarted will, a powerless authority without the desire or ability to inflict a more severe punishment. No harm is done or meant to be done; scolding is a punishment by the harmless of the harmless.

Thus Emily Dickinson presents her relationship with God, and the moral dilemma she experiences as a woman poet in her society, as a daughter-father conflict. Although the backdrop of the poem is light, the issues the poem presents are serious and represent Dickinson's deepest concerns. The little girl who wants to go "over the fence" is torn between her desire for berries (or whatever illicit fulfillment the berries represent) and her sense that going "over the fence" is a defiance of God's will. What is especially interesting about this poem is that the issue at stake is not the berries, the objects of desire, but the "fence" which stands between the girl and the berries. Twice in the space of nine lines we see the phrase "Over the fence" repeated. We must ask the real nature of the proposed crime. Is what the speaker ordered to forswear the symbolic Strawberry (forbidden fruit); or is it what is required to obtain these "berries" (climbing over the fence)? Or is it what is required to obtain these "berries" *if one is a girl*? It develops that the real obstacle standing in the way of gratification is not the fence itself: that, the speaker tells us, she is perfectly capable of climbing ("I could climb–if I tried, I know–"). The real "fence" is God or society's forbidding her to "climb." Presumably, if the berries grew this side of the fence there would be no problem. But "Strawberries–grow–/Over the fence–" and going over the fence is a sin.

As Dickinson wants the reader to understand it, then, she is separated from "berries," not by an innate inability on her part, but by arbitrary restrictions on social behavior. That these restrictions are imposed only upon her sex is made explicitly clear. Boys can climb with impunity; girls, however, have a built-in Apron which prevents them from climbing fences to get berries without being betrayed by telltale "stains." Boys do not have to wear aprons; boys do not have to risk getting dirty; boys can take risks and get all the "berries." It is the wearing of the Apron, then, that serves to keep the little girl from "climbing"; that, and the need for Aprons to be kept clean. One could say that the little girl could simply shed the apron, but the point the poem seems to be making is that the Apron is the emblem of femininity and cannot be discarded. The apron is more than a symbol of woman's dometic destiny which makes such "clean" behavior (refraining from any activity which will "stain" one's "apron") necessary. It is not going "over the fence" per se which is prohibited; it is getting "stained." Since only girls can be "stained," only girls may not go "over the fence" to get the "berries." Even God would not dare to climb unless he "were a Boy."

The poem, with its sexual metaphors implied by apron, berries, stains, and fences, can be read as an allegory of Christian disobedience. The little girl wants to pick Forbidden Fruit in the Garden. She is certain, however, that God will "scold" her if she does. However, she does not consider going "over the fence" to be inherently immoral; any second thoughts revolve around the inevitability of getting caught. The only harm that can result is a stained reputation as a dutiful daughter. She defies her Father by acting unfeminine—climbing fences and getting dirty, literally and metaphorically. She knows that if God were to judge her as a boy, like himself, he would wink at her transgression. Her assumption is that God has a double standard for boys and girls—not unlike her father and society in general.

In one way, the poem is a classic feminist argument against the injunctions against a woman's success. Dickinson criticizes arbitrary laws for social, sexual, and spiritual deportment based on sex. She shows evidence in this poem that she has equal ability to climb fences—a consistent theme from her letters (for example, where she points out that she is every bit as qualified to attend the Whig convention as her father). Since she is not allowed to try to achieve success as a girl and overstep propriety ("fences"), her only recourse is to identify with boys, who represent a kind of freedom. As a daughter, Dickinson encounters numerous "fences"—presumably, writing poetry and expressing her voice is one fence that is all right for boys to climb.

"Over the fence" is actually a pessimistic statement on the nature of a girl's existence and her choices for action. This is why the poem ends on a note of irresolution, with the persona poised on the brink of disobedience; she is only posing the problem of a woman with talent who is being repressed. As in "What if I say I shall not wait!" she is also gaining God's notice by threatening to disobey him. But if this strategy doesn't work, the daughter permits herself one last heretical dig to rouse her Father—the doubt that as a boy God *could* climb the fence like herself: "He'd climb—if He could!" She suggests that only ability, not fear of reprisal, could keep him from doing it: that trying to go over the fence is a natural desire for "boys"—*and* for girls, who are only kept from the attempt by fear of dirtying the Apron. Dickinson shows that trying to keep women from going "over the fence," like shutting them up in the closet, is society's way of trying to keep women from fulfilling their desires.

THE HEAVENLY DAUGHTER

When Emily Dickinson will do "what the Nurse calls 'die'," she hopes Eden will not be "so lonesome/As New England used to be!" (215). But her poetry shows Eden to be a replica of New England—that is, her house in Amherst and the childhood landscape in which she grew up as a lonely child. In fact, her childhood experience in "New England" determines her religious outlook. The earthbound relationship between herself and her Heavenly father is not shown to end at her death; rather, the conflict between the divine bully and the recalcitrant daughter continues in eternity. Just as Dickinson's poetic God is a type of her father, she shows the self who goes to Heaven to be a type of the rebellious daughter; it follows, then, that Heaven is portrayed as the lonesome New England schoolhouse or nursery in which Dickinson lived. Thus Heaven is understood as that "fair schoolhouse in the sky" (193), where she is a pupil being explained the causes of her earthly anguish. In the poem which extends the metaphor of Heaven as a schoolhouse, Dickinson asks, "Won't they scold us—when we're homesick—/Or tell God—how cross we are—" (215). In her early letters from school, Dickinson defines herself as homesick, and her letters throughout her life present a self-image of the cross, cranky child. The nature of her childhood experience, which she uses as a metaphor for her adult

life as a woman, determines her pessimism about the possibilities of any other
type of existence in Heaven.

That Dickinson is conscious of the degree to which her earthly experience
affects her ability to imagine Paradise is shown in "I never felt at Home–
Below–" (413), where she again uses the schoolroom analogy between earth and
Heaven:

> *I never felt at Home–Below–*
> *And in the Handsome Skies*
> *I shall not feel at Home–I know–*
> *I don't like Paradise–*
>
> *Because it's Sunday–all the time–*
> *And Recess–never comes–*
> *And Eden'll be so lonesome*
> *Bright Wednesday Afternoons–*
>
> *If God could make a visit–*
> *Or ever took a Nap–*
> *So not to see us–but they say*
> *Himself–a Telescope*
>
> *Perennial beholds us–*
> *Myself would run away*
> *From Him–and Holy Ghost–and All–*
> *But there's the "Judgment Day"!*
>
> [413]

Dickinson's conviction that her identity as a daughter will continue in eternity
is based on her overwhelming sense of the patriarchal nature of the universe.
Given fathers and their interpretations of femininity (and resulting behavorial
codes for "little girls"), there is no reason for Dickinson to think that God will
be any less a "father" to her in Heaven than he is on earth. Consequently, she
will be just as alienated in those "Handsome Skies" as she is on a "Handsome"
earth.

The voice in the poem is the child's, but this "child" has long since passed
childhood, at least in physical terms—I think we can assume her corporal life
is past altogether. Her use of the past tense in the phrase "I never felt at Home–
Below–" indicates that her earthly existence has ended and she now anticipates
the next stage. By speaking in the voice of the child even now, Dickinson
stresses her sense that her whole life has been lived as the schoolchild. That
this existence is/was alienating for her is shown in her belief that she will be
just as unhappy in a place which only extends her subjection and loneliness.
In a strategy used by science-fiction writers and satirists, Dickinson projects
the future in order to criticize the present and the past. Life for her as a "child"

has been an admixture of Sundays and school, where time is punctuated with "thou shalt nots" and commandments to be dutiful. Heaven to her is a depressing combination of the two, a twenty-four-hour, day-in, day-out stifling. It will be "lonesome" for her just as earth is lonely when Vinnie sweeps the stairs and all her friends capitulate into marriage. We know from Dickinson's letters that duty is "ugly" to her; we can see that the idea of unrelieved duty is intolerable. Thus the child enters the schoolroom in the sky with the sulky pronouncement that she does not "like" it. Since there is no recess, her only hope is that God would "make a visit" or at least take a nap, so that she gets a temporary respite from good behavior. But this hope is futile, for the eye trained on her never blinks; what is worse is that his telescopic vision magnifies her. If it were not for the "Judgment Day" she would "run away/From Him—and Holy Ghost—and All."

The poet's assumption that her treatment on earth will be identical in Heaven would be pessimistic were it not for the use she makes of the child persona. The child can ask questions and make statements that would be considered impertinent or heretical in an adult.[8] The chances of the child speaking heretically are greater, for children are not as aware of taboo topics or inappropriate attitudes as adults, and so enjoy a relative freedom to speak their minds. Adopting the pose of a child, Dickinson can challenge authority by assuming ignorance. Therefore the voice of the child in this poem is not only an emblem of hopelessness. It is also a means of rebellion in itself, for as a child Dickinson can criticize and complain with impunity. For example, Paradise by definition is one of those non-issues. Only an unredeemed sinner could not want to live there or would make its merits a matter of controversy. Saying one does not "like" Paradise is tantamount to heresy; even saying one "likes" it is inappropriate. Condescending and disrespectful, the expression belies an ignorance of religious teachings. The only excuse is that the child does not know better. But the poet does. Her identification of herself as a child and the use she makes of the child persona constitutes rebellion.

Considering her rebelliousness, we may wonder why Dickinson assumes she will be in Heaven at all. But even though Dickinson will portray her speaker as balking at going and wanting to run away once she is there, in no poem does Dickinson imagine herself being any place else. Her consciousness is so dominated by a father figure that she does not conceive of any type of existence in which the father is not present. She has to be in Heaven, not Hell, because the Father lives in Heaven. She will be her father's daughter forever. In the poems she will never portray herself grown up and leaving home for an independent life. She may threaten to leave home as she does in the above poem, but she will also argue against the ultimate logic of so doing: God and his judgment are inescapable.

This does not mean, of course, that she cannot complain. Her poems extend her criticism of her father and his abuse of authority not only to God but to the Church in general. She may want to think that heaven will be different

from earth, so that she will have a protective father and will not be lonely, but
in one of her last poems, she shows why she despairs of this hope:

> *Who has not found the Heaven—below*
> *Will fail of it above—*
> *For Angels rent the House next ours,*
> *Wherever we remove—*
>
> [1544]

According to the daughter construct, Dickinson has internalized her family
structure so that she carries her sensibility as a daughter—and her corresponding alienation and homelessness—with her. This accounts for poems such as
"Away from Home are some and I—" (821) and "Who occupies this House?"
(892). In these poems heaven is a paradigm of alienation for the little girl. In
the latter poem, the speaker tells us that she does not feel "at home" in the
house (which is in a still heaven of "grave" citizens). The owner of the house is
a stranger to her here, like all of "Eternity's Acquaintances." These poems cast
light on Dickinson's feelings about her earthly existence—that she does not
know, and is not known by, the people with whom she lives. The speaker tells
us she would rather be where "Boys were possible." In other words, no "boy"
could live in the heaven—or earth—in which she lives as a little girl. The word
"boy" represents the unrestricted life of freedom, spontaneity, climbing fences—
the opposite of her life as a girl, where it is "Sunday all the time" and aprons
have to be kept clean. Thus we see Dickinson's ambivalence to her identity as
a girl emerge as the primary reason for her homelessness on earth and in
heaven. Because of the nature of her experience as a daughter, she will never
feel "at home" as a little girl. Being a daughter alienates her not only socially,
then, but spiritually. Her rebellious relationship to her father and to God is the
result of their preference for "boys."

THE FAITH OF THE REBELLIOUS DAUGHTER

Emily Dickinson is aware of the role her childhood experience plays in
her religious development: in numerous poems she chronicles the effect the
social and spiritual double-standard for boys and girls has on her entire spiritual
attitude. In the process, she provides a justification for her rebellion as a "girl,"
both on earth and in heaven:

> *I prayed, at first, a little Girl,*
> *Because they told me to—*
> *But stopped, when qualified to guess*
> *How prayer would feel—to me—*

If I believed God looked around,
Each time my Childish eye
Fixed full, and steady, on his own
In Childish honesty—

And told him what I'd like, today,
And parts of his far plan
That baffled me—
The mingled side
Of his Divinity—

And often since, in Danger
I count the force 'twould be
To have a God so strong as that
To hold my life for me

Till I could take the Balance
That tips so frequent, now,
It takes me all the while to poise—
And then—it doesn't stay—

[576]

In the first two lines she describes her initial obedience to society and parental authority: she prays because "they" tell her to—the same ones who shut her up in prose, shut her out of heaven, and scold her when she's homesick. As always, "They" urge conformity upon her. Prayer is the conventional way one reaches God; she does what she is told to because she is a good "little Girl." In other words, to Emily Dickinson being a little girl in itself is symbolic of duty—of being told what to do and doing it. Obedience requires an unquestioning mind. Therefore a "little girl" signifies the triumph of a "sing-song" mentality. In addition, the Puritan mind is taught that it is heretical to question doctrine and religious authority in general. But Dickinson stresses the fact that it is *because* she is a little girl that she is obeying—just as because she is a little girl she is enjoined from scaling the fence. In the process, faith in prayer is subtly reduced to obedience. Turning to God for guidance constitutes an obedience to society's own precepts. As I suggested in my discussion of the Valentine sermon (1), parents, society, and God are seen in conspiratorial alignment enforcing dependence and obedience; being dutiful to one is being dutiful to all. By this reasoning, therefore, Dickinson suggests that when she presents herself having stopped praying, she is rebelling against a social as well as a religious authority. She impugns society's intelligence and sensitivity, and challenges the wisdom of their instructions. She only does this, though, when she is "qualified to guess"—no longer a "little girl." Perhaps the act of defiance in itself alters her status as a "girl"; guessing is a bold activity, for she projects her feelings onto the highest authority and imagines how she would feel as God (see poem 248). Based on her own intuition, she makes a "rational" decision not to pray. Therefore she values and trusts herself more than her parents: Emerson's daughter here, she is self-reliant as well as defiant.

Moreover, she satirizes the premises of prayer, citing parents/society for their "childish" egotism to think that their questions are important enough to be answered. But this stance indirectly faults God, who is again shown to be just as neglectful as her father, who is "too busy with his Briefs–to notice what we do." The child, bewildered because God does not answer her questions, reasons that she must be too inconsequential for Him. Therefore, his attitude toward her and his essential absence lessens her self-esteem, which only reinforces her negative self-image as a child. Pretending to defend God, she attacks his manifest lack of concern. It is a highly effective attack, utilizing the satirist's method of blaming while pretending to vindicate. What she does is vindicate herself, of course. Why should she pray if she is not answered? She does not want to presume on God's important time.

But the wording of stanza three, in which she reasons out her decision to stop praying, gives the impression that Dickinson's final purpose in the poem is not so much to satirize God for his ignorance of her, but to satirize God as He is presented to her by parents and society. She is told to tell God "what I'd like, today," the common and casual parlance of the marketplace. People tell her to approach God as one would a butcher at the meat counter ordering pork chops: an approach she attributes to the Yankee relationship to God. (It is interesting to note in this regard that Edward Dickinson was reproved by his minister for approaching God "like a lawyer.")[9] They want to argue philosophy with him, "The mingled side/Of His Divinity–" as casually as they would discuss issues with a politician. It appears that the ignorance is on the part of society in their sacrilegious approach to God, for the poem satirizes the secular nature of the religion fostered on her as a little girl by a society whose precepts she will no longer obey for duty's sake. She will not approach God through "prose," but through poetry. Perhaps then it is not God who suffers from her refusal to pray, but the God of doctrine and convention promoted and supported by the culture in which she lives.[10]

In the same vein, Dickinson makes fun of the metaphysics of the basis of Christianity itself: the hierarchical relationship between God and Christ, whom people are supposed to go through in order to reach God (357). She speaks heretically in her deliberately casual and satiric presentation of God as a "distant—stately Lover" (357). She makes an analogy between the human-Christ-God relationship and the doomed courting ritual of the Priscilla-Miles Standish-John Alden trio from Puritan history. This analogy emphasizes the absurdity in the enforced Christian procedure by treating spiritual transaction in terms of "a Vicarious Courtship" where God "Woos . . . by His Son," a love quest which becomes sabotaged in the process.

In the second stanza, Dickinson scoffs at how the doctrine is loophole-free:

> But, lest the Soul—like fair "Priscilla"
> Choose the Envoy—and spurn the Groom—
> Vouches, with hyperbolic archness—
> "Miles", and "John Alden" were Synonym—

[from 357]

She feigns admiration for God's legal strategy: he is as crafty in his contract as the men who seek his aid. Thus the God is secularized into a smart Yankee lawyer—like her father. This is the God promoted by his emissaries on earth and the "faded men" who wrote the Bible. The clergy and Bible are "Miles Standishes" wooing her in the name of God. Craftily, she reveals the one loophole in the doctrine: she rejects the substitute suitor (society, parents, Church). Since they all purport to be "synonymous" with God, she rejects—and outsmarts—God. Because she may not actually accept the convention in the first place, she may be seen to merely sport with it to show how it can be abused, exposing it as potentially harmful folly: the courtship can be sabotaged by this process, and God's suit rejected.

This, in fact, is precisely what Dickinson claims has happened (1258). If she has been disobedient to God, she reasons, she attributes it to the way in which society depicted God when she was a child and wanted to know where she stood in relationship to him. When she asked about her relationship to God and Christ she was "portentous told/With inference appalling" (1258). The doctrine that she received only reinforced her childhood experience so that what she was told became quite plausible. She thinks that if God Himself had told her when she wanted to know, and presumably had answered her prayer instead of leaving her in an ignorance of dread, "We better Friends had been, perhaps." As it is, she is convinced that it is too late for any rapprochement. Faith is innocent when one is a child and trusts, but when that trust is abused, when what the world offers is not good, faith can never be on the same solid foundation again.

Dickinson exonerates society somewhat from the responsibility of her alienation by maintaining that it is God's fault for withholding true information about himself, by not making his love felt to offset her "girl's" negatively prejudiced attitude towards him. She faults God for allowing society to misrepresent and taint him—they impart to God the traits of her own father. Her God is therefore a Yankee bargainer, shrewd and secular, every bit as economical as her own natural father. She even calls him "The Thrifty Deity" (724) who is unmoved by circumstances. He has a "Perturbless Plan," inserting here, taking away there, which implies a rigid immunity to prayers.

It is important in this context to examine Dickinson's attitude to prayer, because it is the traditional sanctioned convention by which one reaches God. It requires faith in the precepts that God does intend for people to pray, or that the society that advocates prayer can be trusted. Moreover, it requires faith in

God's ultimate justice, goodwill, and mercy. On these terms, of course, Dickinson is prone to be skeptical. She stands to benefit from prayer; but she
perceives the act of prayer to be a submission to God and society. Prayer
becomes charged with her ambivalence to doctrine, fathers, and conventions
which limit her own destiny. To pray is to be an obedient daughter in spiritual
and social terms; not to pray is to rebel against a secular advocacy as well as
an anti-feminist religious structure. It is interesting, although not surprising,
that George Whicher, Dickinson's first major biographer, should find Emily
Dickinson to be "all woman" when she wrote, like a good daughter:

> At least–to pray–is left–is left–
> Oh Jesus–in the Air–
> I know not which thy chamber is–
> I'm knocking–everywhere–
>
> [from 502]

To Professor Whicher, she was "all woman" because her imploring tone is
evidence of being "overwhelmed by emotion" and lacking "maturer judgment:"
his definition of a woman is one who is immature, hysterical, and naturally
dependent.[11] If she is the apotheosis of true femininity when she humbles
herself to her father figure, it follows logically that Dickinson rejects her feminine role when she gives up praying. In her letters she had written, mysteriously: "Let Emily sing for you because she cannot pray." In poem 576 the
persona renounces prayer, and thus gives up her safe identity as a "little girl."
She flounders in the identity vacuum between little girl and "wife" we see in
poem 199. Spiritual and emotional stability come with being the little girl, but
she has "finished that—That/Other state" because even when she dutifully
humiliates herself, God does not "care."

> Of Course–I prayed–
> And did God Care?
> He cared as much as on the Air
> A Bird–had stamped her foot–
> And cried "Give Me"–
>
> [from 376]

The "of Course," which implies that her first impulse was to be "dutiful,"
anticipates the obedience professed in "I prayed at first, a little girl (576), where
she also describes her rationale for not praying.

In poem after poem she tells us that obedience results in humiliation—as
in "I meant to have but modest needs–" (476). When she prays to go to Heaven
and be "content," Jehovah laughs at her and even the angels come down to
deride her. In response, "I threw my Prayer away–." Disillusioned, she now
regards the skies in the same manner as a child who has been "swindled." God,

in addition to being merely indifferent, mocks her. Numerous poems recount how she came to give up prayer, and the cycle is given momentum by Dickinson's seeming inability to accept the implications of unanswered prayer. In spite of all her previous repudiations, she finds herself begging:

> *Just Once! Oh least Request!*
> *Could Adamant refuse*
> *So small a Grace*
> *So scanty put,*
> *Such agonizing terms?*
> *Would not a God of Flint*
> *Be conscious of a sigh*
> *As down His Heaven dropt remote*
> *"Just Once" Sweet Deity?*
>
> [1076]

God, addressed as "adamant" and stone-hard to appeals, does not answer the prayer. Although she has been put in the position of dependency on God, the fact that he has denied her has taught her "how to starve" on "little love" (690).

To Dickinson, praying only underscores the social pressure to conform in religious terms: as an orthodox strategy to reach God, it does not work. God is either not at home when she calls, or pretends he is not. In being rejected or ignored in spite of her dutiful prayers, the child only becomes further disillusioned and alienated, and the people urging trust in this convention lose credibility. Prayer, ironically, becomes the vehicle by which Dickinson ascertains that she in fact has been rejected. Thus society has provided her the means by which she fails to gain the love, recognition, and security she seeks.

But Dickinson represents herself as left in a quandary, because she has been taught that when in extremity, "No other Art [except prayer]—would do—" (564). She describes a metaphoric narrative about being driven, her previous "Tactics" having failed, to confront God where He lives to know if He exists or not. But when she arrives at his abode, she does not see any sign of him (no face) nor of his house (no chimney, no door). But the revengeful daughter goes farther than "proving" that God does not exist. Instead, she finds his absence to be evidence of his presence: "The Silence condescended." In other words, the Father is known by silence, the sound the absent make. Father, then, *is* absence. Purporting to be convinced in this ironic and tragic way of his "existence," Dickinson presents a rationale for giving up prayer altogether:

> *There comes an hour when begging stops,*
> *When the long interceding lips*
> *Perceive their prayer is vain.*
> *"Thou shalt not" is a kinder sword*
> *Than from a disappointing God*
> *"Disciple, call again."*
>
> [1751]

The Father is impotent, absent, and incompetent: in fact, Dickinson has constructed an argument that God is not "God," and therefore, that prayer is futile. In "My Portion is Defeat–today–" (639), Dickinson describes a pathetic scene that illustrates the tragic futility of believing in a powerful, merciful God—and hence, prayer. On a battlefield, strewn among the "Bone and stain"—all those "defeated" in the battle—are "scraps" of prayer.

Emily Dickinson's campaign against prayer includes attacking the people who told her to pray as "a little girl:"

> *Prayer is the little implement*
> *Through which Men reach*
> *Where Presence–is denied them.*
> *They fling their Speech*
>
> *By means of it–in God's Ear–*
> *If then He hear–*
> *This sums the Apparatus*
> *Comprised in Prayer–*
>
> [437]

Her disillusionment about God is also a disillusionment about society. She satirizes the secular use of prayer; people who use it as a "little" tool. She debases the relationship between God and humanity into a mere transaction, a matter of mechanics. Underlying the satire is bitterness toward The Father for denying people his presence. Similarly, in "Faith is a fine invention" (185), Dickinson accords to faith the same attributes she has given prayer: faith is a useless tool—useless in the way that an electric mixer would be useless without electricity. But faith is designed on this principle—for all those who do not need it. Therefore, when we see the speaker "pray" in the poems, it is more than a dutiful effort on the part of the daughter to have faith in convention: it is a signal of need and distress, a sign that God is absent in her life. [12]

Thus the poem depicting the relationship between Dickinson's speaker and God can be seen as efforts on the part of a "daughter" to achieve her Father's notice. In this sense the poems function as "prayers," if prayer is in itself an acknowledgment of need and a commemoration of absence. Poetry returns God to the speaker in the same way that language brings the reassuring sense of mother or father to the infant; and such "childish" use of language also acknowledges the child's sense of separation from a parental community. In terms of the Daughter Construct, Dickinson's persona cannot conceive that she is not responsible for the separation existing between herself and her parent. If she is rejected by God (1163), she feels she is to blame. So faith manifested by prayer depends upon the poet seeing herself as individually and collectively guilty, and hence deserving of the punishment of parental absence. Since the response is "faith," the speaker's need for faith and a "strong" God also represents a need for absence as well. Her rejection of the socially-known God when he ignores her is not only a symptom of her defiance as a little girl, but a poet's strategy to sustain absence. In a way, the separation she feels *is* her fault because she has created it.

THE BELOVED DAUGHTER

There is another dimension to Dickinson's portrayal of the relationship between the little girl and God in the poetry, and while it diverges from the poems informed by the archetypal rebellious daughter, it perhaps is more revealing about the nature of her ambivalence toward her father. Dickinson has chronicled her rejection by an ineffectual God, which may be a strategy on her part to enhance her singularity and to justify her dissociation of herself from "prose" (reaching God through orthodox means), but in as many poems she casts the daughter in a love relationship with the Father. In the tradition of religious or mystical poetry, the poet of either sex portrays a consummation between speaker and God by making the speaker the bride of Christ. In Emily Dickinson's poetry, the use of this tradition suggests an Oedipal fantasy or "Electra" complex. Positing God as a lover enables the daughter to raise her self-esteem, for she then becomes the desired "wife."[13] The poems then constitute another strategy to gain the father's recognition. On the most elemental level, a loved daughter is a *noticed* daughter: her prayers/cries have literally been answered. But as the poem "I'm 'wife' " (199) makes clear, transcending the identity as unnoticed daughter entails being eclipsed. God can only be known by a total rejection of one's individuality, either in death (being absorbed into a communion with the universe and a sexual union with the deity) or in marriage—which Dickinson defines in her letters as another form of death for women.

We see something very complex, then, that can only be understood as ambivalence on the part of the daughter poet, for whom being singular and single (and maintaining one's identity) is a way to foster God's neglect. The poems are strategies to win God's attention and pity and to earn his punishment; they insist that God is a bungler no daughter could love, and present a rebel daughter no father could love. In a poem which seems to contradict the image of God as a Yankee menace, Dickinson writes:

> *Where Thou art—that—is Home—*
> *Cashmere—or Calvary—the same—*
> *Degree—or Shame—*
> *I scarce esteem Location's Name—*
> *So I may Come—*

> *What Thou dost—is Delight—*
> *Bondage as Play—be sweet—*
> *Imprisonment—Content—*
> *And Sentence—Sacrament—*
> *Just We two—meet—*
>
> *Where Thou art not—is Woe—*
> *Tho' Bands of Spices—row—*
> *What Thou dost not—Despair—*
> *Tho' Gabriel—praise me—Sir—*
>
> [725]

The tone of respect here is strained with the masochism that characterizes Dickinson's letters to her "Master" and other father figures. In these "love" poems, the suffering and deprivation she complains of elsewhere are here interpreted not as rejections but as emblems of love. Perhaps these poems are the most devastating indictments of God's cruelty, because the poet's ingenious mental efforts to perceive herself as loved by the father are pathetic. Dickinson's speaker does not care what happens to her, whether it is incarceration or crucifixion, or in what form God's notice is given (whether it is esteemed status or "Shame"). Her strategy is to transform her deprivation into her sign of election. Thus we see her *asking* to be crucified and incarcerated in Him (384), or asking to lose herself in love to Him (580), or describing "Wild Nights" (249), or consummating their union where she is "Given in Marriage unto Thee" (817), all of which raise her spiritual status to the *Son* of God. It is crucial to understand that Emily Dickinson wants the esteem and possibilities of the son— whether it be the son of her father or of God. She identifies wistfully with Christ, because she wants us to see her as martyred: then we will see that she is important to her Father. Therefore, she feigns "doubt" of her "Worthiness," but she also describes "His beloved Need" of her—just as in her letters she insists that her father needs her, wishing it were true (751). Dickinson also writes poems in which she rejects other lovers because her relationship with God is superior.

But her ambivalence to God as a father-figure comes in when we see that even as a lover, God, "distant" and "stately" like her own father, is a disappointment (357), so that their rocky love relationship takes on the dimensions of the little girl/father prototype examined in the preceding pages. Echoes of the relationship we witness in the letters between Emily and Edward are seen in the way Dickinson's persona desperately protests her love, undergoes rejection, assumes guilt for disobedience, and accepts injustice passively. The following poem describes the aftermath of rejection:

> *He strained my faith—*
> *Did he find it supple?*

> *Shook my strong trust–*
> *Did it then–yield?*
>
> *Hurled my belief–*
> *But–did he shatter–it?*
> *Racked–with suspense–*
> *Not a nerve failed!*
>
> *Wrung me–with Anguish–*
> *But I never doubted him–*
> *'Tho' for what wrong*
> *He did never say–*
>
> *Stabbed–while I sued*
> *His sweet forgiveness–*
> *Jesus–it's your little "John"!*
> *Don't you know–me?*
>
> [497]

In this poem we see the "daughter" describing "trust" in Erikson's terms. Even though she does not know what she has done wrong, like the child she assumes when she experiences rejection (absence) that she has been "bad." Yet Dickinson shows how this parent betrays her trust ("Stabbed–while I sued/His sweet forgiveness"). Conceiving Christ as God makes her plead with a rival brother ("Son") for attention (just as we see Dickinson in her letters plead to her brother for recognition). In the poem, she depicts the neglect of both her father and brother: neither recognizes her loyalty or her true status as a poet or daughter. She is "John," the man to whom God gave the revelations in order that they be given to the world. Does not God know that she is being his poet? Doesn't her father know her true worth? As in the poem "Over the fence," Dickinson tries to show that if she can get God to identify her not as a little girl, but as "little 'John'," he will respect her.

The eagerness to adopt any identity and strip herself of pride in order to please Him that we read in Dickinson's letters to her "master" is repeated in the following poem:

> *You said that I "was Great"–one Day–*
> *Then "Great" it be–if that please Thee–*
> *Or Small–or any size at all–*
> *Nay–I'm the size suit Thee–*
>
> *Tall–like the Stag–would that?*
> *Or lower–like the Wren–*
>
> . . . .
>
> [from 738]

She makes more and more ludicrous offers to change her identity, even as she did mockingly to Austin in her letters, with "just this Stipulus–/I suit Thee–." It is difficult to distinguish between Dickinson's love poems to God and to a more worldly lover because she addresses her lover with the humility, masochism, awe and reverence she would bestow on God—or vice versa. She sees the lover as her "God," transferring the father-image onto both. Therefore she is a persecuted Christ, or "son," to her lover as well as to God:

> 'Twas Love–not me–
> Oh punish–pray–
> The Real one died for Thee–
> Just Him–not me–
>
> Such Guilt–to love Thee–most!
> Doom it beyond the Rest–
> Forgive it–last–
> 'Twas base as Jesus–most!
>
> Let Justice not mistake–
> We Two–looked so alike–
> Which was the Guilty Sake–
> 'Twas Love's–Now Strike!

[394]

Beneath the depiction of a masochistic sensibility ("Oh punish–pray–") a tremendous ego is revealed as the daughter describes her ultimate fantasy. Anticipating the television commercials in which "Brand X" is mistaken for the preferred brand by the surprised expert, Dickinson shows that God cannot distinguish between "The Real one"—his own son, Jesus Christ—and herself. She comes to this conclusion because she apparently feels as persecuted and martyred as Christ. Instead of complaining outright as she does in her letters about being martyred in her family's kitchen, or being demoralized, she frustrates any plans to make her humble by ingeniously (and most wickedly) pretending that her suffering must mean that God has mistaken her for his son. She has to remind him that he has already had his son killed: "Just Him–not me."

Dickinson does even more outrageous things with her poem. Not only does she suggest that God is a trifle forgetful about such matters as the crucifixion, and perhaps even a bit blind or senile, in the tradition of the rebellious daughter exposing her father, but she provides a logic for God's mistake that hinges on her own Christ-like goodness. What has caused God to mistake her for his son, she believes, is her love, which outreaches any other's, including, presumably, Christ's. This, then, she suggests, must be her "crime," and the reason why God is punishing her: "Such guilt–to love Thee–most!" This crime dooms her "beyond the Rest" and makes her the "last" to be forgiven. It is as "base" as

Jesus' crime: in other words, not "base" or criminal at all. Therefore Dickinson exonerates herself from any wrongdoing, for no one can really think it bad to be even more loving than Christ. She cannot help it if she is a more qualified "son." At the same time, Dickinson soothes the divine pride by point out how natural God's mistake was: "We Two—looked so alike" that God could not tell "Which was the guilty sake." It is her son-like "love" which is to blame; if such "love" is a crime, why then, "Now Strike!" Therefore, even though her punishment by God was the result of a case of mistaken identity, the point is that she does merit it: she is Christ's equal—if not better. Proving how she surpasses her rival brother (Austin, Jesus) has been all that the poet has ever really wanted.

Dickinson's need to identify herself with the "favored son" is evident in several poems (see, for example, poems 456 and 553), and constitutes a causology for poems in which she writes, "Joy to have merited the Pain" (788) in which she interprets her pain as a sign of her father's singling her out for special treatment. Her "joy" is that God thinks she "merits" it—that he thinks she is his "son." The poet's strategy, then, seems to be to use God's fatherly neglect and torture as evidence of election, not rejection, for if she suffers, then she must be the son God loves most—as she has been claiming all along.

It is important to recognize, then, that the "love" relationship in Dickinson's poems about father figures who resemble God, and God who resembles father figures, is not a married or sexual love so much as it is a parental love that consists of notice, tenderness, esteem—and yes, neglect and tyranny. I have discussed in "What if I say I shall not wait!" how Dickinson portrays her little girl persona fleeing authority and repression. But in escaping the domination of earthly authority figures, the speaker runs to the ultimate authority, God. This would appear to be a contradiction; but however ambivalently she may feel about fathers, Dickinson seems to crave the father-daughter relationship, or at least to need to perpetuate it in the telling.

If we unravel the narrative of the little girl-God interactions in the poetry poem by poem, a metaphoric account of her experience with God proceeds fairly logically: the little girl needs her father's protection and comfort to ease her privations and suffering on earth (caused by "them"); she experiences additional losses incurred by God (including her own ignorance of her fate); society teaches her to pray for consolation. Either God ignores her or is not there, because her prayers go unanswered. Although both are horrifying possibilities, she can accept the former more easily; preferring guilt to a universe with no "monarch;" she therefore interprets absence as punishment for some unexplained crime. She asks to be forgiven; but since this involves prayer and she does not think he listens, she sets out on various expeditions to find him; but her search only confirms his absence. She scornfully rejects prayer as a means to reach him, and rejects him as the object of prayer. But she is then left in a desolate vacuum, lacking an alternative method to console herself. She considers herself banished from heaven, and stands at the gates in limbo; she rejects heaven as no place for little girls, and rejects society who set up her failure by teaching her trust and prayer; her only consolation seems to be, like Milton's Lucifer, irreverence, jests, and bitter accusations and self-pity. In spite of all this, she still needs a father. In an Oedipal fantasy, she projects herself as his lover, bride, wife, queen (failing to reach him as daughter, she must approach him as her mother does her father), and "Son;" but even as a husband, God is known as a little girl knows her father. She finds glory in his recognition, even if it is only as a sinner or naughty child.

What I have simplified here is a construct that is parallel to the way she describes her experience with her own father. Each poem depicts a stage of the "plot" outlined above. The stages appear more or less randomly in the poetry so that the father-daughter relationship is never seen to develop, evolve, change, or resolve. This tells us that Dickinson's poetic conception of the relationship was already formulated by the time Dickinson began to write her "keeper" poems. The poems reflect her needs and sensibility as a daughter: they function as strategies to effect God's notice; fantasies which assume she is recognized by him as his "Son;" and critiques of God's parental competence that build her own self-esteem.

8

Hunger in the House

In over one hundred poems that serve as culinary companion pieces to "They shut me up in Prose" (613), we encounter the daughter alternately starving, begging, being fed too little and too late, being offered the wrong type of food, and refusing to eat what and when she is offered. Mealtime is a trauma of parental and filial perversity. Given the daughter's predisposition to view dependence as punishment, humiliation, and defeat, and any exercise of parental authority as bullying and abuse, we could anticipate that Emily Dickinson will interpret the necessity of eating as tragic; for it makes the dependent child vulnerable to unreliable, nonexistent, and punitive parents. Emily Dickinson's hunger poems, then, reflect the daughter's hypersensitivity to her dependent role in her Father's House.

The trouble with—and symbolic import of —eating is that it requires the mutual cooperation of parents and dependent child. When harmony does not exist, diet becomes a matter of power politics, a mode of communication, a means of warfare and will. Dickinson's hungry child is both rebel and victim: "I had been hungry, all the Years–" (579); "'I want'–it pleaded–All its life" (731); "God gave a Loaf to every Bird–/But just a Crumb–to Me–/I dare not eat it–tho' I starve–" (791); "Deprived of other Banquet,/I entertained Myself–/At first–a scant nutrition–/An insufficient Loaf–" (773); "It would have starved a Gnat–/To live so small as I–/And yet I was a living Child–/With Food's necessity" (612).

The element of hunger is present in an astonishing number of poems. Oral imagery underlies Dickinson's concepts of fame, hope, home, faith, victory, and defeat in her "definition poems." The poet has hunger in mind even in poems that purport to describe other forms of deprivation or childhood unhappiness: the variant for "homesickness" is "hunger" (215); for "waited," "fam-

ished" (1282); for "live so small," "dine so small" (612). In conceptual poems
about food, over half describe it as not eaten, and the remainder associate food
with a negative unfulfilling experience or disparage it as impure or find it better
when untouched. The food the persona does eat distinguishes her from the rest
of humanity; it is mostly metaphor for the insubstantial (crumb, air, dew). In
poems about "eating" or "dining," the persona does not eat or dine: food is
withheld from her or she renounces it. In poems featuring body mechanisms
associated with eating, such as the tongue, lips, palate, or tooth, Dickinson
describes them as starving. When the poet plays "Yesterday," (728), she describes herself in terms of her "famine." Altogether nearly five hundred poems
(close to a third of all she wrote) are informed by the rhetoric of hunger.

Eating—the act of nurturance—embodies the child-parent interaction at
its most intense. We have witnessed the daughter's uneasy response to any
situation that aggravates her sense of powerlessness. In their earliest stages
children have absolute dependence upon their parents for nurture and even
survival; such total dependence upon figures she claims are absent and toward
whom she has ambivalence, at best, is certainly traumatic for the daughter. We
see her interpret the physiological necessity of eating as an affront to her
esteem, a duty that diminishes her, a "Custom" that must be disavowed. She
will diet with defiance, "tho' I starve." At the same time, Dickinson shows her
persona wallowing in the piteous suffering her dependence causes in order to
stress her predicament as a child of incompetent and cruel parents. Dickinson's
dramatization of the extent to which the child is at the mercy of her parents in
what and how often she eats is explained by Freud in his characterization of the
"oral" stage in a child's development, and further, by Erik Erikson's equation
of the "oral" and "trust" stage, when food is a metaphor for parents and the
outside world they represent.[14] For Dickinson, to refuse food is to say "no," to
these parents and the precepts that govern their raising of her. Refusal is an act
that constitutes distrust, rejection, or a mode of self-defeating rebellion. Such
an expression of will, which requires the temporary putting aside of one's
physical needs in order to assert oneself emotionally, is risky—and full of anger.
Denying nurture can be the child's first exercise of power and autonomy, one of
her only measures of control in a world in which she is otherwise almost totally
helpless and dependent. On the other hand, hunger, the body's warning sign of
physiological danger, signifies a lack of control. The infant can cry and thrash
about but she cannot say, "Very well, then, I'll go cook myself a pork chop."

Emily Dickinson depicts the situation of infant powerlessness with particular effectiveness:

> It would have starved a Gnat—
> To live so small as I—
> And yet I was a living Child—
> With Food's necessity
>
> Upon me—like a Claw—
> I could no more remove

> Than I could coax a Leech away—
> Or make a Dragon—move—
>
> Nor like the Gnat—had I —
> The privilege to fly
> And seek a Dinner for myself—
> How mightier He—than I—
>
> Nor like Himself—the Art
> Upon the Window Pane
> To gad my little Being out—
> And not begin—again—

[612]

In ludicrous images designed to emphasize the absurdity of one's helplessness in the face of hunger pain, Dickinson represents herself at the mercy of the sinister lone Claw of some unnamed creature. The comitragic futility of the effort to remove a Claw or Leech by *coaxing* it or to persuade an equally intractable Dragon to go away stresses our sense of the childlike smallness and innocence of the persona, and convinces us of her inability to deal with the larger, even monstrous, forces restricting her life: she is Cinderella without the fairy godmother. Dickinson contrasts the nightmare quality of a child's predicament with the actual needs of a "living Child" who is too weak even to cast her life away. Her "hunger" here seems to be the consequence of powerlessness. She cannot command food, nor can she "coax" or merit reprieve from those responsible for her needs. The ignominious gnat is "mightier," then, than she, because at least he can escape the house, find his own dinner, or kill himself upon the pane: she cannot. She has neither the "privilege" nor the ability to provide for herself.

Hunger is not only at the center of Dickinson's creative consciousness, but constitutes her dominant metaphor for herself as the powerless, unloved, and angry child. The poems show us that hunger and anger are analogous states for the dependent child, particularly when the hunger is a function of helplessness when parental nourishment is withheld. Although Dickinson does not specify who starves her, the hungry child she portrays suggests the motherless child of her letters ("I never had a mother"). In her poems set at mealtime, she is invariably alone (except in poem 579, when she is joined by "Noon"), clanking her spoon against the void. The birds are her only companions; they share their crumbs and cherries with her. Even when the hunger poems point to the lack of responsibility and compassion in the father figure (690, for example), Dickinson's complaints are still drawn in terms of a malfunction in the mother-child relationship, where at infancy the concepts of mother, child, food and love are one amalgam at the breast. Dickinson's hunger poems could be an implicit indictment of her mother, or a commemorative of her mother's absence in her life. But hunger is Dickinson's way to talk about survival needs and often the "food" she finds being withheld from only her is that which is provided in her culture by male authorities of one kind and another—esteem, knowledge, grace, fame. Thus we see Dickinson despair of God's spiritual food and society's encouragement.

But before we assume that Dickinson's hunger poems convict an adult world which has not adequately nurtured her, it is important to examine the hunger poems more closely in terms of the daughter's expressed needs and strategies. "It would have starved a Gnat—" (discussed above), for me, Dickinson's most effective evocation of hunger, shows her persona to be a helpless victim. And yet she has survived having to "live so small." Beneath the self-pity in this poem is the boast of a wronged daughter who evidently can endure impossible privation. She is a supra-human martyr.

In other poems, the boast—and the blame—are more explicit:

> God gave a Loaf to every Bird—
> But just a Crumb—to Me—
> I dare not eat it—tho' I starve—
> My poignant luxury—
>
> To own it—touch it—
> Prove the feat—that made the Pellet mine—
> Too happy—for my Sparrow's chance—
> For Ampler Coveting—
>
> It might be Famine—all around—
> I could not miss an Ear—
> Such Plenty smiles upon my Board—
> My Garner shows so fair—
>
> I wonder how the Rich—may feel—
> An Indiaman—An Earl—
> I deem that I—with but a Crumb—
> Am Sovereign of them all—
>
>   [791]

Emily Dickinson's poems about her relationship with God have shown that however she may disparage God's fatherly behavior, she will do anything to gain this father's notice and esteem—including a great deal of creative rationalizing whereby abuse or neglect become evidence that she has been singled out for special attention. To the daughter, destiny is less a function of what one is given than what one claims. Within the curious pathology of this poem, which purports to celebrate, even worship, a crumb, we recognize the daughter who is simply carrying obedience and gladness too far ("Too happy" is right) in order to reveal the absurdity and irresponsibility of her authority figures. She acquiesces to the manifest inequality of the "Crumb" without a whisper of Jobian questioning ("Why me?"), and professes to be so grateful for the crumb or pellet that she refuses to relinquish it "tho' I starve."

But underlying the tension between pathos and sarcasm in the poem is the scorn of the triumphant poet who uses her alleged oppression, persecution, or rejection to prove her distinctive identity, and in fact her superiority, over everyone else. The persona deems herself "Sovereign–of them all" for her receipt of the Crumb, her ability to withstand the humiliation and privation the Crumb represents, and her perverse determination to "starve" rather than consume such a talisman of God's esteem. The Crumb may signify God's apparent lack of concern for her, even an aggressive dislike, but to the daughter, any news is good news. Being chosen for disfavor may be more precious than receiving the Loaf along with the multitude; starving and being distinct are better than being common, loved, and fed. In a fashion we have come to expect from the needy, scheming, crafty daughter, then, she first claims discrimination (which is a sign of attention, after all), and then interprets it as privilege—the mark of favor and uniqueness—and thus manages to malign the Father, win pity for her innocent and exuberantly loyal self, and transform deprivation into fulfillment, superiority, and "difference." This is indeed the daughter at work.

We see a similar poetic structure in "It was given to me by the Gods" (454), in which the persona is proud of her "difference," given to her "When I was a little Girl . . . new–and small." While Dickinson does not specify what "it" is, "it" distinguishes her from the crowd, and takes the visible shape of deprivation, for when the persona hears *other* people referred to as "Rich" by "lips at Corners of the Streets," she smarts: "Rich! 'Twas Myself–was rich–." But her wealth is of an invisible sort. Responding to her "gift" in the same exaggerated way she does the Crumb in "God gave a Loaf" (791), she portrays herself as so grateful and so *dependent* upon her insufficiency she would starve or die rather than give it up. Distinction, which "made me bold," is worth more than her life.

While such a poem could convince the reader that the child heroine has indomitable pluck, it also suggests that the daughter does not triumph in spite of such deprivation but because of it: evidently, she thrives on being starved. It appears that hunger is intrinsically related to her sense of self-esteem. In fact, we see that the hungry daughter is not quite the helpless infant wailing to be fed, dependent upon the conscience of her mother; nor is she as passive as "It would have starved a Gnat–" (612) suggests. Although the poems seem initially to portray her as the victim of deprivation, it becomes clear that the daughter takes an active, even aggressive, role in her own deprivation, maintaining her "abstinence" deliberately ("I dare not eat it–tho' I starve") and defiantly. "I had been hungry, all the Years" (579), for example, reduces the persona's life to a pathetic image of oral deprivation:

> *I had been hungry, all the Years–*
> *My Noon had Come–to dine–*

> I trembling drew the Table near—
> And touched the Curious Wine—
>
> 'Twas this on Tables I had seen—
> When turning, hungry, Home
> I looked in Windows, for the Wealth
> I could not hope—for Mine—
>
> I did not know the ample Bread—
> 'Twas so unlike the Crumb
> The Birds and I, had often shared
> In Nature's—Dining Room—
>
> The Plenty hurt me—'twas so new—
> Myself felt ill—and odd—
> As Berry—of a Mountain Bush—
> Transplanted—to the Road—
>
> Nor was I hungry—so I found
> That Hunger—was a way
> Of Persons outside Windows—
> The Entering—takes away—
>
> [579]

In this parable about hunger, the persona's initiation to Bread is less a failure (the ceremony ends in indigestion) than an affirmation of the persona's inability to be common. With physiological accuracy, Dickinson describes the effects of long-term deprivation: subsisting on the Crumb so long has shrunk her stomach to the point that eating normal portions makes her sick. This is a way for Dickinson to prove that "Bread," representing common fare, is unsuitable for her, even if her spirit is willing. But of course, the spirit is no longer sorry to be hungry, for normal food loses its mystique when the speaker finds it available, and she concludes that she prefers the alienation of hunger. To hope for "Wealth," to enter that "Window," to swallow that "Bread," is to become a part of a social or religious structure, and Dickinson, whose identity has been based on her hunger, refuses to give up that which distinguishes her from society. She is no Berry of the Road, and will not let herself be "transplanted" by the act of eating (we note that the poem's narration omits the actual moment of partaking).[15] While hunger, therefore, is important, food itself is not:

> Undue Significance a starving man attaches
> To Food—
> Far off—He sighs—and therefore—Hopeless—
> And therefore—Good—
> Partaken—it relieves—indeed—
> But proves us

> *That Spices fly*
> *In the Receipt—It was the Distance—*
> *Was Savory—*
>
> [439]

The phrase "And therefore—Good—" gives away Dickinson's attitude about fulfillment and her true need or desire to be fed. Her rather perverse aesthetics
prefer the unattainable; again, she posits her belief in maintaining "Distance,"
where Spices retain their flavor. Given this aesthetic, we can judge that her
"hunger" is perpetuated, if not contrived.

Why she values, insists on, and even creates such hunger becomes increasingly clear. We have seen that the Crumb, symbol of her deprivation, is a
"poignant luxury" because it elevates her above the "Rich" and "lips at Corners
of the Streets": "I deem that I—with but a Crumb—/Am Sovereign of them all—".
In every case, wanting makes her superior. In the following poem, Emily
Dickinson introduces a rationale for cultivating *hunger* rather than another form
of deprivation: she suggests that her identity as a poet is linked to her "hunger"
and to her refusal to *satisfy this hunger*:

> *I play at Riches—to appease*
> *The Clamoring for Gold—*
> *It kept me from a Thief, I think,*
> *For often, overbold*
>
> *With Want, and Opportunity—*
> *I could have done a Sin*
> *And been Myself that easy Thing*
> *An independent Man—*
>
> *But often as my lot displays*
> *Too hungry to be borne*
> *I deem Myself what I would be—*
> *And novel Comforting*
>
> *My Poverty and I derive—*
> *We question if the Man—*
> *Who own—Esteem the Opulence—*
> *As We—Who never Can—*
>
> *Should ever these exploring Hands*
> *Chance Sovereign on a Mine—*
> *Or in the long—uneven term*
> *To win, become their turn—*
>
> *How fitter they will be—for Want—*
> *Enlightening so well—*

I know not which, Desire, or Grant—
Be wholly beautiful—

[801]

Dickinson now clarifies the source of her "hunger." Being a dependent woman
in her culture (a "lot . . ./Too hungry to be borne") and therefore estranged from
the nurture to which "independent Men" are entitled, proves to be a valuable
deprivation. Not having been given "Riches" like the "Man–who own[s]" them,
and convinced she "never Can," drives her to comfort herself through "play"—
like a child. The last two stanzas reveal the self-conscious poet turning our
focus on the poetic process before us as she discusses her metaphorically
exploring hands and illuminates what she means in earlier stanzas by "play."
The "hands" of the poet may strike "gold" and become Sovereign, for words
represent wealth, immortality, and power, and are a different means to wealth
than the general public owns. At the time the poem was written, "independent
men" were finding fortunes in the California gold fields. Exploring the recesses
of her female identity with a poet's pen (like the miners who penetrate the
"feminine" earth), Dickinson is in effect "mining" for "gold"—her code word
for poetic immortality. The act of writing poetry confers the autonomy and
satisfaction that otherwise can only be achieved in her culture by the independent man. But poetry is not only compensation, a substitute for "Riches" to
quell the childish "clamoring" for all she feels she lacks as a dependent woman;
it is a means by which the daughter can achieve these "Riches." By virtue of
the fact that she gives them to herself, both her enjoyment and her control over
her wealth is superior to the complacent independent man's. Were not Emily
Dickinson to feel dissatisfaction with her "lot" as a daughter, she would not be
motivated to turn to language to console or "free" herself to become "what I
would be." If she had "Riches," she would not need to "play at" them. She
would have metallic gold but not poetic immortality: "Great hungers feed themselves" (*L*. III, p. 668).

   Hunger is shown to be necessary to Dickinson's artistic fulfillment, specifically, the hunger of the child to whom the word is associated with food and
love. Words take on the function of food for Dickinson as a way to love and
nourish herself, and in this way she can be seen to become a mother to herself
as the poet. Through hunger, mother and child become a self-contained unit in
the poet. Emily Dickinson's persona is the unsatisfied daughter who uses her
hunger to stimulate her literary talents, playing at Riches, or otherwise "enter-
taining" herself: "Deprived of other Banquet,/I entertained Myself—" and while
at first it is "scant nutrition," it grows "sumptuous enough for me" (773).
Therefore, being mother-hungry is actually a requisite for writing poems because the need for nurture promotes the making of words. If she is mother to
herself, she is still in no danger of being nurtured in any way that could subvert
her sense of deprivation. For as I stress in the discussion of Emily Dickinson's
relationship with her mother, the daughter distances herself from her mother

through her use of language in order to dispossess herself of her mother's destiny.

The Aesthetics of Anorexia

Dickinson's hunger strategy employs two methods: either she refuses food, which entails presenting it as being offered, or she claims she is denied food. To the daughter, any news is good news. By showing herself given the Crumb while everyone else gets the Loaf, she can provide evidence of her unique status with the divine dispenser, and hence increase her odds for a unique destiny. When the persona in Dickinson's poems refuses to eat, she is reflecting the poet daughter's strategy to keep herself in the business of writing poetry. But if rejecting food makes the possibility of immortality any more likely, in that it stimulates poetry, it also accomplishes several related goals for Emily Dickinson. She refuses to be nurtured, and thus exerts the child's measure of control over her existence. She would rather starve than take in what society (and her mother) have to offer, not only because she does not want to become a "nobody" like her mother, but because she does not want to be common. From her point of view, what the world offers her is not fit to eat. To eat would be to symbolically ingest "not me"-type doctrine and ideals that would turn her into her mother, and thus to eat, or even to *agree*, is to obey and conform to a menancing mode of feminine duty. In the light of Dickinson's uncertain identity and her determination to establish her identity as unique, she must portray herself refusing the Bread of parents, society, and God. I see Emily Dickinson's deprivation poems, then—like her denials of her mother's existence—as strategies related to her identity quest as a poet. Whether she refuses food that has been offered too little or too late, or whether she complains that it never comes, she uses her contrived deprivation as evidence of her "difference." Her so-called "deprivation," then, is turned into a sign of election, and in this way she transcends convention and attains a superior destiny. Her perception of deprivation is a defense against conformity and the maternal matrix.

Thus the poems which tell how "It would have starved a Gnat–/To live so small as I" (612) are not complaints, but avowals of self-conferred distinction. She defines herself "fitter"—that is, fitter to write poetry—because of her self-imposed diet:

> *I fit for them–*
> *I seek the Dark*
> *Till I am thorough fit.*
> *The labor is a sober one*
> *With this sufficient sweet*
> *That abstinence of mine produce*
> *A purer food for them, if I succeed,*

> *If not I had*
> *The transport of the Aim—*

[1109]

Dickinson's hunger strategy is built on a foundation of commitment and confidence in her poetic career. Her "abstinence" provides a "purer food" (the immortal word) than the kind made in the kitchen ("the food that perisheth"), so that taking in "pure" food (that is to say, no food) insures that the food this mother-poet will provide in turn will be equally "pure." *Her* food, not her mother's, is the nurturing food to eat. As a mother, then, she encourages her reader to "Partake . . . Abstemiously" (994) as well, and refers to the superiority gained by such refusal, pointing to herself as an example of the benefits of following such a strategy ("I, of a finer Famine," 872). Declaring "Who never wanted—maddest Joy/Remains to him unknown—/The Banquet of Abstemiousness/Defaces that of Wine—" (1430), she exalts "wanting." In these references we see her conviction that not eating enhances as well as creates her art, for it is only "Beggars" who can "define" a "Banquet" (313). (See also poems 299, 711, 904).

Emily Dickinson's poems about fame provide insight into how she makes the aesthetics of anorexia work for her. Her determination to be a "Beggar" at life's banquet requires the renunciation of the nurture the parent world can give her. This entails conceptualizing "fame," the longed-for approbation into a "food" which is withheld from her ("Bread," "that Diviner thing/Disclosed to be denied," 1240), or as food unfit to eat ("a fickle food," 1659). And, following her pattern, Dickinson describes herself as a beggar at the "door for Fame," just as she presents herself before God or life's banquet. Dickinson's poems about her repudiation of fame shed light on her hunger poems, for denying fame is a way to gain it:

> *To earn it by disdaining it*
> *Is Fame's consummate Fee—*
> *He loves what spurns him—*
> *Look behind—He is pursuing thee.*

[from 1427]

Dickinson's other representations of fame emphasize its untrustworthiness: it is "the one that does not stay—" (1475), a bee with a sting and a wing (1763). Emily Dickinson's renunciation gains have made her proud:

> *Art thou the thing I wanted?*
> *Begone—my Tooth has grown—*
> *Supply the minor Palate*
> *That has not starved so long—*
> *I tell thee while I waited*

> *The mystery of Food*
> *Increased till I abjured it*
> *And dine without Like God–*

> [1282, rough draft I]

Again we see the longtime hunger; that Dickinson perceives hunger to be an act of punishment is supported by the existence of another draft of this poem, in which the line "That has not starved so long" is replaced by "Thou could'st not goad so long–". This time, the persona does not even try to eat, for she has grown accustomed to subsisting on nothing. Her hunger is so large that her Tooth, symbolizing appetite, has grown to the point where it is insatiable: starving has produced in her a *major* "Palate." Relating her hunger in terms of her mouth's expansion suggests that not only the hunger but the persona herself has grown. She is a physically larger person now; and starving has made her spiritually more consequential. Indeed, "dining without" makes her now "Like God" for she needs nothing: creator, not created: mother, not child.

At issue in the hunger poems is not who starves Dickinson or even what nurture she requires, but the fact that she is dependent on some parental omnipotent figure who has the capacity to fill her needs: this vulnerability seems to hurt the pride of the daughter. Her supposed inability to fulfill her needs herself (like the child), plus her ambivalence towards both nurture and her nurturers, identifies her as the dependent, rebellious daughter who tries to forge a sense of importance for herself out of her renunciation of her maternal matrix. Whatever withholding parents she has in mind have no real opportunity to satisfy her. Her aesthetics demand that she say "no" to any food. For the daughter, this is a way to write immortal poetry and become "like God" in his omnipotence and autonomy. But for the parent involved with this poet daughter, the relationship is what today would be termed a "no win" situation.

Emily Dickinson's use of hunger to define herself as the daughter can best be summed up in a deceptively unremarkable poem about watching the moon (629). There is a wistful note in the speaker's voice as she describes her response to the moon "around the House" as a bodiless woman. The poem continues,

> *–for not a Foot–nor Hand–*
> *Nor Formula–had she–*

> *But like a Head–a Guillotine*
> *Slid carelessly away–*
> *Did independent, Amber–*
> *Sustain her in the sky–*

> *Or like a Stemless Flower–*
> *Upheld in rolling Air*
> *By finer Gravitations–*
> *Than bind Philosopher–*

No Hunger–had she–nor an Inn–
Her Toilette–to suffice–
Nor Avocation–nor Concern
For little Mysteries

As harass us–like Life–and Death–
And Afterwards–or Nay–

. . . .

As we see Dickinson marvel at the moon's independence, autonomy, her uncon-
cern for an "Avocation" or life's "little Mysteries," and her lack of *hunger*, it
becomes clear that the self-absorbed poet is defining the moon in terms of
herself, projecting upon that orb all that she, by sharp contrast, is not—or so
she claims in her daughter poems. For in her psychological, metaphoric portrait
of herself as the poet daughter, she presents herself immersed in her avocation
(her poetry), chafing at her dependence and confinement, and *hungry*. For the
daughter, the sense of hunger is directly related to the woman's lack of power,
independence, and autonomy in her own house and the father's house beyond:
this deprivation makes "Possibility."

9

Let Us Play Yesterday

THE DAUGHTER'S PATERNITY SUIT

For a poem which contains every image of the daughter experience we have been exposed to thus far, "Let Us play Yesterday" should seem familiar. It is an evocation of childhood which features the tormenting savior and daunted daughter and all the accompanying motifs of the daughter construct: famine, imprisonment, dependence, ambivalence, repression, accusation, and craftiness. But for all its echoes, the poem—a major one—is strangely inaccessible, and passed over by Dickinson's critics. Perhaps we cannot believe that the daughter would deliberately summon her past: the poem seems like a ritualistic exercise in masochism, anxiety, and ambivalence. But the real problem is the degree of linguistic distress she displays in going over this territory of trauma— the hypertense structure, syntactic leaps, dissociative density. Indeed, the "Yesterday" she conjures is no sentimental romp through a straw-hatted idyll, or even a snowy Amherst landscape. It is gothic daughterhood:

> Let Us play Yesterday—
> I—the Girl at school—
> You—and Eternity—the
> Untold Tale—
>
> Easing my famine
> At my Lexicon—
> Logarithm—had I—for Drink—
> 'Twas a dry Wine—
>
> Somewhat different—must be—
> Dreams tint the Sleep—
> Cunning Reds of Morning
> Make the Blind—leap—

> *Still at the Egg-life–*
> *Chafing the Shell–*
> *When you troubled the Ellipse–*
> *And the Bird fell–*
>
> *Manacles be dim–they say–*
> *To the new Free–*
> *Liberty–Commoner–*
> *Never could–to me–*
>
> *'Twas my last gratitude*
> *When I slept–at night–*
> *'Twas the first Miracle*
> *Let in–with Light–*
>
> *Can the Lark resume the Shell–*
> *Easier–for the Sky–*
> *Wouldn't Bonds hurt more*
> *Than Yesterday?*
>
> *Wouldn't Dungeons sorer grate*
> *On the Man–free–*
> *Just long enough to taste–*
> *Then–doomed new–*
>
> *God of the Manacle*
> *As of the Free–*
> *Take not my Liberty*
> *Away from Me–*
>
> [728]

As she recites her terse litany, the bold assurance with which the speaker invites our participation in the poetic venture into her childhood disintegrates. The narrative voice is abrupt and there is so little syntactic connective tissue that there is a breathless, gasping quality to the lines. In the process of ritually summoning the requisite images of want and repression, the speaker becomes increasingly distracted. She ends the poem playing "Yesterday"—on her metaphoric knees, humbly begging God: "Take not my Liberty/Away from Me–." Her counterpart is passive, its role being simply the audience of this demoralized speech. The point seems to be that she was, and remains, helpless, dependent, vulnerable, and traumatized.

While the anxiety-producing "play"—it does seem like a ritual—ends in the speaker's defeat, recalling Dickinson's other chronicles of father-daughter encounters, the poem is also a fascinatingly ambiguous allegory of her rebirth as a poet. In setting out the complex relationship of the girl at school, "You," and "Eternity–the/Untold Tale–," Dickinson suggests that the poet needs a consciousness of having been a "little girl" to gain immortality. "Yesterday" is crucial to her as a poet because, like the craving daughter of the hunger poems, she is "easing" the "Clamoring for Gold" (as she expresses it in poem 801) she felt "Yesterday," by feeding herself—as opposed to being fed—words: "Easing my famine/At my Lexicon–." Turning to her "Lexicon," the little girl can provide herself the nurture she lacks: definition. Although Dickinson relied heavily for her poetry on the lexicon provided by her neighbor Noah Webster, her poetry is itself a series of definitions, or more accurately, redefinitions: a private, self-created, largely subversive "lexicon" of the rebellious daughter. Since she feeds herself words (as in "Deprived of other Banquet,/I entertained Myself–"), she is intellectually autonomous, a poet-mother to a hungry daughter-self. Dickinson's reference to herself drinking logarithms helps place her at her desk as a little girl, and contributes to our image of her oral deprivation, but it also helps clarify the intellectual nature of her hunger. The logarithm, a form of reason specifically concerned with the effect of power on relationships, is an apt metaphor for Dickinson's poetry. To recreate her "famine" of "Yesterday" when there is so much she needs to comprehend in her own relationships with powerful figures, and in her own quest for power, Dickinson "plays" with her poetry, and relives the needs that compel her immortal "Lexicon" or "Logarithm."

Dickinson's deliberate reference to her poetry informs the remainder of this litany as she provides what seem to be conflicting dimensions of the poet's necessary schoolgirl existence. After revealing her hunger, even for sleep, she makes an analogy between the schoolgirl and a bird:

> *Still at the Egg-life–*
> *Chafing the Shell–*
> *When you troubled the Ellipse–*
> *And the Bird fell–*

Frequently identifying with birds as both daughter and poet, Dickinson uses the image of the bird's hatching from its shell to symbolize her emergence out of the security and confinement she so often describes herself feeling as the embryonic daughter in her father's house (the "shell" both imprisons and protects). The personage Dickinson addresses as "You" functions as a meddling midwife to precipitate her birth by "troubling" her "Ellipse." The bird (herself, the girl at school) falls. While her dependence has made the schoolgirl "chafe," Dickinson's words "trouble" and "fall" are unusual terms to describe birth, and indicate some ambivalence about her release. Since the bird's emergence is an act of painful independence (it breaks its own shell when it is able), the "girl's" being "troubled" suggests a premature birth in which neither mother nor child is in control. The bird literally falls from the nest: it is noteworthy that Dickinson poses no protective mother bird to catch or save her. The fate of the bird is left unspoken—the speaker assumes the listener ("You") is so familiar with this

tale that her fate is understood—but falling is usually considered an accident
or possibly fatal conclusion, and the omission of the landing details seems
particularly significant.

"Fall" carries with it, of course, the association of Adam and Eve in their
forced eviction from Paradise, and in fact, the situation Dickinson describes
recalls this original "Yesterday." The "fall" suggests the ungrateful, ignorant
disobedience to the father, and the resulting divine punishment of "mortality"
which weighs so heavily upon Emily Dickinson. We are specifically reminded
of Eve's deceptive quest for knowledge of the gods—life's "little Mysteries," as
Dickinson says in poem 629: "Life–and Death–And Afterwards–." Having symbolically fallen from her father's house, Dickinson's "Yesterday" could represent a kind of Eden she could not appreciate at the time because of her hunger
for knowledge and power. Her sense of unrest and rebellion in her father's
house is based on her female identity. It is relevant to remember here that it is
Eve, the daughter, who is dissatisfied with her lack of power and possibility in
the Garden and who agitates for more—or is vulnerable to being tempted for
more—and, furthermore, that she literally feeds herself to get this forbidden
power from the forbidden Tree of Knowledge—just as the schoolgirl in the poem
feeds *herself* with lexicon and logarithm.

Dickinson can be identifying with Eve as the mother-poet dispensing the
word-food, compensating for the lack of God's power or spiritual grace. The
word "fell," as used in the poem, is complex, because it implies the innocence
associated with being out of control; she only "falls" as a result of external
tampering with her shell. Yet Eve, who loses her innocence, has an important
role in her "fall," although she is not wholly responsible for what happens. If
Dickinson interprets her poetic career in strict terms of Christian mythology, it
is the exploitive Evil Tempter who takes advantage of her hunger by telling her
she can be immortal or divine if she writes poetry, feeding herself the forbidden,
powerful fruit that seems unfairly withheld from her. In this case, her "fall" is
not her fault, or even the devil's, but God's who created this hunger in the first
place and leaves her exposed to temptation. We have seen that it is Dickinson's
conviction of God's neglect that "troubles" her and leads her to seek the reasons
behind the withholding of God's Bread in her prayer poems. As the poems in
"The Daughter and the Awful Father of Love" (1204) show, she becomes disillusioned—and subversive—when she seeks out God; she blames him for her
inability to love and trust him, and for being vulnerable to "sin" by wanting to
be "that easy Thing/An independent Man" (801) and to feed herself forbidden
fruit. As "Over the fence" (251) and "I play at Riches–" (801) make clear,
Dickinson feels constrained from fruit or riches not by ability, but arbitrary
mysterious rules imposed upon women. Her self-conscious guilt about writing
poetry derives from a sense that a woman poet sins in the creation process, and
her use of the otherwise unrelated concepts of "fall," the bird's hatching, and
hunger to describe her formative experience reflects her sense that she indeed
sees herself as Eve, as she hinted in her teenage letters, subject to seductive

"evil voices" telling her that she can be "great, Someday"—a poet. Alluding often to her indentification with Adam and Eve's plight, she asks, "and why am I not Eve?" (*L.* I, p. 10). At the heart of her identification with the tragically tempted Eve is Dickinson's ambivalence about the control and autonomy she can practice with impunity as a woman. Describing her emergence by deliberately changing biological facts—making the bird emerge *dependently,* instead of autonomously—shows the extent to which she manipulates being seen as dependent, essentially a victim, in her maturity.

In fact, the next stanza makes clear that the issue of control is the central theme of the poem. It presents her second birth as a happy ending, a release from a prison-shell, not a "fall." While the jail image contradicts the preceding image of the shell being rather prematurely hatched, both images convey the little girl's sense of confinement and release, and both stress her dependence, passivity, and lack of control: her "liberty," like her birth out of the eggshell, is a gift. As a gift, it can be taken away, and while she affirms her obedient "gratitude" for her "liberty," her dependence on her liberator—

> *God of the Manacle*
> *As of the Free*
> *Take not my Liberty*
> *Away from me–*

ironically reduces her to a "beggar" before God, insecure, penitent, humble, and fearful of further punishment. But here is where her bird shell-prison analogy comes in: the bird-poet cannot re-enter the shell because it was necessarily broken in the act of getting out. If her birth really is a function of being "troubled" out of her shell, then her resulting "liberty" cannot be taken away. God is dealing with a very crafty daughter.

Now identified as her passive, silent partner, God is directly addressed as the one actually responsible for her confined punishment ("manacles") and reprieve. The poem-play is a prayer in which she recites her case as before a fatherly judge with the lawyer's reason and logic. "Let Us . . ." review the facts: someone did not feed me, and I had to make do; I was innocently confined until I was "troubled"—by "You"—out of my shell and "fell;" I was released. Each of these circumstances is selected to show her dependence and implicate the judge in what has happened to her so that he will not rescind her liberty. Her rhetorical questions are further designed to persuade him of the logic that the broken shell cannot be entered. She also appeals to his compassion: to take back the liberty would be cruel. But her crucial point is his responsibility for her life. After all, if she can rely on his sense of fairness and show him that he is the one who "troubles" her Ellipse, God must acknowledge his complicity in her birth and experience as a poet. Dickinson has elsewhere discussed her god-given "gifts" as a poet and woman, but in this poem she makes God into the *father* of herself as poet—the goal we saw the daughter strive toward in her poems about God.

Therefore, although "Yesterday" is revealed as the time in which she was starving, unborn, blind, bird-small, dependent, confined, and obsessed with eternity, there is a rationale in thus ritualizing it before her father, for it comprises the nurture on which her poetry feeds, and establishes her as God's daughter. To "play Yesterday" is to remind her father of his role in her life—if not to create it: the poem is a paternity suit filed to accuse, and to win guilty support for the "child" at stake—the poetry. But ironically, playing "Yesterday" is also a means by which the daughter reminds herself of her dependence, so that she ends up on her knees. Dickinson's poetry is seen as coming directly out of the daughter construct. Even the mechanisms of escape and independence are dependent upon a higher authority with power to give and take away. When the parent figure withholds or punishes, the daughter "feeds" herself with words, adopting the maternal savior role for herself and eliminating her dependence upon incompetent parents. The only drawback to her coping mechanism ("easing my famine/At my Lexicon") is that as a daughter she needs a parent to react toward and against, and therefore her means of self-reliance (her "Liberty," her poetry) is dependent upon her sense of a parental figure. This is why it takes two to "play Yesterday"—that is, write poetry. The daughter recites, and the father listens—and listens—to his role in her life for over a thousand such prayer poems.

Thus we see Emily Dickinson's retrospective poetry testify about "Yesterday" over and over:

> *I was the slightest in the House—*
> *I took the smallest Room—*
> *At night, my little Lamp, and Book—*
> *And one Geranium—*
>
> *So stationed I could catch the Mint*
> *That never ceased to fall—*
> *And just my Basket—*
> *Let me think—I'm sure*
> *That this was all—*
>
> *I never spoke—unless addressed—*
> *And then, 'twas brief and low—*
> *I could not bear to live—aloud—*
> *The Racket shamed me so—*
>
> *And if it had not been so far—*
> *And any one I knew*

> *Were going—I had often thought*
> *How noteless—I could die—*
>
> [486]

Or, "I was a Phoebe—nothing more . . . I dwelt too low that any seek—/Too shy, that any blame—" (1009). Thus the dutiful daughter's self-effacement and deprivation is the *poet's*: "A Phoebe makes a little print/Upon the Floors of Fame—." It is as the *poet* that she waves off self-pity for her martyr daughter role of "Yesterday":

> *'Tis true—They shut me in the Cold—*
> *But then—Themselves were warm*
> *And could not know the feeling 'twas—*
> *Forget it—Lord—of Them—*
>
> *Let not my Witness hinder Them*
> *In Heavenly esteem—*
> *No Paradise could be—Conferred*
> *Through Their beloved Blame—*
>
> *The Harm They did—was short—And since*
> *Myself—who bore it—do—*
> *Forgive Them—Even as Myself—*
> *Or else—forgive not me—*
>
> [538]

The daughter goes so far as to assume, first, that God will punish her parents for their treatment of her—surely an indictment of her parents—and, second, that it is through her intervention—like that of the Son himself—that they will be forgiven. None of Dickinson's poems about "Yesterday" omit the mention or implication of her identity and destiny as a poet with special status with God. In "Better—than Music! For I—who heard it—" (503), Dickinson continues a child's interest in the loss of Paradise and her identification with Eve's hunger and rebellion as a daughter and poet. The story told to children is that before the Fall "Brooks . . ./Bubbled a better Melody—." But she hears that "better melody" *now*, the same one that caused "Eve's great surrender." And it is presumably her response to that fatal prelapsarian "tune" that we see in her poetry.

> *Children—matured—are wiser—mostly—*
> *Eden—a legend—dimly told—*
> *Eve—and the Anguish—Grandame's story—*
> *But—I was telling a tune—I heard—*
>
> [from 503]

Her authentic version of "Yesterday," the temptation story, is not one the church
will sanction ("Not such a strain–the Church–baptizes–"), and not one she will
"spill" (except in private "Rehearsal") until she sings "around the Throne." But
in the meantime we are to understand that when she "plays Yesterday" through
her poetry, she is posing a challenge to the "legend" about Eve and the consequent rationale for the punishment that all people have since supposedly merited. This is another way to undermine a father's authority and our confidence
in the "antique men" who wrote the Bible that justifies the punishment Dickinson feels she undergoes as a woman in her culture. She may indeed be "Eve,"
but her retelling of her innocent childhood clears her reputation at the expense
of God's.

Another "Yesterday" poem is "I Years had been from Home" (609), written
when Dickinson was forty-two. The speaker describes her terror and ambivalence in returning to her front door, only to find herself afraid that "a Face/I
Never saw before /Stare stolid into mine/And ask my Business there–," and that
she would discover that the "Life I left" would no longer be there for her to
resume. Jean Mudge cites this poem as a description of Dickinson's first home
on Pleasant Street.[16] But the poem does not describe an attitude towards a
specific house; rather it outlines a renunciation strategy in which a long-denied
fulfillment is renounced. As we saw in "I had been hungry, all the Years" (579),
deprivation is presented as irreversible. After having been starved, she cannot
eat, just as she cannot re-enter her home after having been gone for "years."
As she says in "Let Us Play Yesterday" (728), the lark cannot "resume the
Shell;" leaving home has broken it as the bird's emergence breaks the eggshell.
The change that she fears in her home is unavoidable, given her necessarily
destructive departure in the bird-daughter analogy. The womb or sheltered
house is forever closed to her, and she is a postlapsarian victim, filled with
remorse amd ambivalence about the hunger that led to her intellectual and
artistic growth. Dickinson's having her speaker lean "upon the Awe" as she
lingers "with Before" recalls her statement in her letters: "I always ran home to
Awe when a child, if anything befell me. He was an awful Mother, but I liked
him better than none" (L. II, pp. 517-18). "Awe" is her term for whatever
substituted for her mother's love. We could surmise that Dickinson has left
home because she has "never had a mother," but the poem also presents
compelling reasons for not leaving home in the first place. Dickinson herself
stays home with her mother; it is only that she takes trial excursions in her
poetry in order to prove their folly to herself. Like "Let Us play Yesterday," her
experience in "I had been years from home" (609) is a defeat; she "dares not
enter," and "Lest back the awful Door should spring/And leave me in the Floor–
" she "like a Thief/Fled gasping from the House–." It is as if the experience of
being "outside Windows" that she describes so vividly in "I had been hungry,
all the Years" (579) is enough for her: it is "playing Yesterday," the daughter's
ambivalent, cagey recapitulation of deprivation, alienation, confinement, dependence, and frustration ("chafing at the Shell"). Lest the daughter appear at

cross-purposes like the father she portrays in her letters, we should remember that whether she purports to remember a home-like paradise from which she has been evicted, or a concentration-camp childhood, she takes every opportunity, under the innocent guise of "playing Yesterday," to suggest the divine hand in her dependence, before and after the "fall."

10

The Self-created Daughter

THE VOLUNTARY EVE

Her sense that a writing woman, anathema in her culture, is by the same logic, a sinner, abhorred by God, occupied a great deal of Dickinson's creative energy. Her anxiety about writing made her engage in the kind of tortuous metaphysical loopholing that we see in "Let Us play Yesterday" (728), where she twists herself into contradiction—the dutiful Eve, the passive writer, the dependent bird. But while this anxiety was pervasive, it was not crippling. The poems continued. And in spite of her crafty poems pronouncing her dutiful dependence and lack of autonomy, a number of poems manifest the rebellious daughter not only "chafing the Shell" but vigorously breaking that shell with her poetic feet: she renounces her parents, proclaims herself an orphan, and celebrates her independence through her use of poetry.

We have seen Dickinson's orphan pose used to accuse her parents and stress her sense of isolation as a female poetic genius with no model or tradition. In her letters, Emily Dickinson approached Thomas Wentworth Higginson of the *Atlantic* in the guise of an orphan in quest of a parent who could "instruct" her "how to grow." Speaking as a poet, and guileful daughter, Dickinson claimed need of a "Monarch" to help her organize her "little force"; and she professed dutiful uncertainty about proceeding in her poetry without sanction or instruction. But to a girlfriend who had no power to publish her, she bragged: "I have dared to do strange things–bold things, and have asked no advice from any–I have heeded beautiful tempters, yet do not think I am wrong" (*L*. I, p. 91). She is a shameless, self-confident Eve in writing her poetry, despite her feints of anxiety for her temerity in exercising such autonomy. In "I cannot dance upon my Toes," she boasts about the effects of her "lack of instruction"—in other words, the lack of parental and social care, encouragement, and nurture. To be instructed is to be esteemed, valued, believed in, and hoped for. But she triumphs anyway:

> *I cannot dance upon my Toes—*
> *No Man instructed me—*
> *But oftentimes, among my mind,*
> *A Glee possesseth me,*
>
> *That had I Ballet knowledge—*
> *Would put itself abroad*
> *In Pirouette to blanch a Troupe—*
> *Or lay a Prima, mad,*
>
> *And though I had no Gown of Gauze—*
> *No Ringlet, to my Hair,*
> *Nor hopped to Audiences—like Birds,*
> *One Claw upon the Air,*
>
> *Nor tossed my shape in Eider Balls,*
> *Nor rolled on wheels of snow*
> *Till I was out of sight, in sound,*
> *The House encore me so—*
>
> *Nor any know I know the Art*
> *I mention—easy—Here—*
> *Nor any Placard boast me—*
> *It's full as Opera—*
>
> [326]

This self-conscious self-confidence in her art is one of the most arresting and perhaps novel characteristics of Dickinson's poetry, a direct result of her sensibility as a daughter who fights and fears the odds against her achieving distinction in her culture through her poetic craft. Here she poses her uniqueness as a poet, using the metaphor of "dance." Ballet may be the most prestigious form of dance, but Dickinson will sport with this assumption since her use of language bears little resemblance to the art of poetry practiced by her peers and forebears: in fact, her style is decidedly unfashionable. She says she "cannot" do this "ballet" writing ("upon my Toes") because it requires special skills which must be taught, and she, of course, has "no Man" to teach her. But she does not develop the familiar strain of the pitiful daughter begun in the first two lines. Instead she describes the "glee" that she would feel in her art, were she to obtain "Ballet knowledge." Then she proceeds to display her knowledge of "ballet."

Dickinson's choice of ballet is significant, for balancing on one's toes is not a matter of genius so much as technical practice and training, while her "dance" is original—less taught, less dutiful, and less conforming. Dickinson does dispense with the conventional formalities of poetry promulgated by Higginson, who urges—ever politely—"ballet:" uniform rhythm, rhyme, and meter upon Dickinson's "spasmodic" awkwardness. Such "ballet" is "prose," but just as in her Valentine poem, Dickinson shows that she is not ignorant of "Customs." If she dispenses with them, it is by choice.

Dickinson continues distinguishing between her own poetry and commonly practiced metrics in the definition of her role as performer to her audience. She does not present herself to her reader in the obligatory garb (gauze and ringlets); she is not a public writer; her art is not fashionable. Just as refusing to perform in the style of the day is a rejection of the behavior of society women, refusing to dress poetry in ornaments, poetic fashions, and finery is a rejection of the style of poets who have been "taught." Elevated contemporary poetic "style" is better left unlearned, for it can express only conventional grace, requiring disciplined obedience to rules; as such, it cannot be a vehicle of spontaneous "glee" or emotion. And most importantly, "ballet" is most often a performance composed by someone else. One cannot be expressed as a unique individual by using "ballet." Dickinson's distinctive poetic style can be seen as another part of her strategy to identify herself on her own terms, based on her inability to be a "common" woman and on the failure of literary parents ("men") to teach her or to help her "grow."

Dickinson regards her refusal to perform in public—to broadcast herself—as another rejection of conformity. She does not demean herself by seeking an audience (which presumably expects ballet on-the-toes); her art does not aim to please a crowd ("hop . . . to audiences"), nor does it "dress up" like a woman of fashion. It is uncompromised. Thus she gains no conventional recognition from society; nor having "taught" her, society does not know how to "read" her, not is it capable of recognizing the quality of her art without the stylistic refinements to which it is accustomed.

"It" in the last line refers not to "placard" but to "the art I mention easy here"—that is, her ability to write is self-evident, shown by the lines before us. Her poetry is "full as Opera," complex, rich, dramatic, even if unknown and "foreign" to her culture. The poetry derives its power because it is unknown and because it transcends fashion and technique—because, in other words, she has no man to "instruct" her. The poem champions self-reliance for a poet, giving the stratagem of defiance an intellectual and artistic rationale.

A GOD OF ANDROGYNY

Convinced that her own worth is a function of the lack of "instruction" or nurture, Dickinson secedes from her parents:

I'm ceded–I've stopped being Theirs–
The name They dropped upon my face

> *With water, in the country church*
> *Is finished using, now,*
> *And They can put it with my Dolls,*
> *My childhood, and the string of spools,*
> *I've finished threading—too—*
>
> *Baptized, before, without the choice,*
> *But this time, consciously, of Grace—*
> *Unto supremest name—*
> *Called to my Full—The Crescent dropped—*
> *Existence's whole Arc, filled up,*
> *With one small Diadem.*
>
> *My second Rank—too small the first—*
> *Crowned—Crowing—on my Father's breast—*
> *A half unconscious Queen—*
> *But this time—Adequate—Erect,*
> *With Will to choose, or to reject,*
> *And I choose, just a Crown—*
>
> [508]

The poem functions as the child's fantasy that one can throw away one's parents (and hence, one's dependence, insecurity, and limitation). No longer "their" possession, Dickinson renounces her identity as daughter, symbolized by dropping the name that her parents have given her ("dropped upon my face") in the childhood christening ceremony. Her given "name" embodies her sex-defined and sex-confined childhood lack of possibility as a little girl "Yesterday," and she repudiates the Christian conformity that the baptism process signifies. Her name is discarded along with all the other symbols of a girl's childhood: dolls for practicing motherhood, spools for sewing—those roles and activities that are imposed on her as a daughter. The summary line to the first stanza imparts an almost childish cast to the lines—more stubborn and defensive than determined. A defiant tone results, with the emphasis on "too" functioning as a kind of "so there" to her announcement. Adding a seventh line to the first stanza grants to the line a sense of being added as an afterthought, giving the "too" a pouting emphasis. She implies that having to "thread" has been forced on her; now she can finally admit her distaste. The tone signifies that she is still responding as a child.

What the speaker objects to is that the social/sexual/religious doctrines used in raising her as a daughter have been imposed on her without her consent ("without the Choice"). She suggests that she did not have any alternative to what she would grow up to be, and this concern with destiny is what makes her rebel. Now she is going to give herself a new name, identity, and role, which will give her a unique destiny. That she did not feel sanctified nor important as her parents' daughter is manifest in her desire now to have "grace" and to be named after the "supremest name," which is God. In other words, Dickinson wants a promotion in spiritual status. She wants to realize her full potential as a human being: "called to my Full–." But here the poem reveals on what terms the persona is able to confer a new identity upon herself: she is dead. It would seem therefore that Dickinson is rather pessimistic about one's chances to shed one's oppressive identity and the attendant insignificant roles the identity incorporates. Rejecting external concepts, such as fame, prayer, faith, and even parents, does not eliminate them; because her identity is given by society and therefore tainted with society's restrictions for a daughter, she must renounce herself as well.

But in light of the poet's desire to wear the "crown" of immortality, having her existence defined in terms of "one small Diadem" is a victory. In the third stanza, she has achieved, then, the rank she has sought as a poet (being only a daughter was "too small a rank"). "Crowned" with immortality, she "crows" on her "Father's breast," swooning in rapture at her status ("A half conscious Queen–"). She is born again—an Eve-like daughter-wife to a mother-husband-Adam, out of whom she emerges. The fact that Dickinson says "breast" instead of "chest" for father strongly indicates that Dickinson's recreated parent is mother as well as father, especially since food, her dominant symbol of nurture, is first learned at the mother's breast. Dickinson wants two parents in one. The only possible candidate would be God, the nurturing, powerful One capable of creation. This is what Dickinson herself wants to be, and why, therefore, she must be God's daughter as a poet. The kind of sustenence God can provide (immortality, "Bread of Heaven") is the poet's food.

Even in this poem where the persona apparently transcends the child relationship to the parents and attains a new identity, the persona is actually headlong into another father (mother)-daughter relationship. Apparently, this is what the daughter wanted all along. She has replaced a father who does not notice her and a mother who does not nurture her (intellectually) with one who not only identifies her but loves her sensually, and maternally. What makes the difference in the new relationship is that *she* is "Adequate," or satisfactory (and perhaps satisfied as well: "adequate" here implies both), and "erect," not humble, effacing, or dependent. This is because she is able "to Choose, or to reject." As a poet, she exercises the power of autonomy. What she chooses is "just" immortality, the "Crown" and the "Diadem," symbols of artistic, divine, and royal status. The choice she conceives, to choose or reject, is analogous to the choice we have seen her construe as the daughter: she can obey and fulfill expectations, or she can rebel and say "no." Writing poetry, Dickinson says "no" to a common destiny. Yet she will be dancing around the throne, wearing the immortal crown. As a poet, she is God's eternal child—like Christ. She is still a daughter, but with this identity, and on these terms, she will be satisfied.

Emily Dickinson had written, "How to grow up I don't know" (*L.* I, p.

241). She meant that she had no one to teach her what she wanted to know, which was how to grow up to be *"great,* some day." She wanted a model and she wanted sanction. Therefore, she established relationships with people whom she thought could encourage her "to grow" in the way she desired. She sustained her identity as a daughter, which freed her at least from having to "grow" in the way that people were willing to teach her. What Dickinson learned was that there was no one to serve as a model for her, nor could there be: she wanted a singular destiny. Nor could anyone sanction her desire to have a voice in eternity—her goal was so imperious that no one could have the credentials to sanction or even "forgive" her, except God. She had left the common destiny for the world to teach; what she wanted to learn had to be self-taught. Thus we have her poem which insists that indeed one can grow, in the way one wants to grow. The only thing we need is self-reliance, determination, and a will to succeed. [17] Identity and potential proceed out of the daughter construct:

> *Growth of Man—like Growth of Nature—*
> *Gravitates within—*
> *Atmosphere, and Sun endorse it—*
> *But it stir—alone—*
>
> *Each—its difficult Ideal*
> *Must achieve—Itself—*
> *Through the solitary prowess*
> *Of a Silent Life—*
>
> *Effort—is the sole condition—*
> *Patience of Itself—*
> *Patience of opposing forces—*
> *And intact Belief—*
>
> *Looking on—is the Department*
> *Of its Audience—*
> *But Transaction—is assisted*
> *By no Countenance—*
>
> [750]

In fact, one cannot let obstacles such as social expectations stand in the way of "growth." External influences such as parents ("sun" and "atmosphere") ultimately do not count. One must force one's way up out of the ground and be internally motivated to "grow" or "stir." We cannot realize our potential by waiting for someone to tell us what to do or how to do it. We are alone, and must conceptualize our own "difficult Ideal" and strive to achieve it by ourselves. Over and over, Dickinson stresses that this process is lonely and must be so. To reach her "difficult Ideal" to be great, Dickinson must lead an essentially "Silent life"—the hampered existence of the dutiful daughter in her father's house. The only "condition" for her success is the effort she sustains. This developing identity, "Itself," must be patient of conflict ("opposing forces")— the conviction that she can be great despite what she is told as a daughter, against her internalization of her parents' expectations which preclude immortality, power, or glory. The dutiful and the rebellious daughter war, but the "Belief" that she can be "great" is left "intact." Her audience, whom she has temporarily neglected in order "to grow," will eventually be "looking on," even if she does not publish now. But her "transaction," (that is her *business* to write poetry) must be done in private. This formulates Dickinson's credo as a poet and as a daughter. The two "opposing forces" are reconciled as the daughter gains recognition and autonomy for writing poetry. Dickinson's "difficult Ideal," to transcend a common destiny, necessitates formulating a new identity out of context of the social daughter. The voice of the private daughter in these poems expresses the "Silent life" of the public dutiful daughter which she ingeniously simulates as a strategy to safely "grow."

Emily Dickinson presents her life as daughter governed by a parental, androgynous God (508) whose notice she stimulates by threats of disobedience, avowals of love and loyalty, postures of submissiveness, paternity suits, hunger strikes, and other strategies. She defines herself in terms of this relationship, whether she experiences benign neglect, banishment, or specific sanction. Her poems about hunger and rebellion and repression expose her self-image as daughter, and show that spiritual and emotional security, identity and artistic supremacy arise out of, and in fact depend upon, being a dependent "little girl," albeit a dependent little girl of her own making. The poems encompass a specific strategy to single herself out as this daughter and project the little girl's parents onto the behavioral patterns of institutions and traditional authority. These poems are the direct consequence of the daughter's need to have love and recognition, but at the same time to be an independent, singular person who can write poems and enjoy the destiny conferred on sons.

PART FOUR

The Haunting of the House of Art: The Aesthetics of Emily Dickinson's "Maturer Childhood"

Superiority to Fate
Is difficult to gain
'Tis not conferred of Any
But possible to earn

A pittance at a time
Until to Her surprise
The Soul with strict economy
Subsist till Paradise.

[1081]

11
❧

Perversity, Nerve, and Nervousness: The Consciously Feminine Sensibility

THE ARTIFICIAL DAUGHTER

In her persistent way, Emily Dickinson testifies to chronic daughter distress, yet she stays "at home" as a daughter in her letters, her way of living, and her poetry, cagey, scheming, and full of complaints. Determined to live with what is by her own admission the inadequate and the impossible—a disappointing, petty tyrant, an absent mother—she believes "Power is only Pain–Stranded, thro' Discipline" (252); the rose's attar is the "gift of Screws" (675). From Dickinson's point of view as an artist, pain is not to be transcended, nor merely tolerated as useful for art, but as she declares to Thomas Wentworth Higginson, it is to be deliberately nurtured as an aesthetic strategy: "Nature is a Haunted House–but Art–a House that tries to be haunted" (L. II, p. 554).

On the theory, then, that the persecuted and abandoned child is the cocoon stage of the poet, Dickinson maintains and cultivates her daughterlike sensibility. Her muse appears only to the retrospective and eternal daughter, haunted by the spectral omnipresence of a father and mother who lurk in corridors of memory, forever inaccessible, forever menacing. Extending her childhood hungers and perspectives to court her muse, Emily Dickinson calls her adult poet sensibility a "maturer Childhood": "The Risks of Immortality are perhaps its' Charm–A secure Delight suffers in enchantment–The larger Haunted House it seems, of maturer Childhood–distant, an alarm–entered intimate at last as a neighbor's Cottage–" (L. II, p. 480). Whether or not Dickinson ever experiences the painful childhood she describes in her poetry, she gives us cause to study her poems—and her mind—as a "House that tries to be haunted." This approach to Dickinson's poetry, which deemphasizes the nature of her actual experience as a daughter in her father's house, has been anticipated by scholars such as Thomas H. Johnson, for example, who suggests that Dickinson may have exaggerated distress as part of her method, and by Dr. Harold Shands, who sees Dickinson trying to "irritate" herself like an oyster in order to make "pearls" (*L*. I, pp. xix–xxii).[1] Such theories may serve to relieve us from taking Dickinson's complaints seriously.

But even if Dickinson consciously infuses her art with crisis, it is important to understand the significance of the *kind* of experience which generates her "haunted" poetry: the chronicles of the lifelong, beleaguered daughter. What we have yet to fully appreciate is how her female experience informs Dickinson's aesthetics, the images and metaphors she creates to express pain, the strategies she creates to write, her attitudes toward writing, her preoccupation with her voice, and most important, her need to write poetry at all. Dickinson's reading and her religious sensibility both justly have been given credit for her mode of depicting pain.[2] But Dickinson's own sexual conflicts inform her reading and religious feeling, and may be the primary source of her aesthetics of pain; and we may understand this use of feminine consciousness in terms other than literal sexual frustration or menstrual pain: her experience as a little girl "at School" or in her "father's House" provides Dickinson with her major metaphor of her identity as a poet.

We need to know how Dickinson *uses* her experience as a daughter—which her contemporary, major American poets (males) did not share—for the aesthetics of renunciation and pain she expresses: "Am told that fasting gives to food marvellous Aroma, but by birth a Bachelor, disavow Cuisine"; "The stimulus of Loss makes most Possession mean"; "The finest wish is the futile one" (*L*. II, pp. 350, 485, 500); "The Riddle we can guess/We speedily despise–" (1222). Dickinson's poems about her "art" and its personal significance for her reveal her attitudes toward her sexuality and the extent to which her feminine sensibility affects her representation of pain. Tracing the issues, images, themes, and patterns of these poems will help us identify the elements of the daughter construct that characterize Dickinson's unique poetry and poetics. After identifying the major issues, we can closely examine key poems which illustrate the method in her literary life as a daughter.

The use of a consciously feminine sensibility in Dickinson's poems about art provides Dickinson with the alienated, adversary role she seeks to cultivate as an artist. She interprets her desire to write poetry as the need to defy expectations—or non-expectations—for the dutiful, dependent daughter. Her occupation is portrayed as a bold refusal to identify herself with a common, sex-defined destiny. Not only the pain but the joy of the woman who deliberately flaunts convention are set against Dickinson's self-conscious references to the fact that she "gambles" in being so unfemininely "overbold" (801) as to write poetry. Emily Dickinson will not let her audience forget her sense of disease, defiance, and anxiety in picking up her pen before us; she tells us she will pay for this transgression, and indeed, she does not mind—but meanwhile we must know the cost and significance of her liberties with her voice. Dickinson presents it as an essentially unbelievable fact that in spite of the odds against her, she writes poetry; she cannot take it for granted that her poems exist, and neither must her reader.

Dickinson sets her poetry apart from the male literary tradition by emphasizing her problems in assuming her right to speak. Intensely self-conscious, deliberately so, Dickinson's words are attended with her anxiety about her inappropriate gender, and her consequent feelings of guilt, inadequacy, heresy, risk, and disobedience; these feelings permeate the poetry—in fact, constitute its central theme, and characterize its presentation. Refusal, defiance, risk, secrecy, sin, guilt, doubt: these are creative, purposeful ways of seeing her writing as a woman. Dickinson *chooses* to portray her art from these perspectives, rather than underplay any anxiety, or submerge her sexuality, in order to increase her reader's and perhaps her own, appreciation of the uniqueness of her art. She tells us what it feels like to be a woman poet, a self-confessed "Kangaroo among the Beauty."

"Easier To Die Than Tell"

Emily Dickinson's approach to the subject of "telling" about her poetry reveals her secret, guilt-ridden, and defiant identity as a poet. Underlying her famous formula for success, "Tell all the Truth but tell it slant–/Success in Circuit lies" (1129), is a burdensome, lonely distrust of her audience in whom she cannot freely confide. This distrust makes for an unusual tension between herself and her reader in her prose and lyrics. She exposes her dependence upon her reader to activate her poetic identity, but is vulnerable and defensive, as if her reader is an adversary who can betray her by using her words as evidence against her. She is unable to say like Whitman, "What I assume, you shall assume;" she cannot assume her reader's support or sympathy. Consequently, she protects herself from her reader by only hinting at her "truth" as a woman poet; and yet, since she relies on her readers' continued interest, she arouses our curiosity and frustration by announcing the presence of secrets she cannot reveal.

As to these secrets, she is candidly, forthrightly coy. In her letters, Dickinson alludes to her subversive poetic activity and aspiration dramatically ("but oh! I love the danger!" [*L*. I, p. 104]) without further explanation. Her "sin" is left to her correspondent's imagination. In her poetry, especially her early work, she presents herself as unable to acknowledge that she *is* writing poetry, and her commitment to her poetic career. She reveals herself harboring secrets and even "shutting up" in silences, whether with crucial syntactic ellipses—her stammering effect—or with unnamed "secret" subjects. In the following poem, Dickinson poses the dangers of abandoning the security of conventional behavior for a higher goal, yet the nature of her bold venture remains paradoxically unnamed. Dickinson will risk all, but she cannot tell what for:

> *'Tis so much joy! 'Tis so much joy!*
> *If I should fail, what poverty!*

And yet, as poor as I,
Have ventured all upon a throw!
Have gained! Yes! Hesitated so—
This side the Victory!

Life is but Life! And Death, but Death!
Bliss is but Bliss, and Breath, but Breath!
And if indeed I fail,
At least, to know the worst, is sweet!
Defeat means nothing but Defeat,
No drearier, can befall!

And if I gain! Oh Gun at Sea!
Oh Bells, that in the Steeples be!
At first, repeat it slow!
For Heaven is a different thing,
Conjectured, and waked sudden in—
And might extinguish me!

[172]

In this literary pep rally, then, we encounter the familiar Dickinsonian low-class persona ("poor" and standing to be poorer) on the threshold of a momentous achievement. Aware that she could destroy herself, she urges herself on, for if she succeeds, she will attain a new life in "Heaven," presumably as an immortal poet. Another early poem also describes her "gamble," without specifying the nature of the "game" (139). We know only that "hundreds have lost." But because a "few" have won, she encourages herself to persevere in what the poem suggests is a bid to wear the "crown" of immortality. Of course, the "crown" can also symbolize Christ's crown; through writing poetry, Dickinson gains the spiritual status of the "Son." Dickinson feels that gambling for a more important destiny is saving her from a fate which "No drearier, can befall." Keeping her gamble secret or at least unspoken is crucial to Dickinson's sense of daughterly defiance.

We recall her words to a teenage friend when she announced that she had dared to do "bold things" without taking anyone's advice, ending with the cryptic phrase, "No one *guesses* the joy" (*L*. I, p. 104). No, nor the reason for it, because she refuses to come out and say that she has decided to become a poet. Emily Dickinson continually points her reader's attention to the fact that she is unable to divulge her "secret." In this way, of course, she alerts her reader to the existence of a "secret" and to her fear of disclosure as well as makes her use of her voice the subject of her work. In divulging her inability to divulge, she impresses upon her audience her problems associated with her poetic identity, and aligns her reader with those who do not know her "secret"— with her family, especially her parents—thus becoming daughter to her reader.

Obviously Dickinson expects her reader to know she writes poetry. The pretense of skirting her subject may be used to endow her less-than-dramatic life with the defiance, suspense, and mystery it lacks. Dickinson wants to impress people, to say "I'm not what you think!" In poem 1326 she says that the only reason we tell secrets is "to make each other stare." But to announce a secret and then *not* tell it creates *more* interest. More important, it manifests her sense that she does not possess a *right* to the subject, at least from the parent/reader's point of view. Her exultance in her courage is therefore ironically undercut by her fear of naming her undertaking, and contributes to the reader's understanding of her anxiety in her craft. Perhaps the reader is meant to share or shoulder the responsibility for her lyric nervousness.

Dickinson's insistent refusal to "tell" who she is and what she wants is the subject of an early poem which gives the other side of the "joy" of defiance and secrecy. Note Dickinson's defensive posture before her reader:

> *The Murmur of a Bee*
> *A Witchcraft—yieldeth me—*
> *If any ask me why—*
> *'Twere easier to die—*
> *Than tell—*
>
> *The Red upon the Hill*
> *Taketh away my will—*
> *If anybody sneer—*
> *Take care—for God is here—*
> *That's all.*
>
> *The Breaking of the Day*
> *Addeth to my Degree—*
> *If any ask me how—*
> *Artist—who drew me so—*
> *Must tell!*
>   [155]

Here Dickinson retreats from her claims of boldly taking the initiative in her poetic career, to her stance in the daughter poems of the dependent, passive creature who is acted upon, and therefore, a blameless and unaccountable victim. In Biblical language, her persona "yieldeth"—a very obedient thing for a daughter to do—but to the tempter Bee. If she sins by yielding to the muse (the bee is the symbol of poetic inspiration in many poems), she sins helplessly. Furthermore, it is not her fault that she remains mute and undisclosed in her career; only the "Artist" who "drew her so" can speak for her. She is but a creation, a vehicular possession who is "shut up" by the Artist, whether God or Satan. As in "My Life had stood—a Loaded Gun—" (754), Dickinson's ability to speak is controlled by her master. In poem 1088, God is made directly respon-

sible for her silence; God forbids her to "print." In fact, the "Story, unrevealed"
is *not hers* to tell; she does not own the right to her voice: "Had it been mine,
to print!/Had it been yours to read!" She *wants* to tell, she wants an audience,
but it is not her "privilege." Therefore "shutting up" is obedience to a Father
who wants his little girl "still." In the second stanza of "The Murmur of a Bee,"
we see the daughter persona dutifully draw herself behind a protective master-
father-god who defends her from society's sneering.

But why should society sneer? Or blame? After all, these poems about
guilt, risk, and imminent destruction proceed from nothing more than a woman
sitting at her desk in her white dress, committing words to paper. Any punish-
able offense is only in Dickinson's mind, a product of her sense of female
impropriety, for she would not fear the consequences of using the "metaphoric
penis" as Gilbert and Gubar interpret the nineteenth-century view of the pen in
The Madwoman in the Attic,[3] if she were a man, and if she felt that a woman
poet could be sanctioned by her family or her church. Even if the church does
not excommunicate a woman poet, Dickinson conceptualizes her poetry as a
rebellion against a patriarchy that wants to control her voice. She seeks to alter
her worldly status and opportunity. We have seen in the "daughter-at-work"
poems how she pleads for God's recognition, expresses her dissatisfactions, and
challenges the wisdom of not making her the "son." Titillated with her guilt, *we*
cannot see how she has given herself up to evil influence unless we condemn
her in her own terms for expressing an *unauthorized* voice, or "speaking too
loud" (248).

The question of her authority to write continues as a major issue in
Dickinson's poetry. She presents three interpretations of herself as a poet, then.
If she describes herself as the tempter's victim, we absolve her of some responsibility for her poetry; she becomes like Eve, only pitiable in her feminine
weakness; and if she is God's poet, we can do nothing but "fall on our faces"
when the time comes for her to be revealed as such. But if she has taken this
step on her own volition, and asserted herself in the act of expressing her own
voice on paper, it is, as she interprets her culture's response, "witchcraft."

Dickinson's definition of "witchcraft" is closely allied with her sense of
her own poetry:[4] the art of heretical women in the service of the Evil Tempter—
the very one Dickinson describes in her teens urging her to become "great,
Someday" by writing poetry (*L*. I, p. 202). She had asked Thomas Higginson if
poetry was "untaught," like "melody" or "witchcraft." In "I cannot dance upon
my Toes/No Man instructed me" (326), Dickinson makes much of the fact that
she lacks instruction and is better for it. Perhaps the fact that the poetry she
practices is self-motivated and self-taught makes it "witchcraft." Or perhaps
writing is witchcraft if "no man" (326) has told her to do it. Her brother Austin
is told to make a career, and is given the means to do it, but Emily Dickinson
is told to make bread. Obedience depends upon orders from a sanctioned
authority; if no one orders her to write poetry, it follows that to initiate action is
in effect to disobey. Throughout her poems, Dickinson is afraid of disobeying:

"Did we disobey Him?" (267). Dickinson will undergo metaphysical contortions to find a way to account for the fact that she writes poetry, including saying that she is helpless against the Devil. Her sense of guilt in her poetic career derives not from the activity of poetry itself, but from the idea that it is wrong for a woman to assume such practice. In this sense, any autonomous act of a woman is "witchcraft," a disobedience to the fathers.

But if Dickinson does what she is told, she will write or live "Prose:" thus her dilemma. Accordingly, her resolution-on-paper centers about the morality of her autonomous, powerful craft in a culture where women are told to "obey" by doing little that the world esteems: "Trite is that affliction which is sanctified" (*L*. II, p. 511). Dickinson partially resolves the problem by asserting that she is not acting autonomously when she writes poetry. She exploits the stereotyped image of femininity ("Lie still") in order to diffuse society's antagonism at her assertive behavior. Poem 155 reflects her decision in her own life to be a martyred, unknown, dutiful daughter by day, a woman of "degree" in her night poetry. The mystery in the poem refers to the status she gains at Sunrise, which inaugurates a new day of martyrdom and concludes a night of momentum toward "Possibility." But the poem ends with ambiguity. We do not know whether the speaker is a witch or a divine daughter, and neither does she. All we are meant to know is that she professes to be unable to speak for herself. She has temporarily abandoned the dangerous pose of autonomy in her art. Rather, she now *poses* as dependent and helpless, for writing is, of course, a vigorous practice of intellectual autonomy, and Dickinson's lyrics in theme and style are deliberately and self-consciously independent or even defiant of tradition, convention, and orthodoxy.

Dickinson's efforts to deny her autonomy and assert her obedience by not "telling" reveal the conflict at the heart of her career and the role of her daughter identity in the conflict. A brief additional example can suggest the extent to which this conflict is felt in the poetry. Dickinson's many poems about loss have interested scholars who seek to know what or whom Dickinson has lost as a clue to Dickinson's haunting life story. However, in many of these poems, loss does not concern a person, as biographers and critics suggest,[5] but refers to Dickinson's fear of losing her ability to create.

> I held a Jewel in my fingers—
> And went to sleep—
> The day was warm, and winds were prosy—
> I said, " 'Twill keep"—
>
> I woke—and chid my honest fingers,
> The Gem was gone—
> And now, an Amethyst remembrance
> Is all I own—

[245]

That the valued jewel is poetry, and the poem a metaphoric statement about art is suggested by the emphasis on "fingers" (which write—801), and by the "prosy" winds: the "Gem" is the poetic idea that did not get put down on paper; the word makes her "rich." If Dickinson measures her wealth by her ability to create poems, and if she fears the loss of her poetic powers, she is not autonomous: her wealth is a function of what she is given. In poem 840, Dickinson laments the loss of "it" in the same terms: "I cannot buy it-'tis not sold-/There is no other in the World-/Mine was the only one/I was so happy I forgot/To shut the Door And it went out." Through these poems about loss Dickinson can present a dutiful pose of vulnerability, insecurity, and dependence. The loss poems constitute one more means, then, by which Dickinson tries to deny or diffuse her autonomy.

There is another facet to Dickinson's problem with disclosure, which relates to her sexual conflict in trying to avert her mother's fate. Although Emily Dickinson will try to create an "impregnable fortress" in her "house of art," and although she consistently denies her mother and rejects the maternal matrix, the language she uses to convey her obsessive, public secrecy is often reminiscent of the language of childbearing. For example, as her eyes roam her garden universe for metaphors and analogies that can help define her life, they light on a cocoon: "Stealthy Cocoon, why hide you so/What all the world suspect?/ . . ./Your secret, perched in esctasy/Defies imprisonment!" (129). The cocoon, harboring and nurturing the devouring larval butterfly within, is likened to the obviously pregnant belly which advertises its hidden, but evident, "secret." But the cocoon is an external, autonomous womb. The significance of this image of an independent, *motherless* pregnancy where the birth is self-delivered is compounded when we consider the features Dickinson ascribes to the cocoon: cunning, furtive ("stealthy"); hiding, secrecy; defiance; ecstasy; imprisonment; and a suspecting world. These would seem to bear little relation to each other or the cocoon unless we recognize in this idiosyncratic image cluster the terms in which Dickinson habitually renders her experience as a poet daughter in her father's house. *She* is the cocoon, bursting with words, yet confined and "shut up;" she has a "secret" creation no one can see; her dutiful daughter image contains, protects, and hides her present and future greatness as a poet. In other words, she is, and inhabits, the unlikely cocoon in her masked role—or shell—as dutiful daughter, secretly pregnant with her poetic self.

Just as people assume the cocoon's destiny, Dickinson hopes "all the world" will "suspect" the inevitable butterfly in her, and hence, will liberate her poetic identity. But first, she has to create suspicion. She has to hint of a different destiny, as she does in her poems and letters, and keep herself manifestly swollen with secret. Since she has no visible signs of internal creativity like a swollen belly or poetry manuscripts lying about, she has to suggest the latent butterfly by presenting herself *as a cocoon*: imprisoned and embryonic, motherless and autonomous, awaiting a miraculous transformation and liberation, and stirring with poetic wings.[6] Hence the "daughter" poems.

Therefore, we see Dickinson associate the need to keep her poetry unacknowledged with the requirements of a female identity. Even to Dickinson's confidante, her sister-in-law Susan Gilbert, her poetry is the unmentionable topic, a taboo which is broached by indirection: " 'Power and honor' are here today, and 'dominion and glory!' I shall never tell! *You* may tell, when 'the seal' is opened. *Mat* [her niece] may tell when they 'fall on their faces'–but I shall be lighting the lamps then in my new house–and I cannot come" (*L.* II, p. 340).[7] Resorting to euphemism, Dickinson describes her writing in terms of its effect upon her—the divine and masculine forms of prestige she craves as a daughter. Such an accomplishment is so heretical and subversive that she not only commits herself to indirection, but vows silence unto death ("I shall never tell!"). This "stillness" implies obedience to a code as strict as a nun's—and a similar faith in ultimate reward. It is as if her consenting to being unknown during her lifetime absolves her from her overreaching. In "Ended, ere it begun–" (1088), for example, a poem Dickinson sent Susan Gilbert, she appears resigned to God's will that "The Story" remain unrevealed: she is sure that when she dies ("lighting the lamps then in my new house") she will be rewarded for her obedience. Her poetry will be discovered, and people will recognize her real identity as God's poet. She gives Susan and Mattie permission to confirm this identity. Until then, her "pregnancy" will continue until she dies and she is released from her vow of silence.

Why Dickinson has to keep her avocation a secret until her death is more fully explored in "Rearrange a Wife's Affection!" which fuses the themes of sexual conflict and secrecy with shocking candor. Note especially the last two stanzas:

> *Rearrange a "Wife's" affection!*
> *When they dislocate my Brain!*
> *Amputate my freckled Bosom!*
> *Make me bearded like a man!*
>
> *Blush, my spirit, in thy Fastness–*
> *Blush, my unacknowledged clay–*
> *Seven years of troth have taught thee*
> *More than Wifehood ever may!*
>
> *Love that never leaped its socket–*
> *Trust entrenched in narrow pain–*
> *Constancy thro' fire–awarded–*
> *Anguish–bare of anodyne!*
>
> *Burden–borne so far triumphant–*
> *None suspect me of the crown,*
> *For I wear the "Thorns" till Sunset,*
> *Then–my Diadem put on.*

> *Big my Secret but it's* bandaged—
> *It will never get away*
> *Till the Day its Weary Keeper*
> *Leads it through the Grave to thee.*

[1737]

In this allegory of her life as a poet, Dickinson expresses her daytime existence—a virtual disguise—as a martyrdom which the world will only discover when she dies and her poems are delivered up. Until then, being unknown in her daughter role is a "burden" she must bear: "None suspect me . . ."—and while such anonymity is necessary, it hurts. Once again, however, she reaffirms her faith that her strategy to keep obediently silent will succeed; she can endure the "thorns" of being unknown during the day (just as Christ endures the thorns until his crucifixion), since she will wear the "crown" of immortality.

In fact, her identification with the "Son" is based on more than martyrdom and ultimate paternal recognition. Once her "secret" is out, Dickinson imagines the world performing an autopsy on her identity. Given her poems, society must conclude she is a poet: not a woman after all, but a man. Therefore it will "rearrange" her, making her "bearded," and "amputating" her feminine sexuality (symbolized by her freckled bosom) from its image of her, to make her conform to its notions of a poet's gender. Here Dickinson provides a reason why she must carry her "secret" identity as a poet until her death. If men create poems, she has to relinquish her femininity to write, and since femininity is her true identity, to give it up is to die.

Dickinson harbors two deceptions, then, in her "bandaged" existence. Her life as a daughter is protective camouflage, and her role as a poet remains undisclosed, veiled in euphemism, shrouded in hints. The hidden "wound" is both the secret poetry and her female sexuality: the two are one, and as Dickinson keeps both inviolate, "bandaged," poetry is allied with her deepest and most private sexuality as a woman. Her identity conflict is based more on tradition than experience, for dutiful daughter and poet are mutually exclusive identities only by custom; in reality, Dickinson is both woman and poet. It is her culture's notion about the gender of artistry which necessitates her taking upon herself a mutilated, martyred identity, and her consequent aesthetics of secrecy and self-denial. This is why we see Dickinson try to dissociate herself from her feminine identity by keeping her "clay" (flesh) and spirit from ever being sexually identified; being unknown as a "wife" is the price she has had to pay for her career as a poet.

In her own terms, then, Dickinson is a "Bachelor from Birth"—constitutionally, deliberately singular, masculine-identified in her pursuit of power, "disavowing" the "cuisine" of the non-nutritive maternal matrix which includes, unavoidably, her own femininity:

> *Me from Myself—to banish—*
> *Had I Art—*

> *Impregnable my Fortress*
> *Unto All Heart–*
>
> [from 642]

Acknowledging that her feminine sexuality is her identity, Dickinson portrays the conflict arising from the "woman poet" contradiction which manifests itself in her fear of her mother's destiny. If she could "banish" her threatening feminine potential, strip to an essential neuter self, she would be safe in an "Impregnable . . . Fortress." Her word choice is particularly significant here: "impregnable" is a form of specifically feminine invulnerability which Dickinson seeks;[8] if she becomes pregnant, she becomes the dreaded, crippled, mortal mother. Dickinson must therefore "banish" or deny her pregnability. She cannot change her biology, but she can become impregnable, like an "independent Man," through "banishing" conventional female life and behavior such as love and marriage, keeping "love" from ever "leaping its socket." To Dickinson, poetry, the antithesis of female creation (child-bearing), is an act which nullifies, as it protects, her sexuality and secret source of identity: this "Art" enables her to escape her mother's fate. But she still is a woman, and Dickinson recognizes the absurdity and futility of her desire to escape her femininity:

> *But since Myself–assault Me–*
> *How have I peace*
> *Except by subjugating*
> *Consciousness?*
>
> *And since We're mutual Monarch*
> *How this be*
> *Except by Abdication–*
> *Me–of Me?*

There is no escape: woman and poet are one, and the effort to deny either identity leads to madness and death. In scores of poems, Dickinson expresses the consequences of having to separate her identity from her sexuality: "I dwelt, as if Myself were out,/My Body but within" (1039).

As Emily Dickinson understands it, then, her problem with her self-image as a poet stems from her female sexuality, not what it is but what it signifies in her culture. Instead of fighting the logic of her culture's masculine image of the poet, Dickinson shows the effects a male-poet prototype has upon her. She presents herself as burdened, a misfit at odds with herself as well as society. Her self-image, at best, is a "Wayward Nun" who fails, feigns, and takes "the Royal names in vain" (722). She constructs elaborate rationales that disprove her autonomy and independence as an artist. She shrouds herself in secrecy. She shows herself being successfully "shut up." That is not to say that writing poetry was exclusively a masculine enterprise in nineteenth-century America, or even that Emily Dickinson thought so, "Rearrange a "Wife's" Affection!" notwithstanding. If Emily Dickinson felt herself to be estranged from the male literary establishment, she did have female role models abroad and a distinct literary tradition in which to work. She avidly read George Eliot, the Brontës, and "Mrs. Browning," who gave expression to her own efforts to achieve poetic immortality (Browning's *Aurora Leigh*, for example). Dickinson identified with these sister writers in her letters, expressing her feelings of kinship with them. In her own country, Dickinson knew of Helen Hunt Jackson's success as a novelist and "poetess": Jackson was a local Amherst girl who had made it. But we see the effects of Dickinson's feeling of living against the grain in a country with no great female poets, especially when we see her empathize with other female writers' pain. She reveals her own consciousness of the obstacles confronting any woman writer as she projects upon other women her sense of herself as a repressed little girl who must be "still": "That Mrs. Browning fainted, we need not read *Aurora Leigh* to know, when she lived with her English aunt; and George Sand 'must make no noise in her grandmother's bedroom.' Poor children! Women, now, queens now!" (*L*. II, p. 376).

In fact, Dickinson insisted upon her isolation, even going so far as to deny support when it was offered, as when Higginson invited her to Boston to meet the literary establishment, or when Helen Hunt Jackson tried to help her publish. Jackson repeatedly pleaded with Dickinson to share her work—those were Jackson's terms—only to be rebuffed with polite but absolute resistance. Dickinson did share her poetry with Susan Gilbert and with friends to whom she wrote letters, but she continued to present herself as an isolato. I think that Dickinson's attitudes toward the female as well as the male literary community could be a function of her daughter sensibility. Her curious refusal to be nurtured by the female literary community in particular is related to her similar refusal to be nurtured by, or acknowledge being nurtured by, her mother. Insisting on a self-image as a "kangaroo" was as much an aesthetic strategy as her keeping herself confined within the daughter cocoon. Her sense of alienation seems to be necessary to her art, even if it means the prospect of being resurrected sans breasts.

12
🍎

The Daughter and the Queen "It"

One need not be a Chamber—to be Haunted—
One need not be a House—
The Brain has Corridors—surpassing
Material Place—

Far safer, of a Midnight Meeting
External Ghost
Than its interior Confronting—
That Cooler Host.

Far safer, through an Abbey gallop,
The Stones a'chase—
Than Unarmed, one's a'self encounter—
In lonesome Place—

Ourself behind ourself, concealed—
Should startle most—
Assassin hid in our Apartment
Be Horror's least.

The Body—borrows a Revolver—
He bolts the Door—
O'erlooking a superior spectre—
Or More—

[670]

Dramatizing identity conflicts in modern gothic horror imagery, Emily Dickinson gives a formula for "Haunting" one's "House of Art." One is simply conscious of the true self within: "Ourself behind ourself, concealed." Awareness that one hides this true self creates a schism in consciousness, producing

177

the alienation Dickinson considers so necessary to write. It serves her purpose
to present poetry as a bold, wicked, masculine, and unmentionable activity in
her writing: she gains a double, and thus becomes self-haunted and horrified.
Dickinson's schoolteachers and father may have harassed her about "modern
Literati," as she claims, but she does not appear to have paid much attention
to their criticisms. After all, she did devote herself to writing and exhibited
great faith in her decision. However, if she presents herself writing in spite of
religious, social, and sexual constraints, she becomes heroic in her defiance,
and forces her readers to join her in a contempt for the Puritan sensibility which
would deny her voice.

Dickinson's continual self-consciousness about her gender widens the division in her self-image between woman and poet. Thus identity is presented as
a series of equations in paradoxical opposition: me vs. me, woman vs. poet,
duty vs. rebellion, dependency vs. autonomy. By playing off contradictory identities within herself, Dickinson creates a sense of duplicity in her character.
And her efforts to deny her reality (independent, rebellious woman) only create
confusion about which identity is the true "one." Dickinson's haunting herself
by her consciousness of being a poet in a woman's body is expressed in a poem
where she confronts "That Cooler Host" in a mirror, as two selves emerge face
to face in a horrible, paralyzing encounter.

Like the evil queen who addresses the mirror on the wall, the poet looks
into herself:

> Like Eyes that looked on Wastes—
> Incredulous of Ought
> But Blank—and steady Wilderness—
> Diversified by Night—
>
> Just Infinites of Nought—
> As far as it could see—
> So looked the face I looked upon—
> So looked itself—on Me—
>
> I offered it no Help—
> Because the Cause was Mine—
> The Misery a Compact
> As hopeless—as divine—
>
> Neither—would be absolved—
> Neither would be a Queen
> Without the Other—Therefore—
> We perish—tho' We reign—

[458]

This is a key poem in understanding Dickinson's life as a daughter as it relates
to her aesthetic strategy. It has never been dealt with or explicated (nor has

"Rearrange a "Wife's" affection," 1737), but it serves as an important example of the process of objectification of the creating self for the purpose of art: the self that creates the mask of dutiful daughter is the same self that creates the poetry. The creator is pictured as alienated from what she creates (the mask), and the process of creation is transformed from an active one to a passive state of merely receiving. In this way, poetry is merely a mirror of the conflicted self.

The second stanza makes the analogy more clear: we see that the lines one through six have functioned as an appositive, describing the face she is looking at. The face she "looked upon" sees "Just Infinites of Nought," or an endless and hopeless procession of nothing. At this point in the poem it is revealed that the hopeless countenance she describes is her own: "So looked itself–on Me–." She herself constitutes the "steady Wilderness" which her eyes reflect. The pronoun "it" has been used in the poem to describe what turns out to be a face; but its repetition here is ironic and startling because we are made to realize that the persona is talking with detachment about herself. The pronoun "it" does not only suggest an inanimate object, but one that is sexually neuter. The persona thus indicates that she is alienated from her female sexuality. Her other self is neither woman nor person.

Given that this poem is dealing with an identity problem, the choice of "it" to describe her reflected image is particularly significant when contrasted with the specifically feminine identification of the persona later on in the poem as a "Queen." What becomes apparent is that even though "I" and "it" are established as two separate entities, they formulate a single identity in reality. The persona reveals herself as suffering from a negative self-image. It is only at "Night" that she becomes more than a "Blank."

But the artistic process itself demands a double awareness—the stepping back to describe what one sees. What Dickinson does here is to describe not "reality" or that which is externally verifiable, but the image of herself creating and dealing with the conflicting pressures on her as a woman who wants to write. Writing about herself verifies the reality of her pain in her existence as a creator.

But the third stanza shows that the pain caused by objectifying the self (madness, death, detachment, alienation) through the process of art is not unwelcome to the persona. Although the self in the mirror/poem is still an "it" and suffering, she does not elect to "Help" it "Because the Cause was mine–." "It" is the creative self that has been neutered by the necessity of wearing her mask as dutiful daughter. Since the plight of this self is *caused* by her, she takes responsibility for what she has done to herself. We can understand her unwillingness to help the stricken eyes she sees—the anguish behind the mask—as a function of her belief in her own "Cause" to transcend her inferior destiny as a woman and achieve greatness by writing poetry. We have seen that Emily Dickinson's aesthetic credo insists that misery is necessary for creation.

The fact that she identifies "Misery" as a "Compact" is significant. "Compact" is an old legal term used to symbolize an agreement, a form of social behavior. Dickinson's strategy to become great through her misery is her "compact." That she refers to her plan as both "hopeless" and "divine" shows her doubt that she will succeed, but that the "divine" nature of her mission is to *become* divine and immortal. A self in pain is necessary for her "Cause." In this stanza we see that the persona acknowledges control over herself. "It" is not in rebellion against her after all. "It" is suffering, and "It" is a reflection of herself, so she is suffering.

If she were to "Help" that miserable self she surveys when she looks at herself through her poetry, presumably by denying that self, or not looking (not writing), it would not do any good, she protests. What is implied here is that the miserable self Dickinson sees is created by her in the process of self-examination (writing the poem). The poetry needs that miserable "it" and Dickinson complies. The last stanza emphasizes this point. She presents two reasons (or excuses) for her refusal to forsake this self-image of unhappiness in her writing of poetry and confronting (or "seeing") this self. Both reasons argue in defense of why the unhappy self cannot be helped by her. First, the two selves cannot be separated because they are mutually guilty. "Neither—would be absolved" if she offered to "Help." The word "absolve" suggests that harboring the unhappy self is a crime for which she can be blamed.

Secondly, neither self "would be a Queen/Without the Other–." The admission is that rather than identify herself in the negative terms with which the poem began, the persona feels herself to be a "Queen," possessing social status and inherited rank as well as considerable power as the sovereign figure. Even more significantly, she feels that her status as queen is directly dependent upon seeing herself in terms of "Blank" misery and identity conflict. This poem concludes, then, with an acknowledgment of Dickinson's dependence as a poet on her rebellious, conflicted self. Being a Queen—or a great woman poet like "Mrs. Browning"—is a result of the identity crisis incurred by being a daughter. Therefore, Dickinson gives evidence that her description of her torment in the poetry is contrived by her because she cannot be the Queen without being the persecuted, abandoned, anguished "It" we as readers have been startled to see. She has created a self-image that is instrumental to her designs: she has haunted her house of art.

The self looking at itself in the mirror is a metaphor of the artistic consciousness aware of itself. Without this consciousness of pain, being a "Queen" is impossible. The interdependence of pain and consciousness makes the other "perish" as a singular entity; therefore, consciousness *is* pain. Consciousness and perception cannot be felt without pain and questioning; and pain can only be known through self-consciousness. We can interpret this poem to be about the poet's umbilical cord to the self she expresses in the poetry. The cost of acknowledging the necessity of the mask is the loss of individual identity for the creator: "We perish–tho' We reign–." She is forced to admit that she needs to rend herself in order to exist.

Further, the poem demonstrates the necessary fusion of consciousness and pain in terms of its value in creation. At the end of the poem, "Me" and "it" are fused into "We." There has been a progression from a schism between the objectified self (the mask) and the creating poet self to an affirmation that they are one, and when so combined, formulate an identity of a "Queen–," a poet defined in specifically feminine terms. In other words, a Queen is a daughter and poet in conflict, a woman at odds with her own femininity. The pained woman in the self is no longer banished, but becomes the integral dominant ingredient in the poet's identity. "Reigning" is equivalent to perishing, however, because pain and identity crisis are necessary to produce art. The poem, then, presents a positive resolution to Dickinson's identity conflict as writer and daughter: the daughter with her pain and guilt and sense of inferiority *is* the queen. Thus Dickinson reveals that the identity conflict, guilt, and pain caused by her assumption of the mask of a dutiful daughter is an aesthetic strategy. She needs to pose to write poetry and become a "Queen."

13

Choosing against Herself: Resurrection Pain

To Haunt—till Time have dropped
His last Decade away,
And Haunting actualize—to last
At least—Eternity—

[from 788]

In perpetuating her little-girl, pre-adolescent image, "new—and small" (454) both in terms of worldly and sexual inexperience and social esteem, Dickinson cultivates a role of obedience: knowing her place, respecting the male value on female innocence. For according to Dickinson's aesthetics, she must retain her virginity and obscurity or she will lose her "gifts." Thus we see dutiful renunciation of her body—"I dwelt, as if Myself were out" (1039)—and even of her life: "I cannot live with You—/It would be Life—/And Life is over there—/Behind the Shelf/The Sexton keeps the Key to—" (640); "I have no Life but this—/To lead it here—" (1398). She renounces the satisfactions of a "normal" adult existence to create pain—and art. Thus, "the hallowing of Pain" is obtained at a "corporeal cost": "All—is the price of All—" (772), she says, "The Missing All—prevented Me/From missing minor Things" (985). Over and over, Dickinson declares the unjustified costs of satisfaction and the value of abstinence, isolation, and pain. "'Tis Anguish grander than Delight/'Tis Resurrection Pain—" (984). "Peril" is "Good to bear;" "Danger" is an antidote to "Satiety" (1678). While "Want" is a "quiet Commissary/For Infinity," "Satisfaction—is the Agent/Of Satiety—." Once we "possess," we lose the "Joy—/Immortality contented/Were Anomaly" (1036). "Dominion" and "Possession" last only as long as each is not obtained (1257). On the other hand, "How powerful the Stimulus/Of an Hermetic Mind" (711). Dickinson admits,

I lived on Dread—
To Those who know
The Stimulus there is
In Danger—Other impetus
Is numb—and Vitalless—

[from 770]

> *The Soul's distinct connection*
> *With immortality*
> *Is best disclosed by Danger*
> *Or quick Calamity—*
>
> [from 974]
>
> *Forbidden Fruit a flavor has*
> *That lawful Orchards mocks—*
> *How luscious lies within the Pod*
> *The Pea that Duty locks—*
>
> [1377]

Even stimulus can become routine and lose its effect (1196).[9]

The stimuli which make Dickinson chafe so productively—being considered small, lack of recognition—are temporarily bearable; in the long run, she means to triumph through renunciation. Instead of viewing her femininity as an unfair hindrance, she transforms it into martydom, the cost of the passage to immortality. She cannot write poems—or "conceive"—unless she is a haunted woman, but she has to be a virgin woman. She must "bandage" her sexuality, just as she must "bandage" her poetic genius, and from the pain this renunciation and abstinence produces, she can produce poems. Poems come out of not growing up, out of not mating, out of silence: they come when one says "no."

In her letters, Dickinson credits the world with being "hard to give up," but in the life she actually led and in her poetry, she does not manifest any real desire to participate in society's sewing circles, or to go to church, or to receive callers. What she gives up is far greater, and hence her reward is greater. This is why she can say, "Joy to have merited the Pain" (788). In "Triumph—may be of several kinds—" (455), Dickinson sees her own rejection of the world's offering as a reason for triumph in itself:

> *A Triumph—when Temptation's Bribe*
> *Be slowly handed back—*
> *One eye upon the Heaven renounced—*
> *And One—upon the Rack—*
>
> *Severer Triumph—by Himself*
> *Experienced—who pass*
> *Acquitted—from that Naked Bar—*
> *Jehova's Countenance—*

Dickinson associates the "Rack" with the pain that renunciation brings. At the same time, of course, she is making herself a martyr in the same way that Christ does, and in her poetry she intimates that she, too, will be acquitted, precisely for her refusal to accept the "temptation" of a normal life.

Therefore, while devotion to her poetry is a gamble, Dickinson's renunciation poems show confidence in her abstinences:

> *Renunciation–is a piercing Virtue–*
> *The letting go*
> *A Presence–for an Expectation–*
> *Not now–*
> *The putting out of Eyes–*
> *Just Sunrise–*
> *Lest Day–*
> *Day's Great Progenitor–*
> *Outvie*
> *Renunciation–is the Choosing*
> *Against itself–*
> *Itself to justify*
> *Unto itself–*
> *When larger function–*
> *Make that appear–*
> *Smaller–that Covered Vision–Here*
>
> [745]

We see that Dickinson firmly believes that in order to have immortality, she must "let go" any "Presence," whether it be her mother, her father, God, or any form of recognition or nurturance. In order to achieve immortal fame, Dickinson must choose against herself: renounce her feminine identity and become a neuter, lifeless "it." But the "larger function" of self-denial will make her life on earth as a woman appear "small." She has to "cover" or "bandage" the vision that she expresses "Here" in the poem, by which she means that she obscures her ability to see (or write) from the world, although this ability is implicit in the poem's existence. When she refers to "The putting out of Eyes," I think that she is convinced that her covering of her "vision" blinds other people, not herself. She will not let anyone identify her true identity. All that people see when they look at her is an "ordinary" woman. But she knows that her renunciation makes her different. Being different is a function of saying "no" to what the parent world offers.

Examples of other poems which affirm Dickinson's decision to take the "name of Gold" (454) are "Mine–by the Right of the White Election!" (528) and "I had the Glory–that will do–" (349). In poem 528, Dickinson exults in what is "Mine," although once again she does not tell *what* she owns, only that she has obtained it because she has said "no." She is "elect" because she is chaste ("the White Election"), because "in Vision–and in Veto!", in her "Scarlet prison–/Bars–cannot conceal!", she has had the foresight to reject the world. She is "Titled–Confirmed– . . . "long as Ages steal!" In poem 349, Dickinson insists that she "had the Glory" because "With one long 'Nay' " she has rejected "lesser Fames" which appear to be "Bliss," but in reality are "Deforming . . . Dwindling . . . Gulfing up–/Time's possibility."

In scores of poems, Dickinson shows that she equates her refusal to be a traditional woman with her success in achieving a more prestigious destiny as an immortal poet. She attributes her success to her refusals of conventional fulfillment: "martyr albums" come about by making "such and such an offering/ To Mr. So and So" (38). As long as Dickinson refuses to say "I do" and fuels her identity conflict, she does not have to submit to the destiny her female sexuality would imply. Being "different," to Dickinson, is transformation. On one level, Dickinson does not want a common, limited destiny of a "normal" nineteenth-century daughter. She wants to be a poet and have the attendant power, omnipotence, and glory. On another level, Dickinson does not want to die, to conclude, to "shut up." Death is the "common right" of "toads and men." As a poet, she will have a different destiny from others. Then her renunciation, symbolized by the martyr's crown of thorns, will have been worth it. She would rather "dwell in Possibility" (657), and even risk failure, than lead a normal life of "Prose." Her occupation in this house–this haunted house– is "This—/The spreading wide my narrow Hands/To gather Paradise–." Her hands reap the harvest of her self-denials in her poetry—and her poems are only temporarily "anonymous."[10] Many poems convey Dickinson's faith in her earning "Superiority to Fate," a "pittance at a time," subsisting "till Paradise" (1081). In her faith, she forgets to pose as dependent or humble. Consider the following declarations of self-reliance and confidence her renunciation and poetic achievement have given her:

> *Because 'twas Riches I could own,*
> *Myself had earned it–Me,*
>
> > [from 1093]
>
> *To undertake is to achieve*
>
> > [from 1070]
>
> *Finite–to fail, but infinite to Venture–*
>
> > [from 847]
>
> *On a Columnar Self–*
> *How ample to rely*
> *In Tumult–or Extremity–*
> *How good the Certainty*
>
> *That Lever cannot pry–*
> *And Wedge cannot divide*
> *Conviction–That Granitic Base–*
> *Though None be on our Side–*
>
> *Suffice Us–for a Crowd–*
> *Ourself–and Rectitude–*

And that Assembly—not far off
From furthest Spirit—God

[789]

I made slow Riches but my Gain
Was steady as the Sun
And every Night, it numbered more
Than the preceding One

All Days, I did not earn the same
But my perceiveless Gain
Inferred the less by Growing than
The Sum that it had grown.

[843]

He who in Himself believes—
Fraud cannot presume—
Faith is Constancy's Result—

[from 969]

How sweet I shall not lack in Vain—
But gain—thro' loss—Through Grief—obtain—
The Beauty that reward Him best—
The Beauty of Demand—at Rest—

[from 968]

Dickinson is always conscious not only of the cost of her strategy to haunt herself for art, but of the sure results. By following the rules she sets out, she wins the game.

In her case, because she has not offered herself to any Everyman "Mr. So and So," she defines herself in "royal" terms as the divine immortal poet who has taken the word, not the man:

Title divine—is mine!
The Wife—without the Sign!
Acute Degree—conferred on me—
Empress of Calvary!
Royal—all but the Crown!
Betrothed—without the swoon
God sends us Women—
When you—hold—Garnet to Garnet—
Gold—to Gold—
Born—Bridalled—Shrouded—
In a Day—
Tri Victory

> *"My Husband"–women say–*
> *Stroking the Melody–*
> *Is* this*–the way?*
>
> [1072]

Divinity, wife, royalty she is not; but her steadfast devotion to her muse confers on her "Acute Degree"—a status won by pain. It is in contrasting her life to other women that Dickinson is most wistfully, savagely witty. The "TriVictory" is amibiguous indeed, as a wedding vow is the woman's birth and death. Not only does Dickinson describe the bride as symbolically dead ("shrouded"—in her wedding garments) but in the pun on "Bridalled," Dickinson shows the woman confined and restrained by marriage. *Dickinson's* "husband," on the other hand, is the poem before us; she refers to the line she writes ("strokes" with the pen) as she slyly asks, "Is *this*–the way?"

Lest we come to be taken in by Dickinson's mode of haunting her "house of art," then, we should constantly remind ourselves that the reality behind her daughter-like persona is a mature woman who was confident, even arrogant, about her capabilities and her growth as a poet. She may have expressed doubt from time to time (all writers must), but even at the start of her career she was boasting that her chosen path was the way to immortality. In a letter to her brother, written in 1851 when she was only twenty-one, she writes:

> *There is another sky,*
> *Ever serene and fair,*
> *And there is another sunshine,*
> *Though it be darkness there;*
> *Never mind faded forests, Austin,*
> *Never mind silent fields–*
> *Here is a little forest,*
> *Whose leaf is ever green;*
> *Here is a brighter garden,*
> *Where not a frost has been;*
> *In its unfading flowers*
> *I hear the bright bee hum;*
> *Prithee, my brother,*
> *Into my garden come!*
>
> [2]

Inviting him into her garden of words, Dickinson is a generous, creative, powerful, and tempting Eve, who possesses the key to immortality, a literal "Garden." But—and this is the key issue—she camouflages her self-confidence. Dickinson allows this glimpse into her identity to be overlooked, for this "poem" is "bandaged," "shut up" in literal "Prose" at the end of a letter. It was only later pronounced a "poem" by Emily Dickinson's editors on the basis of its rhyme and meter. Here we see Dickinson's ability to fuse prose and poetry, duty and rebellion, the confident woman and the daughter within, the confident woman and the daughter without. How ironic that she should boast of her poetic powers, to offer to confer her poetic immunity, in "prose." And how emblematic of her poetic strategies throughout her life.

14
❦
The Word as Weapon

When Emily Dickinson told Thomas Higginson, "When I state myself as the Representative of the Verse, it does not mean–me–but a supposed person," she was posing: her poems reflect her consciousness of herself as a woman artist. Her identity as a daughter in her life, letters, and poetry was largely a fiction: "It's easy to invent a Life–/God does it–every Day–/Creation–but the Gambol/Of His Authority–" (724). At times Dickinson's poetry conveys un-abashed attitudes toward her artifice, "gamboling," as she does, with divine authority: "Candor–my tepid friend–/Come not to play with me–" (1537). More often, Dickinson dwells on her sense of secrecy and hiding and the futility (891, 894) and loneliness (903, 1385). While it is "good to hide, and hear 'em hunt!" it is "Better, to be found" and "Best, to know and tell" (842), for she claims: "A Counterfeit–a Plated Person–/I would not be– . . . Truth is good Health . . . How meagre, what an Exile–is a lie,/And Vocal–when we die—" (1453). Dick-inson would rather be solid, pure, not "plated" and cheapened in a pose. But she is taught by society to pose. Being an obedient daughter requires that she deny her feelings and submit to the prescribed mode of behavior for women. This means having a "Covered Vision" (in "Renunciation–is a piercing Virtue–", 745), not permitting herself to be seen as she is, either in flesh or her word; she perpetuates society's blindness regarding her true potential. (It is clear to Dickinson that society values and even insists on the pose.) When she says, "Tell all the Truth but tell it slant–/Success in Circuit lies" (1129), she is reciting society's advice to her on "how to grow," or more precisely, how to live without antagonizing anyone. But Dickinson also protests that "My Country is Truth," implying that the country other people inhabit is a lie. But in this "true" life Emily Dickinson cultivates romantic poses of captivity, escape, humility, and impertinence. Even in her poetry she poses as a martyr on the rack as part of her strategy to "haunt" her house of art. In this pose, however, Dickinson is only practicing what society preaches. She carries giving society what it wants

("I'll be a little ninny, a little pussy catty . . .," "I'll be your best little girl . . .
I'll never be noisy when you want to be quiet . . .") to such an extreme in her
little girl/recluse persona that she makes a mockery of social precepts and
expectations. Thus her obliging "stillness" is a means of rebellion against a
society which insists that she tell the truth "slant."

In the identity poems we have seen the consequences for the persona when
she is being forced to pose, or wear a mask: 1) she feels alienated from her
(public) self; 2) she feels trapped in the pose as if it were a prison or a grave;
3) she feels guilty for having a secret; and 4) she is insecure because the person
society loves is not really herself but a fiction designed to meet its expectations.
The necessity of wearing the mask undermines her confidence in her real identity.
We see Dickinson in her poetry "chafing" at her "shell" (728), or her cocoon
(1099), straining to be released from the unesteemed identity of a little girl which
society has imposed on her. Her mask as dutiful or even mildly rebellious daughter is self-defeating, and only serves to perpetuate society's misconception of
her. But the pose stimulates the tension and conflict necessary to fuel her art,
and it also protects Dickinson from being identified as she really is.

THE RETICENT VOLCANO

Underneath the mask of the daughter who is anxious to please is the angry
child who uses words not only to recreate her nurturing parents (if only to spurn
what they offer), and to establish her autonomy, but to revenge herself on a
controlling world which will not let her be her true self. Dickinson's identification with volcanoes, discussed by Adrienne Rich in "Vesuvius at Home," is
quite explicit. In poem 601 she describes her "still–Volcano–Life," her "quiet–
Earthquake Style–/Too subtle to suspect/By natures this side Naples." She is
smouldering below the surface of a calm exterior, "flickering in the night." Her
poetry needs the dark, and secrecy, and provides the outlet for her anger.
Volcanoes to her are a "Solemn–Torrid–Symbol–" whose "lips . . . never lie/
Whose hissing Corals part–and shut–/And Cities–ooze away–." Her anger,
when her lips part in poetry, annihilates cities. She sympathizes with their
"smouldering anguish" in poem 175. She is a volcano in poem 1677: "How red
the Fire rocks below–/How insecure the sod/Did I disclose/Would populate with
awe my solitude." She is ready to erupt anytime, and no one suspects. In poem
1748, Dickinson discusses the volcano again in terms of its secret (boiling
innards) which are confided to no one. The volcano is "reticent," but Dickinson
asks: "Can human nature not survive/Without a listener?" Without a listener,
she feels her message is locked up. Only the volcano and she keep their silence:
"The only secret people keep/Is Immortality." Again, in poem 1705, Dickinson
announces that volcanoes are closer than Sicily or South America: Vesuvius is
"at Home."

Emily Dickinson kept to her room and wrote private, superficially obscure
poetry, because society would not let her express her real voice, and she was

both wary and awed by the anger and power she felt. Thus the shyness she exhibits in front of her reader/parent becomes an assault as well. The poem is discharge from the active volcano who tries to "keep my lid on" with her silence, but in vain. A poem in which she describes herself as a blacksmith forging her lines asks, rhetorically, "Dare you see a Soul *at the White Heat*?" (365). Like her "White Election," the "White Heat" refers to her renunciation of pain (symbolized by her dressing in white) as well as the extreme heat she creates in keeping the "lid" on her "senses." She does not think her reader can accept the power embodied in her poetry, or the fact her "plated" poems are fueled by anger.

Dr. Chevasse, author of the nineteenth-century household text, *Man's Strength and Woman's Beauty*, claimed that anger in a woman was insanity.[11] It was safer in Dickinson's culture to be considered a childishly harmless eccentric than a powerful and angry woman. Emily Dickinson expressed her anger by cultivating a private self-image as a witch. We have seen her idea that poetry written by an un-taught woman is "witchcraft." She has listened to "evil tempters"; she trusts herself; she is a "pagan." As a poet she can belie her harmless image and acquire power through the magic of words. No one suspects what she brews, but she consoles herself with the notion of her dangerous nature. Poetry is a means to exact revenge on the recipients of the word, when it is used by a woman, and when this woman is a daughter.

For the child, the word is learned as an instrument of power. Theoretically, the child is absolutely dependent, helpless, and powerless, but through the word the child can exert a control over his or her life by calling for nurture and other forms of satisfaction. She can control the love, security, and nourishment coming into her life, and she can likewise reject these forms of "Yes." As a woman who uses the word in the guise of a child, Dickinson can enjoy a magical control over her experience that she is otherwise denied. She can cope with her own powerlessness and lack of a voice in society, and she can limit and circumscribe what happens to her. The word can be used both to create and to destroy. Words not said can make certain "Presences" absent, and words can wound:

> *She dealt her pretty words like Blades—*
>
> > [from 479]

> *There is a word*
> *Which bears a sword*
> *Can pierce an armed man—*
> *It hurls its barbed syllables*
> *And is mute again—*
>
> > [from 8]

In fact, when words are uttered by a witch, their "wound" is immortal. In the following poem we hear the cackling voice of the witch as she yearns for evil skills:

Ah, Necromancy Sweet!
Ah, Wizard erudite!
Teach me the skill,

That I instil the pain
Surgeons assuage in vain,
Nor Herb of all the plain
Can heal!

[177]

The impression of consciously-drawn evil is compounded by the repetition of a sigh of sinister satisfaction ("Ah") and her startling use of the word "sweet" to describe necromancy. Only evil takes pleasure in evil. The witch is the poet, wanting the pain she inflicts to be immortal, incurable, irremediable—as permanent as the word. Trafficking in sorcery and black magic as the poet, her soul given over to evil in trying to determine her future, Dickinson's "necromancy" (the art of conjuring the future by communicating with the spirits of the dead—ghosts) is related to her strategy to "haunt" her "house of art" with her "maturer childhood." She may ordain her future as a poet with her haunting use of words, but she identifies with evil in the process.

Because the word is immortal, its witch-author's power does not diminish: "The absence of the Witch does not/Invalidate the spell–" (1383). Similarly, a word's potency does not diminish. "A Word dropped careless on a Page" can sicken or attack the reader hundreds of years later. The word is so powerful and potentially dangerous or volatile that it must be used with extreme caution:

Infection in the sentence breeds
We may inhale Despair
At distances of Centuries
From the Malaria–

[from 1261]

In another poem, Dickinson provides a rationale for a sadistic use of language:

We will not drop the Dirk–
Because We love the Wound
The Dirk Commemorate–Itself
Remind Us that we died.

[from 379]

The "dirk" (sword) is the pen, which the doubled persona values because of the hurt it causes; therefore it is both the weapon and the evidence of a self-inflicted wound. Her use of the plural "we" suggests that the person using the word/

weapon is also the person who has been rendered lifeless by the word. It is this reminder of hurt—perhaps of Christ's crucifixion or her own martyrdom—that precipitates the poetry. Dickinson could be talking about the fact that she has to feel wounded or to wound herself in order to write. She will not stop using the word, which causes pain, because the anguish is necessary to her art.

Perhaps the most illuminating poem in regard to the child poet's anger is "Mine Enemy is growing old—":

> *Mine Enemy is growing old–*
> *I have at last Revenge–*
> *The Palate of the Hate departs–*
> *If any would avenge*
>
> *Let him be quick–the Viand flits–*
> *It is a faded Meat–*
> *Anger as soon as fed is dead–*
> *'Tis starving makes it fat–*
>
> [1509]

The relation between nurture and love becomes the basis of a relationship between lack of nurture and hate. Dickinson's appetite for anger and revenge abates when she is fed. Anger is put forth as a form of hunger for some primal satisfaction which food symbolizes: the less she is fed, the larger her anger grows. Oral activity—the very act of eating itself—is aggressive, for food is bitten, chewed, and consumed. Food is annihilated by the person who eats it and who gains nourishment in the process. The implication is that we "grow" through recognizing and acting upon anger, dissatisfaction, and need. Dickinson wants to "grow" to be a great poet; her aesthetic which cultivates hunger and pain would seem to imply that hunger-anger is necessary to grow "fat." Therefore, Dickinson cultivates, almost celebrates, anger, and it is possible that the ability to express anger might be a joy in itself, since anger is most often masked: thus "bliss" to Dickinson is "Murder–/Omnipotent–Acute–" (379). Power—specifically, God's power—is fatal. Writing poetry about anger frees Dickinson from her harmless and impotent identity, and enables her to assume a lethally rebellious and powerful identity.

By using the word as weapon, then, Dickinson can un-feed and avenge herself. The use of this strategy is illuminated by the revelations made by another writer, George Orwell, in an essay entitled "Why I Write."[12] Like Dickinson, he dwells on a miserable childhood, admitting at the same time that the desire to "get one's own back" is one of the primary motivations to write. He speaks specifically of childhood as the time when one is most oppressed, and therefore the time one most wants to gain revenge for. It is the experience and resultant hostility of the oppressed child which informs Dickinson's poems where the word is used as food and weapon. Orwell asserts that the writer does not *want* to give up this world vision of oppression acquired in childhood. It would seem that Dickinson's perception of this state of helpless anger that childhood embodies is universal, transcending time, culture, and sex. But because Dickinson is a woman, she not only uses the rebellious daughter's anger at not being able to express her real emotions (such as anger) to facilitate her art, but the guilt the dutiful daughter incurs by expressing her anger also fosters the tension necessary for her art. Even though her "enemy" keeps eluding her because her "wards are laid away in books"—that is in her poetry (1549), she is guilty just the same, for the conscience does not distinguish between thoughts and acts. The guilt mechanism is activated for thinking and writing, as much as it would be if she actually hunted down her foes.

A more extreme example of poetic muscle and anger is "My Life had stood—a Loaded Gun" (754), in which the poet is identified with a "gun" who kills her enemies for her "Master." We get a sinister image of the poet's sensibilities when she smiles sadistically at the annihilation her discharges result in. She expresses pride in her power and the fact that she is a dangerous entity. The last stanza of the poem, in which she says

> *Though I than He—may longer live*
> *He longer must—than I—*
> *For I have but the power to kill,*
> *Without—the power to die—*

shows that it is the word that is being used as the weapon, so that the gun is the poet and the bullet is the word/poem. The word/poem has the power to "kill" or wound, but not the power to die because it is immortal, whereas the poet herself is mortal.

It is interesting to note that the poet/gun is submissive to a man in this poem. It may be that the Master, as I have previously suggested, is the component of her sensibility which feels most hostile and angry. This she identifies as masculine, since a dutiful daughter cannot openly express her anger. What the poem makes clear is the reason why the "gun" writes poetry in secret, so that the fatal bullet does not really discharge her enemies. But it also shows the schism in consciousness which results from her attempt to divide herself into conscience, primary needs, and mode of expression.

What is especially interesting, although not surprising, about "Mine Enemy is growing old" or "My Life had stood—a Loaded Gun" is that Dickinson does not name her "enemy." Her enemy could very well be her parents, whose neglect of her she exploits to create the word. In poem 1509 they grow old: in point of fact Dickinson's hostility to these "faces" she uses as tools in "Myself was formed—a Carpenter—" (488) abated when her mother became paralyzed and her father aged and died. In poem 1509 she is aware that her primary anger at them for starving her of emotional support will lessen after they die, and that their aging will mitigate her motivation to make the word. Her parents' physical death also signalled their death as a presence in Dickinson's dialectic in the daughter construct. Dickinson's poetry production decreased dramatically after the deaths of her father in 1874, and her mother in 1882. As a poet, she was literally hungry for hate and starvation, for she used the word to feed herself and make herself "grow," and she only made the word when she was hungry. Therefore, it seems that Emily Dickinson needed withholding parents and a rejecting society in order to create. Part of her artifice in the haunting of her house of art was the creation of these childhood villains.

The poems which reveal Dickinson's need for anger serve to distance her from the feminine ideal, and they thereby aggravate the conflict she feels about her identity. In her poetry, Dickinson can escape from the bonds of her mask as dutiful daughter, but only at her own psychic peril. She knows it is futile to "banish" her feminine identity; alienating herself from this identity provides conflict which fuels her art. Therefore she writes that "Escape is such a thankful word," especially at night, when Dickinson is writing poetry. She trusts what she feeds herself—or rejects. In other words she trusts deprivation, withholding, rejection, and neglect. Dickinson is grateful for the word because she can use it to get away from her posed conventional life. In this way, she saves herself from a traditional eclipsed identity as a woman. The concluding lines of the poem suggest that Dickinson's trust of "the word" as a poet is specifically because her "head" or intellect relies on the word:

> 'Tis not to sight the savior—
> It is to be the saved—
> And that is why I lay my Head
> Upon this trusty word—
>
> [from 1347]

Dickinson lays her head upon the trusty word to escape the social pretense that she is a "little ninny."

THE CALM BOMB

We may look at the poetry as a form of ingenious resolutions to Dickinson's problems. But it is still not clear why Dickinson insists on retaining the consciousness of a child in the poetry, when her identity crisis will never be healed as long as the impotent and frustrated child informs the poems, *unless* we see that the child persona is a metaphor for how Dickinson feels as a woman. It is important to note that when Dickinson talks about herself in the imperious "I" it is always with a sense of the incomplete; or else it is the past tense, as if a consciousness has previously existed but now is ceased: for example, "I died for Beauty," (449), or "I heard a fly Buzz—when I died" (465). "I'm 'Woman' now" (199) describes her plight as being unable to go back to her childhood state. If the poems are informed by the child, then, they speak of an identity that is no longer available to her, one that she has indeed lost—and one that

she needs as a poet. If she plays "Yesterday" (728), and goes back to the time
when she was a little girl, she returns to the stage of consciousness in which
she has not yet "lost" her gift. This gift, as I have shown, is the parental
deprivation she experiences as a child which motivates the word. In "A loss of
something ever felt I," Dickinson claims that "The first that I could recollect/
Bereft I was–of what I knew not/Too young that any should suspect/A Mourner
walked among the children" (959). She bemoans a lost dominion, feels as if she
is the "only Prince cast out–." Her earliest memory, then, is of being unloved,
cast off, alienated. Dickinson can be talking about maternal deprivation; her
ability to write poetry is directly related to her sensibility as a child: "I find
myself still softly, searching/For my Delinquent Palaces–."

For the child, the word is the tool by which one gains love and independence. In order to get the same results a child does when it uses the word, the
poet has to retain a child's consciousness of pain, frustration, and rage, as well
as the indignity of being "least," small, and insignificant. Therefore the symptoms of identity crisis in Emily Dickinson's poetry are strategies to keep the
child, and "Great Hungers" alive, and the poet herself on the edge of madness,
raging and craving attention: I'm bigger than you think! The strategy is to
remain a daughter and keep the self in crisis: only then is the child motivated
to make the word.

A poem which encapsulates her attitudes as a poet and her consciousness of
her needs as a woman and poet is "I tie my Hat–I crease my Shawl–":

> *I tie my Hat–I crease my Shawl–*
> *Life's little duties do–precisely–*
> *As the very least*
> *Were infinite–to me–*
>
> *I put new Blossoms in the Glass–*
> *And throw the old–away–*
> *I push a petal from my Gown*
> *That anchored there–I weigh*
> *The time 'twill be till six o'clock*
> *I have so much to do–*
> *And yet–Existence–some way back–*
> *Stopped–struck–my ticking–through–*
> *We cannot put Ourself away*
> *As a completed Man*
> *Or Woman–When the Errand's done*
> *We came to Flesh–upon–*
> *There may be–Miles on Miles of Nought–*
> *Of Action–sicker far–*
> *To simulate–is stinging work–*
> *To cover what we are*
> *From Science–and from Surgery–*

> *Too Telescopic Eyes*
> *To bear on us unshaded—*
> *For their—sake—not for Ours—*
> *Therefore—we do life's labors—*
> *Though life's Reward—be done—*
> *With scrupulous exactness—*
> *To hold our Senses—on—*
>
> [443]¹³

We recognize the self-conscious woman speaking candidly about her "bandaged" life as a woman poet: the themes of enforced duplicity, the dutiful daughter's martyrdom and madness, the divided, plural self, the future of "Miles of Nought," the self-stimulating strategies, the shyness, the underlying latent explosive power. Dickinson takes us into her domestic sphere for a rare view of the "little duties" she performs as a dutiful daughter—mindless, petty, meaningless activities she does with conscious precision and intensity as if they were important to keep herself from going crazy: tying one's hat, creasing one's shawl, throwing old flowers away. Some crisis has ravaged her sense of existence—she is a stuffed doll whose "ticking" (stuffing and her ticking heart) is punctured. Yet she is suspended in life, unable to conclude her life, and forced to go on with her charade as dutiful daughter. She knows that this is only a lull in between future crises, for there may be "Miles on Miles of Nought—" left to endure. That is, she will be busy with "Infinites of Nought," (as in "Like Eyes That Looked on Wastes" [458]) meaningless trivia and prescribed dutiful behavior that adds up to nothing. This recalls Dickinson's description of emptiness and loss when she is twenty-four and is missing Susan Gilbert: "I rise, because the sun shines, and sleep has done with me, and I brush my hair, and dress me, and wonder what I am and who has made me so, and then I wash the dishes and anon, wash them again, and then tis afternoon, and ladies call and evening, and some members of another sex come in to spend the hour, and then that day is done. And prithee, what is Life?" (*L.* I, p. 304).

But the persona then reveals that her existential crisis may be contrived: "To simulate—is stinging work—". In her poetry, she simulates pain, crisis, and deprivation as an aesthetic strategy, and her art is in large measure a function of her ability to create or recreate pain. She must construct an attitude, a pose which will "cover what we are" (powerful, poetic, rebellious) from "Eyes" that cannot accept her truth. She does not pose for herself, she says, but for others who would be startled to see her truths. As we have seen, many of her "truths" are hostile, defiant, and aggressive. In "A Pit—but Heaven over it—" (1712) Dickinson again discusses her necessary camouflage. She knows that she lives precariously near a "Pit." "To stir would be to slip—/To look would be to drop—." The "Pit" would startle them—the same people who could not bear her truths. So Dickinson is actually stronger emotionally and intellectually; she dares to front the existential chaos within, in her role as dutiful daughter, a life as a "Calm Bomb" or a "Loaded Gun." But the calm that society infers is a veneer, for she is trying desperately not to explode. She does "Life's–labor" just to cope. But she also does it to keep herself aggravated enough to write. Sustaining her pose is simulating, and therefore, "stinging work."

Dickinson's sense of "posing" as a dutiful woman is integrally related to her own sense of power and anger in her role as a poet. She sums up her poetic career with the lines, "I took my Power in my Hand–/And went against the World–" (540). But she changes the Biblical story: when she aims her pebble at Goliath, she, the little one, is the one that "falls." She is a "Martyr Poet" (544) who has "wrought [her] Pang in syllable–" by simulating the pose of the daughter, covering up what she is, and constructing a suitable past for a woman who resists a common, mortal fate.

It seems that the world never had a chance with Emily Dickinson. She felt it would not give her fame; therefore she scorned fame and preferred, she said, to be "Nobody." It withheld recognition; she would not allow anyone to identify her. It hurt her, so she insisted being hurt was requisite for immortality and used her "wounds" as evidence of her "election." If it valued the pose, she would lie; if it devalued women, she would fragment her sensibility. Dickinson turned the world's neglect into fodder for her growth as a poet and in the process exposed the world as being as "mad, and *silly*," and futile as her father. Anything that happened to her could be interpreted as a sign of her singularity.

The only thing the world could not do was love her, nourish her, teach her to grow, or recognize her genius. This she could not permit, for in her aesthetics, less is more, small is greater, hunger is satisfaction: "Great hungers feed themselves, but little Hungers ail in vain." (*L*. III, p. 668). Emily Dickinson's only problem was to keep her "Great hungers" for power and immortality alive. Adopting the daughter persona enabled her to keep herself angry, neglected, small, starving, guilty, and constantly in crisis.

Both daughters, the dutiful and the rebellious, are necessary for the manufacture of poetry, then. Dickinson's role as dutiful daughter may have frustrated her, but keeping herself outwardly "still," refusing to disclose her ambitions, yet hinting of her great secret built a tension between her two lives, her dutiful days and her rebellious nights. It was such *daughter's* pain and guilt for her various refusals and disobediences and secrets in her life as a poet that she disciplined into "Power" to make her poems. Poetry was the Wild No to the Awful Yes she was expected to live, even if she wrote in a closet of her own making, at night, in secret, in her bedroom. Her secrecy made the daughter cocoon into the martyr's hairshirt. But this was Possibility, where Dickinson took her power in her hand and went "against the world." In her seclusion, she could be free, develop her voice. The Closet in which she shut herself was not Prose, but a refuge from Prose, a place to nurture a strategy to keep her in the kitchen of the House of Art, busily cooking up the food which does not perish, and getting plump and saucy on her own immortality.

Notes

Introduction

1. See Millicent Todd Bingham, *Ancestor's Brocades: The Literary Debut of Emily Dickinson* (New York: Harper, 1945), pp. 166–67. Archibald MacLeish said "most of us are half in love with this dead girl" in "The Private World: Poems of Emily Dickinson," *Emily Dickinson: A Collection of Critical Essays*, ed. by Richard B. Sewall (Englewood Cliffs, N.J.: Prentice-Hall, Inc.,), p. 160. The cult of "our Emily" was being complained about as early as the 1920s—Bingham's work was an antidote to Martha Dickinson Bianchi's reminiscences in *Face to Face* (Boston: Houghton Mifflin, 1924). The cult was discussed by Jay Leyda in *The Years and Hours of Emily Dickinson*, 2 vols. (New Haven, Conn.: Yale University Press, 1960), pp. xx–xxi; and Richard B. Sewall, *The Life of Emily Dickinson*, 2 vols. (New York: Farrar, Straus and Giroux, 1974), p. 4. References to Dickinson most often have been merely the familiar "Emily" or the polite "Miss Dickinson" in writers such as Allen Tate, Conrad Aiken, Austin Warren, George Whicher, and so on.

2. Clark Griffith, *The Long Shadow: Emily Dickinson's Tragic Poetry* (Princeton: Princeton University Press, 1968); Ruth Miller, *The Poetry of Emily Dickinson* (Middletown, Conn.: Wesleyan University Press, 1968), p. 87.

3. William R. Sherwood, *Circumstance and Circumference, Stages in the Mind and Art of Emily Dickinson* (New York: Columbia University Press, 1968), p. 138.

4. John Cody, *After Great Pain: The Inner Life of Emily Dickinson* (Cambridge, Mass.: The Belknap Press of Harvard University Press, 1971), a "psychography" that uses the poems as evidence for a "case study," pp. 25–35.

5. For example, see Jean Mudge, *Emily Dickinson and the Image of Home* (Amherst: The University of Massachusetts Press, 1975), p. 197. An evaluation of these points of view is summarized by Phyllis Jones in a 1979 MLA paper, "This Was a Woman Poet: New Directions in the Criticism of Gender Identity," and discussed by Sandra M. Gilbert and Susan Gubar in their introduction to *Shakespeare's Sisters* (Bloomington: Indiana University Press, 1979), pp. xvi–xx. Mudge's work is the first full-length study that even considers Dickinson's sensibility as a woman from a sociological and psychological point of view, although Mudge is more interested in situating Dickinson's sense of place within a philosophical framework.

6. *The Letters of Emily Dickinson*, ed. Thomas H. Johnson and Theodora Ward, 3 vols. (Cambridge, Mass.: The Belknap Press of Harvard University Press, 1958), II, p. 460. Subsequent references to this edition will be cited in the text as *L.*, followed by the volume and page numbers.

7. Leyda, p. xx.

8. *The Complete Poems of Emily Dickinson*, ed. Thomas H. Johnson, 3 vols. (Cambridge, Mass.: The Belknap Press of Harvard University Press, 1955), poem 613. Subsequent references in the text to the poems will cite the Johnson number (he has dated the poems and arranged them in chronological order).

9. John Stuart Mill, *On the Subjection of Women* (1869) in *Essays on Sex Equality*, ed. by Alice Rossi (Chicago: University of Chicago Press, 1970), p. 156.

10. Friends of the Dickinson family included Samuel Bowles, editor of *The Springfield Republican*, Josiah Gilbert Holland, editor of *Scribner's*, and Judge Otis Lord of the Massachusetts Supreme Court. Ralph Waldo Emerson was a visitor, and Thomas Wentworth Higginson repeatedly invited Dickinson to attend a literary gathering in Boston where she would have met the noted writers of her day. Helen Hunt Jackson, who was considered one of the leading female writers of the day, grew up in Amherst. Her work was published by Dr. Holland and praised by Emerson, and like Dickinson, she had Higginson for a mentor. When she found out about Dickinson's poetry, she wrote Dickinson letters urging her to publish, and even arranged for and stubbornly carried through the publication of one of Dickinson's poems for the No Name series, in spite of Dickinson's ambivalence about cooperating. See Sewall, pp. 577–92; *Letters* II, p. 545; and III, pp. 841–42.

11. Sandra Gilbert and Susan Gubar, *The Madwoman in the Attic* (New Haven and London: Yale University Press, 1979). Rev. by Rosemary Dinnage, "Re-creating Eve," *NYRB*, 20 December 1979, pp. 6–8.

12. Taggard, Genevieve, *The Life and Mind of Emily Dickinson* (New York: Knopf, 1930) p. xii.

13. Adrienne Rich, "Vesuvius at Home: The Power of Emily Dickinson," *Parnassus: Poetry in Review* 51, No. 1 (Fall-Winter 1976): 44–74.

14. Leyda, "Late Thaw of a Frozen Image," *The New Republic*, 25 February 1955, p. 24.

15. Charles Anderson, *Emily Dickinson's Poetry: Stairway of Surprise* (New York: Holt, Rinehart, and Winston, 1960), pp. xii-xiv.

16. David Higgins, *Portrait of Emily Dickinson* (New Brunswick, New Jersey: Rutgers University Press, 1967), p. 27.

17. Sewall, *The Life of Emily Dickinson*, p. xi.

18. Inder Nath Kher, *The Landscape of Absence* (New Haven: Yale University Press, 1974), pp. 1, 3.

19. Suzanne Juhasz, *Naked and Fiery Forms, Modern American Poetry by Women: A New Tradition* (New York: Harper and Row, 1976). For example, see Cody, Griffith, and Taggard.

20. George Whicher, *This Was a Poet: A Critical Biography of Emily Dickinson* (New York: Charles Scribner's Sons, 1938), pp. 81ff.

21. David Porter, *The Art of Emily Dickinson's Early Poetry* (Cambridge, Mass.: Harvard University Press, 1966). p. xii; Kher, pp. 3–4, citing Northrop Frye, *Fables of Identity* (New York: Harcourt, Brace, 1963), pp. 193–217.

22. This point of view is supported by Albert Gelpi in *The Tenth Muse: The Psyche of the American Poet* (Cambridge, Mass.: Harvard University Press, 1975), p. 227; Robert Weisbuch, *Emily Dickinson's Poetry* (Chicago: University of Chicago Press, 1975). p. xxi.

23. Sewall, p. 49.

PART ONE. THE CASE: THE IDENTITY POEMS

1. Erik Erikson, *Childhood and Society*, 2d ed. (New York: W.W. Norton, 1962), pp. 209–14.

2. George Whicher sees this poem as a "protest of constancy" and as an "astonishing" metaphysical conceit which "holds good" for five stanzas: then, he says, "the poem falters to an obscure and inappropriate close. . . . Whatever the meaning, the stanza is a collapse, not a conclusion" (pp. 278–79). Genevieve Taggard says the poem, about Dickinson's renunciation of love, concerns an outlaw and his bride, that it is evidence that "words, kisses, vows" have been exchanged and renounced (pp. 30–37). Charles Anderson does not ascribe any biographical relevance to the poem, but his ideas about it are close to Taggard's idea of an outlaw-and-his-bride motif. He sees the poem as a "ballad-narrative" in the "tall-tale mode of Western humor," where the owner is the pioneer lover and the gun is the frontier sweetheart. But reading the poem as a "romantic troubadour theme" leads, again, to a dead end. Unable to relate his discussion to the last stanzas of the poem, he says that the poem itself "does not quite come off" (pp. 172–76). For Louise Bogan, the entire poem "defies analysis" (Louise Bogan, "A Mystical Poet," in *Emily Dickinson: Three Views* (Amherst, Mass: Amherst College Press, 1960), pp. 27–34. Thomas Johnson discusses the poem superficially as a testimonial to her dedication to her art. John Cody analyzes this poem as a symptom of Dickinson's Oedipal problems and of her "acceptance of the masculine components of her personality" (pp. 398–416). Cody, however, discusses the problems with previous interpretations persuasively. His own interpretation of the poems is based on his conviction of Dickinson's bisexual, hostile nature and masculine identification from the psychoanalytical point of view. Recently Gelpi has given an extensive analysis of this poem in "Emily Dickinson and the Deerslayer: The Dilemma of the Woman Poet in America," *San Jose Studies*, 31 May 1977, pp. 80–95. See also Rich, p. 65.

3. Scholars such as John Emerson Todd feel such poems express "The persona's serious psychological disorder" (p. 84); Dr. Cody uses poem 937 to support his conclusion that Emily Dickinson was psychotic: "The foregoing references—this snarl in the brain, the broken plank in reason, and the cleavage in the mind—appear to be sufficient justification in themselves for concluding that the crisis in Emily Dickinson's life was a psychosis" (p. 294). The important aspect of the poem to stress is not whether what it describes is true for Dickinson, but that the persona is engaged in the process of describing this disintegration with full possession of her poetic faculties and sense. As Sewall points out, "She seems as close to touching bottom here as she ever got. But there was nothing wrong with her mind when she wrote the poem" (p. 502).

PART TWO. THE DAUGHTER CONSTRUCT

1. Higgins, p. 27.

2. An abridged version of this section has been published as "I Never Had a Mother: Reconstruction in Emily Dickinson's House of Art" in *The Lost Tradition: A History of Mothers and Daughters in Literature*, ed. E. M. Broner and Cathy N. Davidson (New York: Frederick Ungar Publishers, 1980).

3. Millicent Todd Bingham, *Emily Dickinson's Home* (New York: Harper, 1955), discusses the significance of Mrs. Dickinson's "tremulous fear of death" (p. 4); Whicher mentions her on her husband's arm as they stroll down the street (p. 6) and discusses her relative insignificance (pp. 28–29); Higgins characterizes Mrs. Dickinson as a background figure in the life of her family: "pious, quiet, dutiful" (p. 30); Klaus Lubbers, *Emily Dickinson: The Critical Revolution* (Ann Arbor: The University of Michigan Press, 1968), cites Dickinson's father, sister-in-law, brother, and sister in his index to the kind of work that has been done on her, and makes no reference to any approach to Dickinson that would made her mother important enough even to

be mentioned (p. 328). Whicher discusses the importance of Edward Dickinson, and Griffith's *The Long Shadow* is premised on the dark role the father played in Dickinson's life; Sewall, in his two-volume biography, *The Life of Emily Dickinson* (New York: Farrar, Straus, and Giroux, 1974), notes that "tradition has it that Emily Dickinson's home was dominated by her father" (p. 44). John Cody's *After Great Pain* is the first full-scale study of the role Emily Norcross Dickinson played in her daughter's life and poetry. Following this work, we have Jean Mudge's study, which discusses Mrs. Dickinson at more length in the study of Dickinson's sense of "place."

4. Leyda, I, p. 21. The words were spoken as Emily and her Aunt Lavinia traveled on horseback from Amherst to Monson and were recorded in a letter of her aunt's. Mudge cites these words to prove that Emily Norcross Dickinson "seems to have been an affectionate mother" (Mudge, p. 31). Cody reminds us that this visit was a rather traumatic occasion for the two-year-old, for her mother was forced to send her away in order to recuperate from the birth of her second daughter (pp. 15, 50).

5. This letter is followed by, "I suppose a mother is one to whom you hurry when you are troubled"; see also II, pp. 517–18; and, in this context: "Awe is the first Hand that is held to us—" (III, p. 800).

6. Cody, p. 2; Erikson, p. 288. In a letter Dickinson explicitly connects her childhood experience with the sense of loss of a mother: "No Verse in the Bible has frightened me so much from a Child as 'from him that hath not, shall be taken even that he hath.' Was it because it's dark menace deepened our own Door? You speak as if you still missed your Mother," (*L*. II, pp. 751–52). She was afraid because she was one of those who "hath not," and she was afraid she would be further ravaged. She cannot "conjecture a form of space without her timid face" (III, p. 753).

7. For example, she said in reference to her sister, "I have no parents but her": allegedly her sister dressed her (*L*. II, p. 508).

8. Richard Wilbur, in "Sumptuous Destitution," in *Emily Dickinson: Three Views* (Amherst: Amherst College Press, 1960), pp. 35–46, points out that Emily Dickinson never allows her reader to forget that she has been deprived. We see deprivation of love described in terms of food in the letters. For example, "The supper of the heart is when the guest has gone" (*L*. II, p. 452); "You have so often fed me" (II, p. 543); "Do you find plenty of food at home? Famine is unpleasant" (II, p. 355); when she refuses Judge Otis Lord's marriage proposal, she writes, "It is Anguish I long conceal from you to let you leave me, hungry, but you ask the divine Crust and that would doom the Bread" (II, p. 617). See also John Cody's list of poems in which food and love are equated, p. 145.

9. Erikson, pp. 79–80. Erikson contends that the unity with a "maternal matrix" which is destroyed by the coming-in of the baby's teeth and the mother's subsequent withdrawal is the "earliest catastrophe" we know. Likening the loss of the breast to our being evicted from the Garden of Eden, Erikson emphasizes that a drastic loss of mother love (experienced when the mother rejects the biting child, for example) can lead to mourning for the rest of one's life. "At best," he says, it results in a "primary sense" of evil and doom, and a nostalgia for a lost paradise, each of which characterizes Dickinson's letters and poetry. I do see at most a fine line between the two concepts of "absence" and "rejection" in the child's mind.

10. Cody, p. 7. Cody sees Emily Norcross Dickinson as "in some critical way a failure" (p. 41). Her villainy included being a "habitually complaining woman," "emotionally shallow, self-centered, ineffectual, conventional, timid, submissive, and not very bright . . . subject to depression and hypochondria" (p. 42).

11. Erikson, p. 288.

12. *L*. I, p. 77. Sewall, p. 83.

13. For example, Austin complained to his fiancee that "I have never *before*

received *any* [tenderness] from any *body* . . ." (Leyda, I, p. 315). Edward Dickinson was ambivalent and patronizing (John Cody gives a revealing analysis of his letters home in this regard, pp. 66–70). Mabel Loomis Todd writes, from what she has gathered from Austin, that the mother died "without giving a perceptible ripple on the surface of anyone's life, or giving concern to any of her family," that her "poor little attempts . . . [to make anyone happier] . . . failed sadly" (MSS Todd-Bingham Archive; in Sewall, p. 287).

14. Sewall, p. 76.

15. Ibid., p. 78

16. Ibid., p. 76.

17. See Mudge, p. 29. In her attempt to restore the elder Emily Dickinson, Mudge quotes the obituary written about Dickinson's grandmother and says it is descriptive of her mother as well: "When individuals who are pious, amiable and useful are removed from us by death we may justly lament the event. . . . Few have sustained with greater fidelity and propriety the duties of her station than Mrs. Norcross, humble and retiring in her disposition. It was in the bosom of her family and among those who observed her in domestic life, that her prudence, and affection, regard to the happiness of all around her, appeared most conspicuous" (Leyda, I, p. 11; quoted by Mudge, p. 29).

18. Mudge, pp. 41–42; Cody, pp. 83, 71–84.

19. In a discussion of Dickinson's identity and her relationship to her mother, Jean Mudge makes reference to Emerson's "Me" and "Not Me" but with a different emphasis and conclusion:

> *Actually, the terms identity, inscape, and imagination appear to have a core meaning in common, though each may develop in separate directions from this shared center. Considering identity as "at homeness" in the world, psychologists and psychosociologists have increasingly recognized the importance of a realm of reality lying between the subjective and objective, a third "transitional" or "intermediate" area in which the first two are fused. Here Emerson's "Me" and "Not Me," man and nature, coalesce, and fantasy and fact unite.*
>
> *Psychology sees the mother's role in reaching this transitional realm to be a crucial one; she must mediate between inner and outer worlds to preserve her infant's illusion of subjective creation of an object to a degree short of nurturing solipsism but extending to the vital function of fostering self-confidence in a world which shows itself potentially hostile. It is hard not to see the affinities this analysis has with concepts of inscape, as just described, with the classic views of the imagination.*

20. See also Adrienne Rich, *Of Woman Born: Motherhood as Experience and Institution* (New York: W. W. Norton, 1976). Phyllis Chesler writes in *Women and Madness* (New York: Avon Books, 1972): "Modern women are psychologically starved for nurturance and role-models, i.e., for female heroines and protective goddesses" (pp. 168–69, Plate 1). Chesler makes this point throughout the book and gives reasons why mothers reject daughters and daughters reject mothers.

21. Sewall, pp. 58, 87–88.

22. Helene Deutsch, *The Psychology of Women*, vol. 1 (New York: Grune and Stratton, 1944), p. 3 passim.

23. Although Emily Dickinson theoretically went to Mount Holyoke for education, the "end and aim" of all Mary Lyon's efforts was to "make the seminary a nursery to the church," in the words of Edward Hitchcock, president of Amherst College (Hitchcock, *The Power of Christian Benevolence Illustrated in the Life and*

Labors of Mary Lyon [New York: 1858] pp. 210–211. Cited by Higgins, p. 45). Higgins describes revivals "moving like thunderstorms" across New England during Dickinson's early years. At her school, those who would not confess their life to be Christ's were publically reproached, and the religious fervor was taken up by Dickinson's friends so that her friendships depended in great measure upon their agreement about religion. Faith was not a personal but a public matter for the record. (See Dickinson's early letters in this regard.) Legend has it that at one point Dickinson was the only person who stood up in school assembly and counted herself as "lost."

24. Cody, pp. 92, 120–21, 151; but Cody suggests that her religious crisis is not a function of her identification with her mother but of her identification with Austin—that it is a homosexual crisis (pp. 174–78 ff.). But this homosexual crisis, as he understands it, is a response to her "cruel rejection" *by* her mother (p. 182).

25. Erikson, pp. 235–36; p. 240; p. 245; pp. 247–51.

26. Martha Dickinson Bianchi, *Emily Dickinson Face to Face* (Boston: Houghton Mifflin Company, 1932).

27. The boxes of Dickinson material at the Houghton Library contain poems written by Lavinia Dickinson late in life, after she discovered her sister's poetry. This suggests that Vinnie may have suppressed any creative urges in being the *real* "dutiful daughter." It bears further study. She may not have been all that happy with her cats and posies.

28. Cody, pp. 85–92.

29. Sewall, pp. 44–73.

30. Sewall, p. 49. See also Chase, pp. 89–95 and pp. 6–20.

31. Klaus Lubbers discusses Whicher's influence on later biographical studies in *Emily Dickinson: The Critical Revolution*, pp. 166–67. He contends that Richard Chase and Thomas J. Johnson (*Emily Dickinson: An Interpretive Biography*, Cambridge, Mass: Belknap Press of Harvard University Press, 1955), "hardly went beyond the line drawn by *This Was A Poet*." Furthermore, Chase's biography (1951) "is based entirely on Whicher."

32. The argument against taking Emily Dickinson at her word is presented by David Porter, p. 1 passim. He argues that we should not study Emily Dickinson in the context of her life (p. xii) because he feels that she maintained a pose throughout her life. Therefore she never talked about *herself*. Thus he dismisses her pose to Higginson, for example, as contradictory, "pitifully small and ridiculous," "a pervasive humility, an artlessness" (pp. 6–7).

33. Whicher, pp. 27–28.

34. Sewall, p. 49.

35. The diary of Lavinia N. Dickinson is in Box 8 of the Dickinson family papers at the Houghton Library, Harvard University. Because of its size (about 3″ x 4″), entries are necessarily brief, but usually she gives a summary of the day's activities in shorthand: "Tutor Howland. Bought new ribbon. Visited . . ."

36. Leyda, I, p. 328.

37. Bingham, p. 233.

38. The plate incident is recorded by Taggard, p. 8, and by Bingham, p. 112.

39. Taggard, p. 82. Genevieve Taggard's analysis of the father-daughter relationship is intuitive and perceptive. Her work on Dickinson, while not "scholarly," needs to be re-evaluated. It has been almost completely dismissed.

40. Her brother Austin had been sent "With orders from head-quarters to bring me home at all events." Her words and next resort, "woman's tears," unavailing, Austin was "victorious" and "poor defeated I was led off in triumph" (*L*. I, p. 65).

41. Leyda, I, p. 42 (when Dickinson was eight).

42. *L*. II, p. 427. For the books which Edward bought Dickinson, see Jack L. Capps, *Emily Dickinson's Reading* (Cambridge, Mass.: Harvard University Press, 1966), pp. 14–15.

43. Higgins, p. 31.

44. These relationships have been documented and discussed in several studies. The relationship with Lord came to light in *Emily Dickinson: A Revelation* (New York, 1954) when their letters were published. Leyda put forward documentation of Dickinson's relationships with the Hollands, the Bowleses, Newton, and Higginson. Whicher discusses Newton as an intellectual friend and Reverend Wadsworth from Philadelphia as a spiritual advisor, disputing both Bianchi's contention that Dickinson loved Wadsworth and Taggard's argument for Newton and Gould. Bowles is discussed especially by Higgins and Sewall. (See also Winfield Townley Scott, "Emily Dickinson and Samuel Bowles," *Fresco* [Detroit] 10, no. 2 [Fall 1959]: 7–17.) Sewall devotes a chapter to each figure in Dickinson's life.

45. Sewall, pp. 642–49.

46. David Porter gives a useful discussion of why Dickinson felt that Higginson could help her, judging by his published remarks. She may have thought that he liked "bright women" because he said that "few men in all their pride of culture can emulate the easy grace of a bright woman's letter" (Higginson, "Letter to a Young Contributor"). Also, Higginson presented himself as a father-figure: "To take the lead in bringing forward a new genius is a fascinating privilege" (pp. 3–15).

47. Cf. William Robert Sherwood (p. 208) who says that her letters to Higginson are distinguished by their *lack* of coyness and equivocation.

48. If she makes a mistake, ". . . the Ignorance out of sight—is my Preceptor's charge–. . . ." (*L.* II, p. 415). "You say 'Beyond your knowledge.' You would not jest with me, because I believe you–but Preceptor–you cannot mean it. All men say 'What' to me, but I thought it a fashion." In this same letter she writes that her dog would please him because he is "brave" and "dumb." How far Higginson was off in his assessment of Dickinson may be seen in his stubborn: "You must come down to Boston sometimes. All ladies do" (II, p. 462). Dickinson had told him firmly three times that she would not leave her father's house, and he should have guessed by 1869 that Dickinson was not a typical lady. I believe that Higginson actually did know better at this point. He simply found her studied eccentricity difficult to live with.

49. Griffith, p. 169.

50. *L.* I, p. 94. "When people die, Heaven gets large, the earth gets smaller, and she lonely: this is when God is "more 'Our Father' and we feel our need increased." Also, "It will never look kind to me that God, who causes all, denies such little wishes" (II, p. 376).

51. Richard B. Sewall, *The Lyman Letters: New Light on Emily Dickinson and the Family* (Amherst, Mass.: University of Massachusetts Press, 1965), pp. 70–71.

PART THREE. DAUGHTER AT WORK: THE POEMS

1. Jean Mudge cites this poem as one that enlarges "architectural fact to fit Emily's mood" (p. 5) and later discusses it as an example of a case in which she uses Robert Browning (p. 125). Mudge sees Dickinson's poem as a statement of her obligation to stay home because of her eyes, her fears, and her mother's illness; but staying home, in these terms, is not "Possibility," and does not illustrate how Paradise is gathered.

The majority of the poems I discuss previously have not been dealt with in any substantive way, and several of the key poems have not been discussed or cited at all. These include poems 1204, 564, 394, 659, 454, 1292, 728, 1659, 1240, 1427, 1314, 1475, 1763.

2. Poem 790. We have "To the bright east she flies" (1573) about Dickinson's

mother, which Dickinson wrote in a letter about her mother's recent death (L. III, pp. 770–71).

> *Fashioning what she is,*
> *Fathoming what she was,*
> *We deem we dream—*
> *And that dissolves the days*
> *Through which existence strays*
> *Homeless at home.*

Other poems that reveal her sense of living with strangers on earth who drive her to seek God's notice point to a female rather than a male. We cannot say without qualification that any poem deals with her mother. There is poem 1318, for example, which could be about a mother:

> *Frigid and sweet Her parting Face—*
> *Frigid and fleet my Feet—*
> *Alien and vain whatever Clime*
> *Acrid whatever Fate.*
>
> *Given to me without the Suit*
> *Riches and Name and Realm—*
> *Who was She to withhold from me*
> *Penury and Home?*

A profound ambivalence is expressed toward that Face.

3. John Emerson Todd finds in this "playful" poem that consciousness is the moralizing part of herself (p. 75). But if we consider that alien self to be Dickinson's conscience, it would represent her superego, or internalized parents. Therefore the child would be trying to rid herself of her mother and father. But the rest of the poem makes clear that it is the feminine she needs to banish because she does not want to be "pregnable." If she won her battle with herself, she would be peaceful, impregnable, and unconscious: neuter or dead. John Cody discusses this poem as the result of the repression of violent impulse (p. 331).

4. Porter, pp. 72, 125–26. He cites Richard Chase in support of faulting her for her "rococo" manner in which ornamental motifs are ends in themselves (Chase, pp. 221, 226): "The interest here of course is in the profusion of examples of pairings fitting for a valentine but hardly charged with any profounder intent." According to Todd, the poem is "frivolous," "thoroughly commonplace in thought," and it reveals none of the qualities characteristic of Dickinson's "finest" poetry (p. 2). He uses this poem as a basis for his judgment that Dickinson's "poetic art was slow to materialize and that she indulged in the "sentimental tastes of the age." (The rules of the day for poetry can be defined as what was being published. See Sewall, pp. 671–71, 674, 742–50.) Todd also takes her parody seriously when he refers to her "long, rather tedious succession of hexameter couplets. . . ." (p. 1).

5. Jean Mudge sees this poem as evidence that Dickinson's parents so punished her, p. 43. See Leyda, II, p. 483. Also, see Cody, pp. 78, 218.

6. Actually, as far as I can determine, Higginson seems to have been most circumspect and respectful. But Dickinson responds to him *as if* he treats her as a wayward child. She does it to perpetuate her daughter role, of course, but also, she may interpret his silences and tacit criticisms of her poetry as admonishments and disobediences. We can ascertain his criteria for poetry by his calling attention to Dickinson's irregularities, and further proof of his attitudes lies in his regularization

of her poems when he edited the first volume of poems after she had died. In 1903 he wrote: "Emily Dickinson never quite succeeded in grasping the notion of the importance of form" (Thomas Wentworth Higginson, *Reader's History of American Literature*). Cited in Sewall, pp. 573–75.

7. This poem is discussed by critics in terms of its biographical portraiture. For example, Whicher believes that the two she "lost" were Leonard Humphrey and Ben Newton who each had early deaths. The third loss is Wadsworth's departure (Whicher, pp. 107–8). But the poem was written before Wadsworth had departed. George Whicher could not have known this, for his biography was written before Thomas Johnson established the chronology. But the point is that trying to make a biographical paraphrase of a poem does not illuminate the poem's essential meaning. Similarly, Thomas Johnson, pp. 206–6, specifies the poem as referring to the death of Sophia Holland. See also Sewall, p. 492. Again, in the biographical vein, the poem is discussed as an elegy to Frazar Stearns or as evidence of Dickinson's exasperation at not being published by Samuel Bowles or as her offering to be his friend no matter how he treats her. See also Chase, pp. 102–3; Sherwood, pp. 34–35; Todd, p. 21; and Porter, pp. 48, 163–64.

8. Susanne Langer, *Feeling and Form* (New York: Scribner's 1953). She discusses "the question" as a statement that contains an answer and an assumption about that answer. See also Edwin Mosely, "The Gambit of Emily Dickinson," *University of Kansas City Review* 16 (Autumn 1949):12; and Todd, p. 9.

9. Leyda, I, p. 178.

10. It is not surprising that Mabel Loomis Todd writes in regard to these poems that society and the Church took great offense at them. See Sewall, p. 290. It would seem that the poems were correctly interpreted by the reading public, who felt the venom of the satire which was aimed at them. However, Mabel Todd tried to convince them that Dickinson was not "irreverent." This may have been true in some ways, but Dickinson was irreverent towards *society*, and that is usually what people mean when they say that someone is "irreverent."

11. He says that in poem 376 she gains a sense of perspective, bringing "her emotion under control" in "maturer judgment" (p. 272). He seems to perceive the little girl as the apotheosis of femininity: "all woman." As she detaches herself from her feminine sensibility, she "matures" into objectivity.

12. For an especially fine discussion of Dickinson's attitude towards faith, see Charles Anderson's discussion of "Faith is a fine invention" (185), pp. 34–35.

13. It seems that Dickinson is aware of a special problem in regard to her female identity in relation to God. That the Creator is masculine has been taken for granted, but the implication of this interpretation of the Deity is profound for women. It means that God does not have, and does not need, a wife. His only relation is a "son." Therefore, if Dickinson wants to be close to Him, she must be his "son." But since she is a woman, she can only project being a "wife." In this context, her relationship with God is a cross between a wife and a son, a martyr and a lover.

14. Erik Erikson, pp. 78–85.

15. Cf. Sherwood, p. 158, who sees the poem as a discussion of the communion sacrament (but does not see it as a rejection of that sacrament). Rather, deprivation enables one to have communion (p. 159). For Todd, this is a "sentimental" poem in which she approaches the "heavenly table." (p. 67). Cody gives this poem an in-depth psychosexual analysis (pp. 44, 129–33, 138–42, 144).

16. Mudge, p. 50. See also Todd, pp. 80–81; Cody, pp. 129–33, 36–38, 44–46; Sewall, p. 467 n.; Miller, pp. 298–303.

17. Robert Sherwood says that Dickinson's notion of self-reliance and the will to succeed is closer to Horatio Alger's than to Emerson's (p. 174). I agree. I think Emerson is filtered through Dickinson's father and becomes Alger.

PART FOUR. THE HAUNTING OF THE HOUSE OF ART: THE AESTHETICS OF
EMILY DICKINSON'S "MATURER CHILDHOOD"

1. Johnson, p. 56 (but see *L*. II, p. 388). Dr. Harold Shands is another practicing psychotherapist who is interested in Emily Dickinson as a "case study." His unpublished manuscript focuses on her narcissism and its relation to her creative impulse. Dickinson does refer to "pearl" in several poems and it is possible that she considers herself an oyster (rough and plain on the outside) in her shell as dutiful daughter.

2. See especially Whicher, pp. 206–224; Chase, pp. 206–13; Richard B. Sewall, pp. 668–705; Capps, p. vii *et passim*; Higgins, pp. 71–76; Johnson, pp. 98–100; John E. Walsh, *The Hidden Life of Emily Dickinson* (New York: Simon and Schuster, 1971); and Sister Mary T. Power, *In the Name of the Bee* (New York: Sheed and Ward, 1943).

3. Gilbert and Gubar, pp. 3–4.

4. Dickinson's poems on the woman poet as witch include "I think I was enchanted" (593), which describes her initiation as a "sombre Girl" to Elizabeth Barrett Browning. In this poem, "The Dark–felt beautiful–", she cannot tell whether it is "noon at night," she loses her power, her mind is converted, " 'Twas a Divine Insanity–/The Danger to be Sane . . ./'Tis Antidote to turn–'"

> *To Times of solid Witchcraft–*
> *Magicians be asleep–*
> *But Magic–hath an Element*
> *Like Deity–to keep–*

See also, in this regard, "Witchcraft has not a pedigree" (1708) and "Witchcraft was hung in history" (1583).

5. See note 7, Part Three, on the critical response to "I never lost as much but twice" (49). For the following poem, see Whicher, p. 94, Chase, p. 102. But also see Porter, pp. 50–51.

6. The secrecy aspect of Dickinson's identification with the cocoon is present in other poems concerning the cocoon. Poem 1099 begins, "My Cocoon tightens–" and shows her chafing at the shell as in "Let Us play Yesterday" (728):

> *I'm feeling for the Air–*
> *A dim capacity for Wings*
> *Demeans the Dress I wear–*

She is claustrophobic in her shell, restless to emerge, to fly ("A power of Butterfly"). She is able to fly, which makes her outward role (dutiful daughter) demeaning. Her sense of disguise in her cocoon embryo is explicit in the last stanza, where the theme of secrecy and mystery is suggested by the words "baffle," "hint," "cipher," "Sign," and "clue divine."

> *So I must baffle at the Hint*
> *And cipher at the Sign*
> *And make much blunder,–if at last*
> *I take the clue divine–*

Perhaps the divine clue is that she *can* fly—or write poems, if she only interprets her longing for "Air" correctly. The restless daughter is given a "Sign" she *may* emerge.

In poem 66, the cocoon is compared to a bulb which "will rise–/Hidden away, cunningly,/From sagacious eyes," confounding "*Peasants* like me."

See also poems 453, 517, 970.

7. "Mat" is Martha Dickinson, the daughter of her brother and sister-in-law. Dickinson is referring to Revelation 7:11 in which the angels fall on their faces before God. She is suggesting that her poetry is "God" which people will revere, as well as the idea that people will be surprised to discover her identity as a poet.

8. For other poems dealing with the notion of "impregnable," see poems 1054 and 1351. In the former, impregnability comes about through a consciousness of the faith others have in your ability not to be vulnerable. Impregnability is not "strength" but comes only by avoiding one's "weakness," through "artifice."

9. For examples of other poems in which Dickinson discusses her need for pain, danger, etc., see poems 708, 711, and 904.

10. In thanking someone for the gift of peaches, Dickinson wrote: "I wish I had something as sumptuous to enclose to her–I have, but it is anonymous–" (*L*. II, p. 669).

11. R. P. Chevasse, *Man's Strength and Woman's Beauty* (Cincinnati: Jones Brothers and Company, 1879), pp. 15–22.

12. George Orwell, "Why I Write," in *Such, Such Were the Joys* (New York: Harcourt, Brace and Company, 1945), pp. 3–11.

13. This version of the poem reflects the recent scholarship of R. W. Franklin in "The Houghton Library Dickinson Manuscript 157," *Harvard Library Bulletin*, July 1980. It differs from the Johnson edition in that poem 443 (Johnson) includes five lines that belong to the ending of poem 1712 ("A Pit–but Heaven over it–.")

Index of Poems Cited

Poems are indexed by the number assigned them in Johnson's variorum edition of the poetry, which arranges the poems by probable date of composition (poem 1 is the earliest, from 1858; poem 1617 is "late," from 1884). The poem numbers are set in boldface; those preceded by an asterisk are quoted in full.

210

General Index